AT THE CHASE

AT THE CHASE

THE INSIDE STORY OF SAM MUCHNICK AND
THE LEGENDS OF PROFESSIONAL WRESTLING

LARRY MATYSIK

ECW Press

Published by ECW Press
2120 Queen Street East, Suite 200, Toronto, Ontario, Canada M4E 1E2

LIBRARY AND ARCHIVES CANADA CATALOGUING IN PUBLICATION

Matysik, Larry
Wrestling at the Chase: the inside story of Sam Muchnick and the legends
of professional wrestling / Larry Matysik.

ISBN 1-55022-684-3

1. Muchnick, Sam. 2. Wrestling promoters — United States. — Biography. II. Title.

CV1196.M82M38 2005   796.812'092   C2004-907052-5

Editor for the press: Michael Holmes
Typesetting: Wiesia Kolasinska
Production: Mary Bowness
Photos: All photos from the collection of Larry Matysik
Printing: Marc Veilleux Imprimeur

This book is set in Joanna and Stone

The publication of *Wrestling at the Chase* has been generously supported by the Ontario Arts Council, and the
Government of Canada through the Book Publishing Industry Development Program.
We acknowledge the support of the Canada Council for the Arts for our publishing program.

Canada

DISTRIBUTION

Canada: Jaguar Book Group, 100 Armstrong Ave., Georgetown, ON L7G 5S4

United States: Independent Publishers Group, 814 North Franklin Street, Chicago, Illinois 60610

PRINTED AND BOUND IN CANADA

ECW PRESS
ecwpress.com

for Pat and for Kelly

AT THE CHASE

On "Wrestling at the Chase" I interviewed all the champions, including Harley Race

FOREWORD

As this book was coming together, Larry Matysik casually mentioned that he'd like someone to write a foreword — something objective, he stressed, that put both his words and the stories he's sharing into context. As his editor, I agreed. Having someone introduce his accomplishments, explaining how central he is to the magical world of St. Louis wrestling, as well as how important he is to the contemporary history of professional wrestling in general, made good sense.

Besides, to booksellers, this kind of thing is gold. When publishers attach recognizable names to serious works of non-fiction — the more famous the better — the books become a bit "sexier" to the media, an easier "sell." In wrestling terms, think of the way promoters, for generations, have used "the special guest referee." Whether he's Jack Dempsey, Joe Louis, Muhammad Ali, or "Iron" Mike Tyson, the principle's essentially the same: expand the market, widen the base.

Accordingly, thinking like a promoter — a book promoter, but a promoter nonetheless — my mind raced. A dream list of possible, approachable personalities came to me, fast and furious. It included former world champions, famous sportscasters, and today's leading wrestling journalists. I also knew that they'd be only too happy to do it if asked — after giving so much to the sport he loves, Larry Matysik has earned that kind of respect.

This "Foreword" was going to be so cool. . . .

But then I was stopped dead in my tracks. My author, a guy who knows as much about the right way to promote wrestling as anyone on the planet, had other ideas.

And then he went and asked *me* to write something for his book.

In hindsight, I shouldn't have been surprised. Although he's a central character in the pages that follow, Larry was always downplaying his own part in the action. In fact, he's so self-effacing that at times I actually had to remind him to include himself in his own story. To him, this book was first and foremost about St. Louis and its wrestling, and especially about the man who shaped that heritage, Sam Muchnick. Of course, he'd also concede that *Wrestling at the Chase* is a book about the wrestlers — names like Thesz, Funk, Brisco, Kiniski, Baba, Murdoch, "The Bruiser," Flair, and Brody are just the tip of the iceberg here — who helped Muchnick create this legacy.

No, Larry Matysik didn't write this to "put himself over."

That's not the point, I can almost hear him, gently, but excitedly, saying. *It's about something bigger and more important. . . .*

Like everything professional wrestling means to those — whether they've put their body on the line in the ring or just watched, mesmerized, from the cheap seats — who love it.

He's right, of course. Wrestling is at its very best when everyone involved, on both sides of the ropes, willingly embraces what they have in common. Distinctions blur and disappear when performer and audience become one and. . . .

All that remains is the fact that we're all fans.

As I've said, many, many others are better suited, more deserving of this responsibility and honor. But I know why Larry asked me, and it's representative of everything that makes this book (and its author) unique: I'm qualified to write this foreword *because* I'm "just" a fan.

In so many ways I'm the typical product of my time and its culture. One of the very first things I remember is being confused by a news broadcast, an anchorman talking about the day's events in Viet Nam. But TV played a part in some of my happiest and most powerful childhood memories, too. And the very best of those moments? Sitting with my dad and brother, on a lazy Saturday, yelling at the screen, watching wrestling.

Growing up in Toronto, I was fortunate. The city was, as it is today, a wrestling hotbed — and local fans were schooled in the sport by a diverse catalogue of grappling greats. Over the years, a number of different promotions found their way onto local airwaves. I clearly remember exciting battles from Calgary's *Stampede Wrestling*, and wild, often shockingly violent action out of Montreal. ("Sadistic" Steve Strong, breaking a stubby glass beer bottle over his own head, was "hardcore" years before Paul Heyman marketed the term.) Of course, the wonderful Tunney- (and later, WWF-) produced *Maple Leaf Wrestling* shows, broadcast out of Hamilton and hosted by the ubiquitous Billy "Red" Lyons (to me his voice, and his trademark "Dontcha dare miss it" are an important part of Canadian television history) always seemed to be playing. But my family's favorite wrestling show, hands down, featured the stars of Verne Gagne's AWA.

It was there that we discovered LOD and "The Crusher," and howled at the antics of "The Living Legend" and "The Brain." Those shows taught us to strut like "The Body," and growl like the "Mad Dog." And because I was the kind of kid who always loved the heel — it was there that I found, as I once told Larry, "my" World Champion, Nick Bockwinkel.

Later, of course, as the wrestling universe evolved, so did what I loved about it. But whether it was watching, disbelieving, with the guys in my punk band, "King Kong" Bundy threatening to flatten a handful of midgets; or my real sense of national pride as Bret Hart became the champ; or having DDP celebrate his victory over local-boy Christian on my chair at WrestleMania 18; or watching, backstage in Nashville, Sting and Lex Luger getting ready to enter an NWA-TNA ring together for the first time; wrestling has always, at its best, been able to make me feel like a kid — thrilled, content, and utterly happy.

I mention all of this because I want to make something perfectly clear: after talking and working with the author of this book, and watching the classic St. Louis wrestling tapes he's generously made available, and especially after reading his words, I understand, sadly, what I've missed. I recognize, today, that there was something very special about Muchnick-era St. Louis wrestling. Through some of the performers I saw on AWA programming, I was introduced to the magic — but in *Wrestling at the Chase* I've been invited to become a part of it. Larry has shared many valuable insights with me, taught me more about the business of wrestling and its history than I thought possible, and for that he will always have my gratitude and friendship. But for the rare gift he makes of this book for wrestling fans everywhere he deserves something more. The subtitle of this work explains that it's about the "legends of professional wrestling," and that's fitting — because I want to be among the first to acknowledge (no matter how much he's going to protest) that Larry Matysik is one of them.

Michael Holmes, Editor, ECW Press

Gene Kiniski dethrones Lou Thesz, January 7, 1966

CHAPTER 1

HOOKED

In the beginning, there was this tiny brown box enclosing a thick glass screen. It was the phenomenon of the time — a television! Shadowy, black-and-white figures moved about. One ghostly character had curled white hair and was tossing something from within a squared area surrounded by ropes.

A strong voice from inside the box barked, "It's the famous Gorgeous George throwing golden bobby pins to the crowd."

Another body, this individual nothing less than a titan, jumped between the ropes. He was lean, hard, dark, handsome, powerful. A warrior king.

The voice from the box was awed: "There is the great Lou Thesz, being saluted by the fans."

Suddenly action detonated — Thesz and Gorgeous George began flying from corner to corner in a savage ballet. The crowd roared, screamed, howled, exploded. That little box literally shook and pulsed — I sat transfixed by the spectacle.

Man, I was hooked. Immediately. A seven-year-old addict. A wrestling junkie.

That was the first St. Louis wrestling show I remember. It was televised on Channel 5 from the St. Louis House. Did the little boy I was then have any idea that this crazy business, or sport, or whatever it is, would dominate his professional life forever?

Twenty-six years later, on August 8, 1980, I was the ring announcer at steaming Kiel Auditorium when David Von Erich, a Huckleberry Finn in tights, won the "battle of the claws" against Baron Von Raschke, whose face and bald dome contorted like a stretchy rubber mask. That packed crowd rumbled and thundered so loudly that my brain rattled inside my skull.

Then, to the squared circle came the special referee for the next match. It was none other than Lou Thesz, the idol of my innocent youth. He moved close, grabbed my forearm with his right hand, and held out his left hand palm up.

"Isn't it great when you have them right in the palm of your hand?" whispered the greatest champion in wrestling history. "You helped build this. And it's the most satisfying, exciting feeling in the world."

And now, some 49 years after my first introduction, as I struggle to explain why this magical, bizarre, heart-breaking, exhilarating sport still has me in its claw, I cannot help but think of Thesz's words.

Like that moment in 1954 when I really thought the television was alive, other memories pop up from the warm haze of childhood: a poster on which Verne Gagne was pictured demonstrating basic holds and maneuvers, a television show called "Texas 'Rassling with Vess Box," a colorful magazine entitled *Wrestling Revue*.

When "Wrestling at the Chase" burst onto the scene on May 23, 1959 — what a moment! Here was Joe Garagiola, an established baseball personality, joking and describing the actions of Rip Hawk, Bob Orton, and "Whipper" Billy Watson. And there I was, ready and eager to feed my passion for the spectacle. I started keeping detailed records of what happened every week in journals that even today make me smile.

Back then it was a simple joy for me to write stories about baseball, basketball, and football. I dreamed of becoming a sportswriter or of somehow being involved in wrestling. Obviously, nobody was about to hire a junior high kid with a flat top to cover the Cardinals or write for *The Sporting News*. So, the path of least resistance and most opportunity seemed to be sending a story to *Ring* magazine. I must have sensed that *Ring*'s wrestling section took contributions from unknown sources. The subject was a Texas "death match" between Watson and Gene Kiniski on March 4, 1960, at Kiel Auditorium.

Amazingly, the article was printed in July. I sent another piece; *Ring* printed it, too. This was cool, and my teachers seemed impressed that this skinny pipsqueak was a "published writer." By my sophomore year in high school, I had what I naturally felt was a pretty impressive résumé. But I wanted to do features on individual wrestlers, and I wanted to earn something in the process. Didn't sportswriters, even the ones covering wrestling, get paid?

Rather than risk my relationship, such as it was, with *Ring*'s legendary editor Nat Loubet, I wrote to another writer, one Earle Yetter, who reviewed action around Buffalo and Toronto. In an eye-opening reply, Yetter praised my writing and warned me to get as far away from wrestling as I could. He claimed wrestling was a nasty, horrible business, filled with double crosses, and that my efforts would best be directed elsewhere.

Well, phooey on Earle. I wasn't discouraged, though definitely surprised, and decided to write to none other than Sam Muchnick, who promoted the St. Louis action and was the president of the National Wrestling Alliance. After all, *Wrestling Revue* said Sam Muchnick was the most powerful man in professional wrestling. So did Joe Garagiola.

Doggone if Muchnick didn't send me a long and friendly letter. He mentioned his own writing background and said he liked my work. My ego expanded accordingly. Finally, he invited me to come, with my parents (at 15, I was not yet old enough to drive), to his office to discuss conducting interviews with his wrestlers.

An audience with the king. For me. I set forth to meet the grand ruler of wrestling and begin a long, mind-bending journey — what a surprise it was to learn that God had an office at the Claridge Hotel.

September 28, 1980: David Von Erich was always charismatic

THE NEW MASTER OF THE IRON CLAW . . .

DAVID VON ERICH

"Spider" was what "King Kong" Brody teasingly nick-named David Von Erich. "All arms, all legs, no body," Brody would needle, and David would laugh harder than anyone. Brody, though, would be the first to point out how much pure athleticism David had.

The second oldest son of Fritz Von Erich, David made his St. Louis debut beating Seki, a short and stout Japanese wrestler, on February 17, 1978. But Sam Muchnick had devious reasons for bringing David in at that time. The next evening a group of wrestlers were to play basketball against a sportswriters' team as part of the halftime show for a St. Louis University game. Sam was the wrestlers' coach, and he had two goals.

First and foremost, he wanted to call a time out — since there were no time-outs in wrestling. Good friend Al Ferrari, a former star for the St. Louis Hawks, was enlisted to make sure Sam picked the right spot. Second, of course, he wanted to win.

David, standing 6-7, had been an All-State basketball player in Texas. Ron Fuller, at 6-9 and a former college basketball standout, was added to Sam's roster with

Verne's son Greg Gagne, a collegiate football player who had played plenty of basketball, and Evan Johnson, a national amateur wrestling champion who also had basketball experience.

The final ingredient was a gentleman dubbed Chuck O'Connor (real name John Minton); 325 pounds on a 6-9 frame, he was soon to become "Big John" Studd and had also played college ball. I was the announcer and sat next to the scoreboard operator.

Von Erich and Fuller put the ball in the hoop. Nobody dared drive the lane to try a layup against the soon-to-be Studd. The wrestlers got almost every rebound. Sam won handily, he got to call a time out, and the sportswriters had fun getting to know the wrestlers. To celebrate, Sam hosted a victory meal at the popular Ruggeri's restaurant.

At the time, David was concerned about putting weight on that lean, slim frame of his. "Big John" said that it would be easy. "Eat like I do, Spider. Order everything on the right hand side of the menu."

Inside the ring, though, David needed only experience. Some young wrestlers just have "it," whatever "it" is. And anyone could tell David Von Erich had "it" in spades. Completely comfortable, and working with actual joy, David was smooth and explosive and naturally connected with fans of all ages.

Ted DiBiase agreed: "David deserved the push he got. He was a natural in the ring. He understood the psychology."

In 1980 Lou Thesz said, "David has a real aptitude for wrestling. It comes easy for him. I can see that he likes what he is doing and he'll burn the midnight oil because he enjoys what he is doing. He is real championship timber."

After a grooming period in St. Louis (where he worked many prelims) and Texas, the big moment came May 27, 1979, on "Wrestling at the Chase," when David and his father Fritz were placed against National Wrestling Alliance champion Harley Race in a handicap bout. Race had to win one fall from each opponent or he'd lose the match. The actual idea was brought to Sam by Fritz, and Muchnick thought it was terrific.

Fritz never got in the ring except to congratulate his son. After a furious struggle, David trapped Race in the "Iron Claw" invented by his dad years earlier. Race's head was split open. With the champion bleeding and incoherent, referee Eddie Smith stopped the action and awarded the verdict to David. It was a history-making performance by both performers. Tapes of the duel went all over the country and, later, even to Japan. Almost instantly, David Von Erich became a superstar.

David never did oust Race from the throne, but he was so young and his every battle was so intense that results meant nothing to his rise to the upper echelon. Among their blistering duels was a grueling one-hour draw on January 4, 1980, at Kiel Auditorium. Von Erich headlined thrillers against the likes of Brody (both were disqualified), Ric Flair (won one, lost two), Von Raschke, Lord Alfred Hayes, and Sgt. Slaughter.

He once told me, driving to the office after we had done an interview for a television station, "I'm not a great wrestler, but I love it up there. I won't quit, I *love* the comeback, and when I hear that crowd, man, I just work harder."

David had to work hard when Mickey Garagiola and I took him to a celebrity softball game put on by local businessman and character Steve Mizerany for the Police Relief Association. The contest, on July 14, 1980, pitted members of the media against athletes from hockey's Blues, pro football, pro soccer, as well as other sports figures from the area. Played at Francis Field on the campus of Washington University, the game drew well over 10,000 people.

David did not let us down. He belted a double. And all the other athletes, plus the media types, were charmed by his personality. The shrieks of teen-age females were ear-damaging every time David set foot on the field. After the game, all the athletes signed autographs and mingled with the fans. What was really amazing was that community superstars like the Blues' Wayne Babych were ignored, while David was swamped.

Luckily the police came to our rescue, somehow getting Von Erich out of the eager hands of the young ladies. When we got to my car, David's shirt was ripped and he'd lost his cowboy hat. He didn't care. "Oh, man, Larry, ain't this sooooo much fun?" David raved.

A year later, we had David's charismatic younger brother Kerry at the same charity event. Kerry was movie star handsome and built like a young Hercules. Having learned a lesson, security protected Kerry better than they had his brother. With Kerry, however, there was another concern.

At Sunday's TV taping, Kerry had asked me to bring a glove for him to wear in the field. When we drove to Washington University on Monday evening, I gave the glove to him and he shyly asked, "What hand do I wear this on?"

When I told him it was for the hand opposite to the one he threw with, an embarrassed Kerry said, "I never really played ball. Dad always wanted me to do football, track, and wrestling. I've never really thrown. Or swung a bat."

That was perhaps my first real experience with the strange dynamics that dominated the Von Erich family. We stopped in Forest Park for some quick softball/baseball instruction. Kerry was worried he would make a fool of himself. We worked out a spot where he'd muscle up for the big crowd, but then bunt when he came to bat.

The girls squealed and everyone got a huge kick out of powerful Kerry Von Erich bunting and then taking a spectacular bump as he flew across first base. Kerry was such a natural athlete, he did just fine, even making a nice catch on a pop-up. His simple, pleasant nature was a hit with other athletes, the media, and fans alike.

But that flash of panic and insecurity should have warned me of Kerry's eventual fate — when later the ravages of drug use and the after-effects of a crippling motorcycle accident took hold of him. Only a few months before his suicide in February 1993, while both Kerry and I were working for the World Wrestling Federation, we talked in the dressing room in Cape Girardeau, Missouri. Kerry told me how depressed he had been, that he had thought of taking his own life.

Shocked, I talked about all he had to live for and that he had fought through many difficult times. He perked up and reassured me: "I have found religion and I know it's going to be okay now." A few months later, Kerry Von Erich was dead by his own hand.

Back in 1980, however, there were good times for all of the Von Erichs (including Kevin, the oldest of the brothers). They were all on fire in the squared circle, particularly David. At The Checkerdome on October 3, 1980, Race managed to sneak by David before 15,464 totally psyched spectators. The girl who would be David's wife was his guest that night and sat with my wife Pat. David's lady was cheerleader beautiful, full of pep and life, and thrilled at their future together.

On the way home, Pat told me, "I hope they make it. They are both neat kids, but I don't know if she understands what David's life as a wrestler is like."

The night of Sam's farewell card January 1, 1982, David was a big part of the lineup before a sellout of 19,819. He was even more delightful afterward, though, as we had a private party to honor Sam in the Dome Club. Pat was seriously pregnant, just a few days away from giving birth to our daughter, Kelly. I was running all over as the master-of-ceremonies, trying to coordinate the introduction of wrestlers, promoters, politicians, and sports and media figures. But there was no need to worry about my wife — David had appointed himself her valet.

Pat still laughs about it: "Are you okay? Want a drink? Should you sit down? Should you stand up? Do you need Larry? Can I bring you food? He would tell me jokes and was just a gentleman." It was David Von Erich being his most sincere, natural, charming self. He even offered to be Kelly's godfather, which we would have considered had there not already been an equally good choice in my childhood friend, Dave Kraus.

The wrestling business was in turmoil by late 1983. But David had slipped away, somewhat, from his father's influence — wrestling in Florida as a "heel." By all accounts, he was terrific in that role, too. Plus, he was earning respect from wrestling insiders for his sharp mind and independent nature.

It was Jack Brisco who convinced David that he needed to be out on his own. Jack was so impressed with his ring savvy that he put him over clean. "He was a terrific heel," Jack said.

Life, though, was taking a toll. David and his wife had a baby — but they lost the child to crib death after just two months. The road ate the young couple alive and they soon split. David was depressed, and his body was feeling the demands of a difficult schedule. He was drinking too much and, as we all came to learn, taking painkillers.

On his first tour of Japan, on the night of February 10, 1984, David failed to show up at the arena. Brody was on the same trip and he joined referee Joe Higuchi to rush to the hotel when David did not answer their calls. They found him dead on his bed.

A shaken, tearful Brody called me from Tokyo and said, "I don't want to believe it. He had so much to live for. This had to be an accident." History records that this was the first of many tragedies to befall the Von Erich sons. And today only Kevin remains.

Brody is also, sadly, gone now, so I can relate what he told me. It doesn't change anything. Terrible accident or horrible tragedy, either way, David Von Erich was dead.

Brody found a bottle of painkillers and a few remaining pills in the bathroom. Having himself been trained by Fritz, and also being a close friend of David's, he made a snap decision. Later, he told me there was no reason for the media and the business to cause further agony for the family or to David's memory. He flushed the pills down the toilet and tossed away the bottle.

Like Brody, even today I want to believe David's death was an accident. He still lives in my memory — young, vibrant, full of energy and joy, with just the hint of a smile when those fans would erupt to cheer.

Kevin Von Erich demonstrates his body scissors, October 14, 1979

The father of professional wrestling, Sam Muchnick

CHAPTER 2

SAM

To call Sam Muchnick the father of St. Louis wrestling would be a gross understatement. Rich Banahan, a St. Louis policeman, once told me that Sam took what was a crazy, bizarre, dirty business and made it a real sport in our town. Nobody who recalls the glory days would disagree. Sam was a true Damon Runyan character, larger than life.

Rotund and alert, Sam always wore a suit and tie in public. He was comfortably rumpled, like an expensive, favorite pillow slept on many times. Sam was as he appeared, an amicable, successful businessman. His innate toughness was concealed by his genuine enjoyment of people. A lover of good food, he could swap stories and make friends with those from all walks of life. His antenna was always up, alert to what people were saying and thinking.

From the time I first met him at the age of fifteen, I never lost respect for what he had accomplished and what he taught me. It was about more than just wrestling — from Sam I learned how to deal with individuals, and with the public in general. At one Kiel Auditorium card when I was perhaps twenty-one, he took me into

Committee Room A where his box office crew, led by Dick and Arline Esser, was counting money. Sam picked up a dollar bill and waved it at me. "Look at this. It's green. And I have no idea who spent it to buy a ticket, maybe a doctor, or maybe a thief. The value doesn't change, and whoever spent that on us deserves a great show and our respect."

A native of Russia, born in 1905, Sam moved to St. Louis as a toddler. He could spin yarn after yarn about the neighborhood he grew up in, at 14th and Franklin. After a stint at the Post Office, in 1926 Sam became a sportswriter for the St. Louis *Times*. What an education he must have had, eventually traveling with the Cardinals and the famous Gas House Gang. Sam ran with the likes of Dizzy Dean, Frankie Frisch, and Pepper Martin.

"I wasn't the best writer, not by far," he'd chuckle. "But I was the best reporter. I knew how to dig out a story."

During that same period, Sam became friends with a famous wrestler named Ray Steele — they played handball in Harry Cook's gym at 6th and Pine. As time passed, he became buddies with grapplers like Lou Thesz and "Strangler" Lewis, who also trained at Cook's. Through these connections, wrestling promoter Tom Packs took a liking to the young Muchnick.

When the *Times* suddenly folded in 1932, Packs offered Sam a job. His understanding of wrestling grew from there. Eventually, Muchnick was entrusted with important duties. Nine years later, he was basically running the promotion. At the same time, he learned how the business of wrestling was structured. He also soon realized that his stature as a baseball writer helped bring respect to wrestling — especially when dealing with St. Louis media and politicians.

But Sam eventually had to spread his wings and fly solo, no matter what the odds. He broke from Packs and promoted his first card on March 27, 1942. World War Two stalled his plans, however, and it wasn't until December 5, 1945, that he really got going. It's true that history repeats itself — because the same pressures and rumors I felt and heard when running independently in 1983 plagued Sam in the forties. Like me, years later, he was told he'd never get talent and that he'd be devastated by no-shows.

Instead, Sam thrived. He kept adding talent and helped form the National Wrestling Alliance, a cooperative of nonaligned promoters around the country. On February 4, 1949, Sam had his first sellout at Kiel for a card featuring Buddy Rogers battling Don Eagle. It got even better when he sold more than 17,000 tickets to the throng who got to see Rogers clash with Lou Thesz on March 16, 1951.

The National Wrestling Alliance was the "master stroke," according to Thesz. "It was very creative and just what wrestling needed at that time. Many promoters had come from the carnival era and never got out from under the tent. Sam had a sports background and he rose above what wrestling had been. He brought credibility to the business."

With Tom Packs down for the count, a deal was struck in an effort to keep two St. Louis promotions alive. As far as the public knew, one was run by Sam Muchnick, while the other was operated by Martin Thesz, Lou's dad. Lou — obviously — was instrumental in brokering the deal. Only a select few, however, knew the whole truth; Sam had 50% control in each business and basically called the shots for both companies.

While Sam and Lou may have butted heads over the years, their friendship never wavered. "I was his fan and he was mine," Lou said. "We had each other's backs. We devoted our lives to wrestling. We were doing what we loved."

Even back then, the business of professional wrestling was unpredictable — and just like today, promoters had to survive a roller coaster ride of turmoil and intrigue. The Dumont Network began presenting wrestling on a national basis (yes, before Vince McMahon, Jr. went coast-to-coast in the 1950s). During the 1950s, the sport came under some heavy scrutiny from the Justice Department; the investigation addressed the issue of whether or not wrestling had become an illegal monopoly.

Sam, through his growing political connections, essentially saved wrestling by negotiating a consent decree. It was never discussed publicly, but Sam had serious influence with the government because of his relationship with Illinois Congressman Mel Price. Like Sam, Price was a former sportswriter; their friendship was strong and enduring.

By the late 1950s, things had again changed. Wrestling had disappeared from television and was suffering through hard times. Sam often reminisced about this era, telling me, "It was tough, but we never lost money here."

Then came the momentous plane trip. On the flight, Sam sat next to Harold Koplar, the owner of both the Chase-Park Plaza Hotel and the fledgling television station KPLR. The idea of presenting a locally-produced wrestling show from the gorgeous Khorassan Room sprung from their chat. Yes, the legend is true. Koplar and Muchnick sketched out the deal on an airplane napkin and sealed it with a handshake.

Immediately, the two local promotions merged to form the St. Louis Wrestling Club; Sam Muchnick was the president and controlled more than half the stock. Also included in the mix were promoters Frank Tunney from Toronto, Eddie Quinn from Montreal, and former champions "Wild Bill" Longson, "Whipper" Billy Watson, and Bobby Managoff.

The mid-air meeting kicked off something special — a magical time for wrestling both in St. Louis and around the world. Other promoters got their product on television, but rarely with the kind of deal that Sam had struck.

KPLR-TV paid the St. Louis Wrestling Club $1500 per taping day in return for 5% of the net receipts from each Kiel Auditorium or Arena card. Production expenses were covered by the station. Wrestling also received numerous on-air promos prior to house shows. Advertising revenues belonged to KPLR. No money changed hands until the end of the year. Basically, the deal was a wash, although Sam always said, "If I write KPLR a check, that means we've had a heck of a year at the box office."

In their eagerness to get on TV, other promoters often paid stations for air time and had to cover their own production costs. One particularly expensive arrangement was made by Jim Barnett when he was promoting in Detroit with Johnny Doyle. "It sets a bad precedent," Sam told me, complaining about Barnett's deal. "Stations should pay us for our product if it's good, not the other way around."

Better than good, "Wrestling at the Chase" broke new ground. It was the talk of the industry. Chandeliers, tuxedos, evening gowns — and wrestling! The Khorassan Room was home to St. Louis society's biggest events, which now, apparently, included grunt-and-groaners.

Colorful and witty Joe Garagiola was the program's first announcer. It was a perfect choice, not only because Joe was quick and funny, but also because it solidified Sam's ties with the accepted — and acceptable — sports community. A hometown boy made good, Joe had played major league baseball and at the time was Harry Carey's color commentator on Cardinal broadcasts.

Eventually, Joe became the longtime host of the *Today* program on NBC-TV, in addition to doing baseball's *Game of the Week*. He even guest-hosted *The Tonight Show* a few times — a remarkable achievement for a kid from the Hill. Joe Garagiola is one of the most underrated television talents of the past fifty years. The opportunity to grow and mature as a performer on "Wrestling at the Chase" clearly helped him establish his credentials.

At first, however, Joe was skeptical about his ability to call wrestling. "We'd grown up watching and loving the matches, but I really didn't know one hold from another," he said. "Harold Koplar believed in me, though, and said, 'Just be yourself. Whatever comes to mind, say it.'"

Sam Muchnick believed in Joe, too.

"The kid can do it," Joe chuckled. "That's what Sam always said about me. I'd known him from my baseball days, because it seemed like Sam came in with Abner Doubleday. He was just a really nice man, and all the rookies loved him. Sam would be extra nice to us kids and help us fit in."

And Joe Garagiola more than "fit in." His humor added still another unique twist to "Wrestling at the Chase." The perfect example? Once, when Johnny Valentine won a decision with an elbow smash to an opponent's head, a baffled Joe called it "an arm-and-hammer baking soda elbow." Ring announcer Eddie Gromacki checked with Valentine and announced Johnny as the victor with "a series of brainbusters." As Valentine had his hand raised, Joe mused: "Boy, Valentine must be a tough guy. Did you ever try to bust a brain?"

Thesz, who had been up and down the road since the mid-1930s, said, "It was a joy to come into the Khorassan Room. Just wonderful! Men in black ties and ladies in evening gowns. It was a civilized place after wrestling in tank towns with a lousy ring and a ten-watt bulb. Here it was, under chandeliers. It was elite and became the hallmark for wrestling around the world. If you gave one hundred percent normally, this inspired you to give an extra ten percent."

Mickey Garagiola, Joe's older brother, remembered that many ladies were tricked into becoming wrestling fans. "It was such a big deal to go to the Chase in those days. A husband or boyfriend would say, 'Let's go to the Chase tonight and get something to eat.' Well, they could get food in the Khorassan Room during the bouts and then the gal would realize she was at a wrestling match! Next thing she knew, *she* was yelling at Gene Kiniski or rooting for Pat O'Connor."

Joe described finding out about "closet" wrestling fans. "All of a sudden," said Joe, "we had lawyers and politicians and doctors at ringside. I saw the mayor of St. Louis there one night. Everybody was excited and having a great time. We used to drive by the Chase and wish we had enough money to go inside. Now, thanks to wrestling, it was the place to be. It became a social event."

Mickey called the show "wall to wall" wrestling. He added, "And now we've got class!"

Once again, whether or not anyone believed it was "real," everyone respected what phenomenal athletes like Lou Thesz, Pat O'Connor, Rip Hawk, Gene Kiniski, and "Cowboy" Bob Ellis could do. "I saw Johnny Valentine pound the daylights out of Buddy Rogers right on my table one night. Valentine wasn't holding anything back on those wallops!" Joe remembered.

Those were heady days for wrestling, and St. Louis led the pack. Stations in other markets saw the resounding success of "Wrestling at the Chase" and struck deals with other promoters. Studio doors swung open, though no one had a product quite as attention-getting as St. Louis. The NWA, under Sam's guidance, became omnipotent.

Ted Koplar, Harold's son, who became both occasional director of "Wrestling at the Chase" and owner of KPLR, insisted that, "Sam was amazing. He deserves more credit than he got for making the sport an historical event. He was Mr. Wrestling. He believed in it."

In Koplar's words: "St. Louis was a catalyst for wrestling. St. Louis helped make the whole phenomenon happen. It was born here; it was bred here. Something you don't hear a lot about is, if this town had never accepted it the way it did, wrestling might never have become a national success. Sam was recognized nationally. He was the Vince McMahon of his day — around the world."

I was like so many others, never missing a show and getting to almost all the Kiel cards. Little did I know I was becoming a disciple of Muchnick and the St. Louis wrestling operation.

Most promoters, including Sam, had bookers who put together matches. Some had more power than others. Sam, however, ran a slightly different ship in that he laid out the overall plan and decided who got the title matches and main events. He decided how those wrestlers would move up or down the ladder. A booker really just colored inside the lines he had drawn.

In addition, Sam cultivated a business rapport with stars who could draw crowds and provide the solid, athletic main events he loved. Sam once told me, "I couldn't stand Buddy Rogers. He was a pain in the butt and hard to do business with — but Rogers was a great performer and a terrific drawing card."

Then, he gave me a shrewd look. "A great promoter has to work with everyone. Nobody says you have to be buddies and go out eating together. You just have to do business together, and I did with Rogers."

Got it, Sam, a lesson learned.

Rogers and Sam were involved in one of wrestling's "history-making" moments in 1962. Then the NWA king, Rogers was slated to duel "Cowboy" Bob Ellis at Kiel on September 14. An angle was shot on "Wrestling at the Chase" where Ellis announced he could reverse Rogers' figure four grapevine. Ellis flopped on the floor of the Khorassan Room for Rogers to try the hold, but instead Buddy booted Ellis in the head. A donnybrook ensued.

Naturally, their September 14 feature sold out, but Sam had a fit when just two days before the event "Big Bill" Miller and Karl Gotch battered Rogers in a Columbus, Ohio, dressing room. Rogers begged out of the St. Louis showdown with Ellis, claiming an elbow injury. Except for knowing that Miller and Gotch truly hated Rogers, he would not have believed Buddy's story.

Sam had been having problems with Rogers regarding dates, in part due to Buddy's tight relationship with New York promoter Vince McMahon, Sr. (yep, Vince Junior's pop), and Vince's partner, "Toots" Mondt. Rogers was tired of all the travel as NWA king and McMahon had plenty of large, nearby towns he wanted to use the champion in, more often than he was available.

At any rate, to save the St. Louis show, Sam lured Thesz from semi-retirement to face Ellis. The two had a fabulous struggle, and it led to Thesz becoming active again. Sam decided that Rogers had to go as champ — before Buddy and his cohorts pulled some trick and McMahon wound up controlling the title.

Soon, a showdown between Thesz and Rogers was booked; it would take place in Toronto, Canada, on January 24, 1963. The entire business knew that there was serious heat between the two, and that Thesz, for years, might have truly been the toughest guy in wrestling. It led to a famous dressing room story, which Lou personally guaranteed me was true. It happened as the referee was giving his pre-match instructions. Thesz told Rogers, "We can do this the easy way . . . or the hard way." Rogers chose wisely. They had an exciting scrap (though Lou typically maintained that it was a poor contest) and Thesz was again crowned the NWA champion.

Years later, Lou explained, "I respect a guy who can face the barrier and look you in the eye. Let's see who the best man is. Buddy didn't want to do that." Joe Garagiola claimed that a wrestler once told him: "Rogers has a heart the size of a pea." Thesz would always add, though, "Rogers was a terrific performer."

McMahon, however, did not acknowledge or announce to fans in the New York area that Rogers had lost the crown. He had been preparing to leave the NWA and form the World Wide Wrestling Federation (it was the birth, in fact, of today's World Wrestling Entertainment). Sam was tipped off. McMahon's title would go to Bruno Sammartino. And he quickly worked with his friend, Toronto promoter Frank Tunney, to book a match between Bruno and Thesz — which Thesz won. Because of his foresight, magazines like *Wrestling Revue* acknowledged Lou Thesz as the real champion.

Sammartino then whipped Rogers in New York's Madison Square Garden and became the first WWWF (or WWF, or WWE) titleholder. Sam, though, was unconcerned. As he told me many times, wrestling was booming — so much, in so many places — and no one champion could make all the important dates. Having Bruno working in the Northeast corridor actually took some of the pressure off the NWA. So no, Sam's heart wasn't broken by McMahon's departure.

In the end, Sam and Vince Sr. remained friends and, often, allies. Sammartino even wrestled in St. Louis on occasion. McMahon (until many years later, when his son was calling the tune) never stepped on any toes or tried to expand into a new town outside of what his territory already controlled. Eventually, he even rejoined the NWA. And, ironically, it was Sam Muchnick who made the suggestion and sent Bob Backlund to McMahon to become the WWF champion in the late 1970s.

All of these moves were brilliantly orchestrated by a skillful politician and non-traditional promoter — and history shows that Sam's influence may have been more important at the time than anyone realized. He kept the business of professional wrestling stable for almost two decades.

Over the years, Sam employed many bookers, including Frankie Talabor, Bill Melby, Billy Darnell, Bobby Managoff, Bobby Bruns and, eventually, Pat O'Connor. Often promoters would try to lure them away, figuring that they had put together the cards that drew such huge crowds in St. Louis. But once those men — solid wrestling guys in their own right — left, they never came close to replicating the success they had with Sam. Bruns, in particular, is a great example; he bounced like a rubber ball from Buffalo to Omaha to Kansas City.

On the other hand, Sam kept doing sellout business with whoever became his new booker. So, what was the one constant? Sam Muchnick's vision.

Lou Thesz explained it: "Matchmaking is not just an accident, not just picking names out of a hat. For it to work inside the ring, the right opponents have to be put against each other. To be as successful as Sam has been says something. Matchmaking is an art form, just like what wrestlers do. Sam is very artful."

Another way Sam garnered respect was with his honesty. Take a look at the many wrestling books recently published — almost all of them feature stories of how promoters cheated the talent.

Not Sam, not in St. Louis.

Muchnick paid off 32% of the gate after tax was deducted. The main event performers divided 16%. If there was a single main event, each man got 8%; for a double feature, each received 4%. The remaining 16% was divided between the undercard, depending upon where in the lineup a wrestler was booked. Of course, transportation costs were always covered.

Dick "The Bruiser" told a great story about how he learned to trust Sam. "I was in the main event and my payoff was to be something like $825.16. In those days, the 60s, Sam always paid cash. In my envelope was the box office statement, the tax breakdown, a bunch of bills — and sixteen cents. After that, I never worried about Sam's payoffs."

Years later, Ted DiBiase headlined a title card at The Checkerdome and claimed it was his biggest payoff for years. Ted had topped slates around the country and even early closed circuit shows. "Eventually, of course, I got more money for the big pay-per-views, but that St. Louis show was number one for me for a long time," Ted remembered.

"Sam always did it right. He was one of the very few promoters respected across the board by all the wrestlers. St. Louis was almost the only town where you would see young business executives and their families at ringside.

"I always loved St. Louis, because I knew as a wrestler I would be respected and appreciated," DiBiase emphasized. "It was the way Sam presented it like a sport. There was depth to every match and it mattered who won and lost."

Perhaps one of Sam's proudest moments came in 1953. At the last second a Kiel Auditorium show had to be cancelled when a jurisdictional dispute between two unions effectively shut down the building. His wrestlers were already in town when Sam refunded the ticket sale money to fans. He called the performers to his office at the Claridge Hotel so he could pay them despite the cancellation.

He waited. And waited. And waited. Finally, the rough and rugged Hans Schmidt (who was in the main event) knocked at his door. "Sam, all the boys got together and we realize this cancellation is not your fault," Schmidt explained. "We won't take a penny from you. You've always been honest and that's not going to change."

Sam's philosophy of booking even extended to the referees. "Keep your hands off the ref," Sam would warn. And his bookers enforced the code: "Put the referee over. Nobody makes money beating up a referee or an announcer." Naturally, Sam recognized that once every so often a referee might be in the middle of a situation, so he wanted it to mean something.

Superb officials like Joe Schoenberger, "Babe" Martin, Eddie Smith, Joe Tangaro, Lee and Ed Warren, George O'Brien, Chuck Riley, Henry Costa, Johnny Ramirez, Charles Venator, Milo Occhi, Finis Hall, Walter McMillan, and John Turner appreciated Sam's edict. Again, his choice of these men reflected Sam's desire to earn respect for wrestling — they all had a substantial place in the community.

Of course, in the early days of "Wrestling at the Chase," Sam occasionally became flustered. Gene Kiniski and Rip Hawk often took verbal shots at Garagiola and once even chased Joe around the ring — to the delight of the Khorassan Room audience. Sam was ready to go nuclear on the two grapplers, but that very night, when he stopped for a bite to eat at the old Redbird Lanes (at Hampton and Gravois, it's a Walgreen's now), he saw Joe bowling with his attackers.

Sam immediately confronted the group, who got sheepish.

"Aw, Sam, we were just trying to have some fun," Kiniski mumbled.

Joe, not wanting either Hawk or Kiniski to get fired, backed them up.

"Sam, the fans liked it!"

Muchnick just shook his head.

The feud between Hawk and Joe began when Hawk overheard, while trapped in a headlock, Joe quip, "In the old neighborhood, if that head came out of a sewer, two soccer games would start!"

Hawk jumped out of the ring and came after Garagiola. "I was running for my life," he said. "But we became great friends, like two bench jockeys in baseball. Rip would be flexing in the ring and I'd say that Hawk thinks those are muscles, but it's really just the air from his head blowing up those arms. The fans seemed to like it and Rip would growl at me."

Kiniski was another Garagiola favorite. His gravel-voiced rants would make Joe say, "That's how someone sounds gargling with razor blades." Going into a restaurant with Kiniski was always great fun, because, as Joe recalled, "Gene looked like he was 9-foot-8 and 400 pounds with 2% body fat. If you put laces on his head, you could use it for a football. Gene loved to let me needle him. He was just a big, lovable guy, and I treasure his friendship."

Lou Thesz was somebody else Joe truly respected. "I'd grown up watching him become a great wrestler and seeing guys like Jim Londos and 'Strangler' Lewis. It was a genuine thrill for me any time I was next to Thesz."

Since nobody else could get away with Kiniski and Hawk's shenanigans, the skits stirred talk all over town. Sam believed you had to keep the match in the ring. Then along came Dick "The Bruiser," Dick Murdoch, and "King

Kong" Brody. Some criticized Sam for looking the other way, but he had again created an outline that allowed a few unique individuals to be even more effective.

Terry Funk was one grappler who found out how serious Sam was about his "Keep it in the ring" guidelines. On the February 10, 1973, broadcast, Funk defeated Johnny Valentine. Sam was at a charity luncheon and had to miss part of the taping, but he'd already decided that Terry would take the Missouri State Championship. With only the details remaining to be worked out, he left Pat O'Connor, his booker, in charge of the show.

Lo and behold, Funk used a chair to batter Valentine's leg — right in front of referee Joe Schoenberger. Then Funk clamped on his spinning toehold for the victory. When Sam got back to the Channel 11 studio where the program was being taped, fans were enraged. Sam viewed the footage and I can vouch for his reaction. It was one of the few times I ever saw him truly angry.

O'Connor nearly lost his job. Funk caught a serious dose of hell. The entire booking sequence was rearranged so a rematch could take place on March 16 at Kiel. Without question, the belt was going back to Valentine. Fate got in the way, though, as Valentine was hospitalized with heart trouble in Houston the night before the rematch was to take place.

Sam got the call at 11:30 p.m. I was handling all the publicity by then, so Sam instructed me to notify everyone about what had happened. That still left him with a problem. How would he fill the main event on short, almost impossible, notice? Fritz Von Erich had a show in Dallas, so he was out.

My wife Pat heard us talking, read the situation, and in her debut as a booker whispered, "What about Kiniski?" Dutifully, I repeated her words to Sam. He loved the idea. And while I notified everyone from the Kiel manager and the box office folks to the *Globe Democrat* and the *Post Dispatch* and every radio station I could find, Sam called "Big Thunder."

Kiniski drove from his home outside Vancouver to Seattle, caught a flight at 3:15 a.m. and arrived in St. Louis around 7:30 a.m. The Warwick Hotel manager let Gene into our office, where he was dozing — in my chair — when Sam and I came in around 10 a.m. "Where have you guys been, for crying out loud!" Kiniski roared.

By the way, Kiniski won. Funk relinquished the Missouri crown.

I learned so much from that sequence of events. First, Sam made it clear what could and could not be done in St. Louis — and that, no matter what, he was the boss. Second, we only had to refund $60 worth of tickets that night — testimony to the fact that Sam's honesty in dealing with the substitution was recognized. Third, Sam had earned a loyalty with the talent that few others in the business could claim.

Kiniski, for one, had proven his mettle well before his short-notice substitution for Valentine. On January 31, 1958, Gene was slated to challenge NWA champion Dick Hutton for the crown at Kiel. A blizzard struck the Midwest, dumping 11 inches of snow in St. Louis, and forced Kiniski's plane to land in Kansas City around 5 p.m.

Kiniski called Sam from the airport, rented a car, and began the treacherous trip to St. Louis. Twice Gene drove off the highway and once had to actually push his vehicle back onto the road by himself. Every time he found a pay phone, Gene would call Kiel and have the operator tell Sam where he was.

Sam delayed things as much as he could — even adding a match to the card — but finally, a decision had to be made. Reluctantly, he sent "Big Bill" Miller out to face Hutton. About twenty minutes into the match, Kiniski ran into the building, dropped his bags at ringside, jumped into the ring and — in street clothes — attacked the champ. After order was restored, Kiniski changed into tights and finished the time limit, going to a draw with Hutton.

That, by any definition, is loyalty.

As president of the NWA for 21 years, plus five terms as executive-secretary — which meant Sam still ran the show — he eventually burned out on dealing with wrestler demands and settling disputes between promoters. During that time, Sam's loyalty and professionalism were tested time and again.

At one point, for example, Sam was unable to use "The Bruiser," who had become a close friend, for almost two years — because Dick, who did not belong to the Alliance, was involved in a promotional dispute with NWA member Eddie Farhat. "The Bruiser" and Farhat, better known to fans as The Sheik, were battling for control of Cincinnati and Detroit in 1972 and 1973. Other members watched Sam intently, wondering where his loyalties would lie. He chose to stick with his Alliance, but the situation still hurt him personally. To Dick's credit, "The Bruiser" understood and never complained.

Being the NWA president meant he was also responsible for booking the World Champion. Sam became frustrated as member promoters cut corners, broke rules, asked the champion to do things not in the best interest of the business, and complained about the small booking fee the president made for handling the titleholder. A couple NWA titleholders even went into business for themselves — conducting their professional affairs based on personal interest and causing Sam no end of problems. Lawsuits would sometimes pop up — most notably in Atlanta in the mid-1970s — that vexed Sam tremendously. Wrestling had many rambunctious personalities and many sought power.

When Sam stepped down as president, Fritz Von Erich replaced him for a year; then Eddie Graham of Tampa took over for two more. Finally, Bob Geigel of Kansas City stepped in. Jim Barnett, by that time in Atlanta, was named secretary-treasurer — but he was basically in control.

Barnett got into the NWA essentially because Sam recognized ability and was not in the least prejudiced about sexual preference — or anything else. When Barnett worked for Chicago promoter Fred Koehler in the 1950s, other NWA members did not even want him at their meetings. Sam, however, realized that Barnett was an educated man who understood the growing power of television. He made him the recording secretary.

Along with the likes of "Toots" Mondt and Vince McMahon, Jr., Barnett would become one of the smartest and most feared manipulators in wrestling history. With such different and difficult personalities in power over the years, I always wondered how Sam Muchnick, who was a kindly and friendly grandfather figure to most of St. Louis, could command so much respect — and even fear — within such a dog-eat-dog world.

Whatever went down in the 1940s and 1950s, Sam must have consolidated power. He was always a great negotiator, finding a way for both sides to think they had won. His reputation for honesty, along with the disciplined way in which he operated his own town, obviously helped. Sam never tried to start a promotion in another territory, never attempted to take someone else's city. For whatever reason, until he simply got tired, and the natives became restless in the 1970s, Sam Muchnick held the NWA and the business itself together.

Nick Bockwinkel has a unique take on why Sam was held in such esteem by his peers: "This business is so much about huge egos and muscles, all this male macho stuff. With Sam, though, there was nothing physically challenging or threatening. His background was sports, business, politics, and writing.

"Sam was from a different world than the wrestling people. He had an aura, a demeanor, that everyone from wrestler to promoter respected. Egos didn't bother him in the least. Sam was logical, a true pragmatist. It was hard to argue with someone as logical as Sam."

A perfect example lies in the way he responded to the occasional knock from an unknowing wrestler who'd say, "Someone who never took a bump doesn't know the business." His logical counter was that a wrestler never negotiated a television contract, booked building dates, wrote press releases, or did television production.

As wrestling journalist Dave Meltzer says, "You mean I don't know what a good meal tastes like just because I've never been a chef?" The truly successful promoters, whether they had wrestled or not, brought much more to the table. Sam, perhaps, brought more than anyone else ever had.

Sam often thought about writing a book. He was urged to do so by Baseball Hall of Fame sportswriter Bob Broeg. In the end, though, he told me, "I know every kink, every quirk, every success, every failure of every single promoter in the world. There isn't a story I haven't heard or seen. If I wrote the book honestly, I'd make too many people angry. And I can't write it if I don't write it honestly."

In St. Louis, his reputation was formidable. As a child, Bob Hyland, the famous owner of the powerful KMOX Radio, learned how to score a baseball game sitting with Muchnick in the press box. Years later, the airwaves of mighty KMOX were pretty much open to Sam whenever he wished.

Muchnick was awarded the Campbell Award for meritorious service to sports by the famous Elks Sports Dinner in 1972. He joined the likes of Hyland, Jack Buck, Bob Burnes, Bob Broeg, Bob Bauman, and August Busch, Jr. Sam spent hours on charitable work, especially with the Buddy Fund (named for Bud Blattner), which provided sports equipment for underprivileged kids.

Sam was a regular in the press box for baseball games at Busch Stadium. He also kept up his membership in the Baseball Writers' Association, and always cast his ballot in the annual Hall of Fame voting. Eventually, Sam was awarded the organization's Number One card because he'd been a member longer than anyone else.

Sam's friendships were boundless. Once part owner of Cahokia Downs Racetrack, Sam loved going to the horse races. He had many laughs with racing expert Tommy McMahon, who was also the bartender at the Press Club and Jack English's joint in Belleville. The lunches at English's were famous. Of course, walking in with Andre the Giant would do that for you. The weekly meetings of the 1-2-3 Club, where every single sports personality of note belonged, were Sam's glory, because he was a founder — along with famed Cardinal traveling secretary Leo Ward — decades earlier.

Eddie Moran, a highly-respected police captain, was a near and dear friend, just one of many from the law enforcement community. Yet Sam also got along famously with local characters from the other side of the fence. One, who was eventually killed in a car bombing along Interstate 55, asked Sam a question that always made him laugh. (The gentleman in question was speaking with Sam after leaving the wake of a local politician.)

"The priests always talk about going to heaven," the guy said. "Think of how many people are up there now! Sam, do you think they have room for all of us?"

Sam Muchnick earned respect and affection because he gave so much of it himself.

Gene Kiniski signs the contract handed to him by Sam Muchnick to defend his title on June 16, 1967, against Edouard Carpentier (standing, left). Looking on are former World Champion "Wild Bill" Longson (center) and Bobby Bruns

WELCOME BACK TO THE SPOTLIGHT . . .

"WILD BILL" LONGSON

If you wonder how popular professional wrestling was during the early years of its history, consider the drawing power of "Wild Bill" Longson. Beginning in 1941, Longson headlined 58 events that drew 573,671 fans in St. Louis. That translates to nearly 10,000 per card — better than 90 percent of capacity — for *four* years. Now, add to that the tremendous business "Wild Bill" was doing in Houston, Toronto, Atlanta, and several other major markets . . . .

Lou Thesz described him as "A fighter first. He was not a sophisticated wrestler and didn't pretend to be. He was, however, a legitimate tough guy who would put knots in your noggin in a heartbeat. Bill had a great career."

Orginally a Golden Gloves boxing champ from Salt Lake City, Longson gravitated to wrestling and made St. Louis his base. He quickly picked up the nickname "Wild Bill," because he regularly thumped foes. The piledriver he made famous was a vicious weapon. In fact, he was an early "heel" who could infuriate his opponent (and emotional fans) by running around the ring and launching himself high over the top rope to avoid getting whacked himself.

On February 19, 1942, Longson took the World Heavyweight Championship from Sandor Szabo in St. Louis. Later that year, on October 7, he dropped the gold belt to Yvon Robert in Montreal. "Wild Bill" battled back to the top by dethroning Bobby Managoff in St. Louis on February 19, 1943. He enjoyed a red-hot four-year reign before being beaten by "Whipper" Billy Watson on February 21, 1947, again in St. Louis.

"Wild Bill's" final stint as kingpin began November 21, 1947, when he knocked off Thesz. In a legendary battle, Thesz regained the title from Longson in Indianapolis on July 20, 1948. After a brutal brawl, Thesz had "Wild Bill" on the run and Longson launched himself over the top rope. Unfortunately for him, "Wild Bill" landed with a foot inside the ice bucket of a beer vendor at ringside. His ankle was broken and Thesz got the belt.

By the 1950s, Longson had become a partner in the promotions controlled by Sam Muchnick and Thesz. When "Wrestling at the Chase" got rolling, Thesz dropped out, but "Wild Bill" was a part owner and office operative for Sam at the St. Louis Wrestling Club. Fans loved when Longson and Bobby Bruns came charging into the ring to break up brawls between Gene Kiniski and "Cowboy" Bob Ellis, or Rip Hawk and Buddy Rogers. Thesz jokingly called Longson "Sam's internal bouncer. Bill would smack anyone around, no matter who or how big he was."

That role, in fact, led to Longson's final match. After a four-year absence from the ring, during a post-match squabble between Ellis and Kiniski, Longson was swatted by Gene. He immediately knocked Kiniski cold with a piledriver. Longson then asked for a chance to put the young, aggressive Kiniski in his place. On January 8, 1960, Kiniski was awarded the decision over Longson due to a leg cramp suffered by "Wild Bill" — once again after tumbling over the top rope. Two weeks later, "Wild Bill" had his final bout as he joined forces with "Whipper" Watson to lose a bruising tag tussle against Kiniski and Rip Hawk.

Fans at Kiel Auditorium cards would spot Longson puffing on his giant cigars and joking with the likes of Joe Millich during bouts. When action threatened to get out of control, Sam would usually send him down to ringside — just to take a look.

What few if any knew, however, was that Bill was also in charge of paying the talent. As he walked through the excited spectators on his way from Committee Room A to the dressing room, Longson's pockets were stuffed with thousands of dollars in cash.

Inside the bowels of Kiel, "Wild Bill" directed traffic. Jack Brisco said he knew he was in St. Louis when he saw Longson puffing on a cigar and in a chair at the top of the steps leading to the dressing rooms.

Bill made sure wrestlers saw the doctor and got their license from the athletic commission. He collected bills for their transportation and got everyone into the correct dressing room. Like Sam, "Wild Bill" had an aura that helped keep many grapplers in awe of the entire operation. Plus, he loved to joke with the likes of Dick Murdoch and Rocky Johnson (father of current movie and wrestling star The Rock).

He was another great teacher for me. "Wild Bill" understood wrestling and why St. Louis, under Sam's direction, was different. And what a character! When we shifted the office from the Claridge Hotel to the Warwick Hotel, the moving company was having trouble pulling out the drawers of the file cabinets. "Wild Bill" just gave one cabinet a bearhug and lifted the entire thing, including the drawers filled with files. He carried it through two offices and into the hall to put on the dolly. The young movers were stunned. "Wild Bill" thought nothing of it and moved six more cabinets the same way.

At the Warwick, "Wild Bill" had a small office off the room I used. One day I saw smoke pouring from his cubbyhole. I looked around the corner to see Bill's chest on fire! He had dozed off and ash from his cigar had his shirt and thick chest hair smoldering. I yelled and Bill began giving himself Ric Flair chops to put out the conflagration. He laughed and said, "I guess I was bored."

"Wild Bill," though, had many lessons to teach. Quietly, Bill could describe how the politics of wrestling worked. He had great respect for Sam, but he made it clear that Sam could be ruthless in getting other promoters to toe the line. "We have easy rules in St. Louis," Bill claimed. "Show up on time, ready to work. Always give one hundred percent. We don't care what you do in your private life, but *always* close the hotel door. Never bring the business any bad publicity, or you're fired."

Longson understood the psychology of the ring perfectly: "Listen to the crowd and feel their emotion. It's a roller coaster. Go up and down. Build to a climax."

He also had a great eye for young talent. During the 1950s, it was Bill who engineered bringing a hot young tag team to St. Louis. Joe Tangaro and Guy Brunetti had a terrific run in the Midwest. Tangaro eventually stayed in St. Louis. He became a referee and a successful restaurant owner, once more adding to the substance of wrestling in St. Louis. Eventually, before passing away, Joe gave Lou Gehrig's Disease perhaps its most difficult battle. The courage and determination Tangaro showed was an example of the quality and class of that generation.

To me, Bill Longson was a gentle bear and a terrific friend who took the time to guide a green teenager. And just as Sam had the esteem of his community, "Wild Bill" was a respected character. If there were ever any dispute, as Thesz said, Longson would put a knot in someone's noggin.

"Wild Bill" Longson taking advantage of Steve Martin at Walsh Stadium in 1946

John Paul Henning, my first interview

CHAPTER 3

SAM & ME

PART I

What an amazing relationship it turned out to be. Sam and Larry. Eventually, the old *St. Louis Globe Democrat* did a weekend magazine feature on prominent local mentor-protégé pairs: Sam and I were pictured on the full-page cover.

Clearly, working with Sam opened many doors, both in the St. Louis community and even more so in wrestling. Not long after I had started full time in the office, colorful manager Bobby Heenan and wrestler Lars Anderson stopped by before a card. Sam introduced me as "the next great promoter" in a way that was gently kidding but softly serious. I could see both Heenan and Anderson snap to attention and take a hard look; after all, it was Sam Muchnick talking.

Back in 1963, though, I was just happy to get a few interviews. I also got advice: finish college; save money; and do not be a hero-worshipper or ask for autographs. Finally, I'd regularly get a couple of tickets for the Kiel Auditorium cards and a press ticket for myself, so I could sit at the hallowed ringside press table.

My first interview, by my request, was with John Paul Henning, a main event regular in the early 1960s and the master of the bow and arrow hold. What a disappointment! Henning certainly was polite, but he was also very uncomfortable with the idea of talking about himself. He might be the only wrestler I've ever met I could say that about. Somehow I got enough material for a story and eventually sold it to *Ring* magazine.

Next I interviewed Pat O'Connor, a guy who, over the years, would became such an important part of my career. Pat was definitely more articulate than Henning, but also apparently not too crazy about having to do an interview with a high school kid. In time, I realized Pat was cautious in personal situations — until he trusted you and opened up. He had an incredibly profound knowledge of what happened inside the ring.

Many years later, after O'Connor's death, I was speaking with Nick Bockwinkel about him. Nick was a native of St. Louis, as was his rugged wrestler father, Warren. The fortunes of the business led Nick out of the area — and he eventually became Verne Gagne's American Wrestling Association champion. Nick described O'Connor's mind-boggling ability as a worker: "I was just starting out, but getting a push, when I met Pat. I was nervous, but Pat said, 'Just pay attention, listen, and follow me.' Before it was all over, we had the crowd roaring. What heat!

"Believe me, it was all Pat O'Connor, because he put me in positions where I was pounding on him and spots where he was twisting me like a pretzel. I would have no idea how Pat did that."

Bockwinkel laughed, "His ability to move me into the proper situation and to understand the crowd was just sensational."

Nick does, perhaps, underestimate his own work; he too was a remarkable ring performer. Of course, learning from a master like O'Connor undoubtedly helped polish his abilities.

At any rate, my third interview was with "Big Bill" Miller and I finally got over the hump. Miller, who had played on a Rose Bowl-winning football team at Ohio State and was an equally successful amateur grappler, was open, funny, and interesting. He spoke of his early days in the play-for-pay business, when he wrestled with a mask in Omaha (he was later to perform as "The Crimson Knight" for Sam in St. Louis), and his personal goals.

He recalled teaching blind kids to wrestle at the YMCA in Columbus, Ohio, showing the softer, human side I really had not recognized in grapplers as a teenager. I knew the story would be a gem. When Miller finally left wrestling, he became a prominent veterinarian in his native Ohio.

Actually, my first visit to the press table was on October 11, 1963; I was to learn how to call the results into the *Globe Democrat*, the *Post-Dispatch*, and KMOX Radio. My teacher was none other than Ray Gillespie, who was an editor at *The Sporting News* and a longtime baseball writer. What a fine gentleman he turned out to be: patient, kind, and full of great baseball stories.

Ray was out of town two weeks later, so I was on my own. I was only sixteen, but I knew enough to wear a coat and tie. Brother, this was the *major* league. Sam's partner, "Wild Bill" Longson, visited with me before the card began to make sure I knew the names of the finishing moves. I did an interview with Rip Hawk that was all sorts of fun. The National Anthem played, dignified Johnny Curley did the ring announcing, and the action began.

My memories of the night? "Cowboy" Bob Ellis over Dick "The Bruiser" on disqualification. Fritz Von Erich and Rip Hawk beat Ronnie Etchison and John Paul Henning. Karl Gotch popped Dan Plechas. Midgets: Sam Thomas defeated Jim Baker. Ladies tag team action: Jessica Rogers and Mars Monroe over Ann Regan and Jean Antone. "Bulldog" Brower (not Brown, but Dick Brower) topped Joe Blanchard. Joe Tangaro went to a draw with Angelo Poffo. Emile Dupre beat Frank Altman.

It wasn't as simple as it sounds. The first call to the *Globe* came at intermission, then another quick update came after the Ellis-"Bruiser" scrap, and finally I contacted everyone after the concluding Von Erich tag match.

Naturally, Ellis and "The Bruiser" ended up in a back-alley brawl. Dick destroyed the ring steps and used a piece of wood to get Ellis bleeding. Ellis finally turned the tables, got the weapon, and whacked "The Bruiser" until he too was bloody. This was followed by a bulldog headlock from Ellis, but Dick foiled a second attempt and rammed Ellis' head into the turnbuckle. "The Bruiser" started to mount the top rope for his atomic drop, but referee Milo Occhi blocked him since coming from the top rope was illegal. Dick jumped anyway and decked Occhi. A disqualification was called for, and a real riot between Ellis and "The Bruiser" erupted — until Longson and Bobby Bruns helped the referee separate the two.

Think adrenalin was popping my ear drums? Somehow I must have made sense to Harry "Slug" Mitauer, the grizzled and noted reporter taking my call at the *Globe*. After I phoned in the final bout, I apologized for being a "little" excited. Mitauer growled, "Hey, kid, you did fine."

Whatever test this was, I must have passed. No doubt, knowing how detailed Sam was, he checked with Mitauer and KMOX to make sure I did acceptable work. Sharing that table with someone like Ray Gillespie through my college years was nothing less than fascinating. Having access to the mysterious dressing room area would also give me goosebumps. Watching the NWA title change hands from Thesz to Gene Kiniski on January 7, 1966, is something I'll never forget.

Priceless moments came fast and furious. Who could forget Johnny Valentine defeating and unmasking "Hercules," who was Bobby Graham, on February 21, 1964? Or how about Fritz Von Erich taking a Texas "death match" from Dick "The Bruiser" on April 17, 1964, before a sellout crowd of 12,000 at Kiel? Or Lou Thesz retaining the title in a one-hour match with Pat O'Connor on February 5, 1965? Or Thesz and O'Connor joining forces to win a tag match from Kiniski and "The Bruiser" on May 6, 1966? And imagine this one — on January 5, 1968 — Buddy Rogers, of all people, officiating a main event in which Kiniski kept the championship by beating Edouard Carpentier, the "Fabulous Flying Frenchman." I watched an endless parade of superstars in mat classics, time after time.

Letting all that atmosphere and awesome wrestling soak in from right up close, visiting regularly with Longson and Sam in particular, and going to all the "Wrestling at the Chase" tapings was like a carefully directed educational program — designed by Sam Muchnick, especially for me.

My budding friendship with Gillespie led to another fascinating experience: the Elks' Sports Celebrity Dinner. The event brought together all of St. Louis's sports celebrities for a huge and glitzy banquet at the Khorassan Room of the Chase Park-Plaza Hotel. When I was in college, Ray arranged for me to handle the publicity and media voting for award winners.

Bob Bauman, Sam's very close friend and longtime trainer of the Cardinals and Browns, was one of the key organizers, along with business leaders Hank Siesel, "Bud" Horan, and Gene Wrobel. This was exactly the kind of event with which Sam wanted wrestling associated. The bonus, for me, was that I came into regular contact with folks like Jack Buck and sports editors Bob Broeg and Bob Burnes about something other than wrestling. An added attraction was going to the hospitality suite after the dinner and talking to Stan Musial, "Red" Schoendienst, Lou Brock, Joe Torre, Larry Wilson, Buddy Blattner, and former Cardinal general manager "Bing" Devine — plus many, many others. It was a fun event that went on for years, until the Elks finally turned the affair over to the Multiple Sclerosis Society. Then, the likes of Rex Redfern and Carol Westfall helped me keep the tradition alive.

Over time, I discovered how valuable the public perception of Sam was to wrestling in St. Louis. When I sprained an ankle playing basketball or dislocated a knee being thrown from the ring by Dick "The Bruiser," Sam sent me to the Cardinals' clubhouse at Busch Stadium. Bauman, a first-class gentleman and trainer, helped heal the aching joints. I spent one summer sharing a whirlpool with Redbird great Ozzie Smith.

A call on behalf of Mr. Muchnick to the mayor's office or the police chief went right through to the head honcho. The general managers of the local CBS and NBC affiliates were just as happy to hear from Sam as the owner of a small weekly newspaper. Buying a new mat cover for the ring at KPLR or a typewriter for the office was always fast and easy — everyone I spoke with either knew Sam or recognized his name. Dinner reservations at the best restaurants were made with the establishment's owner, who would inevitably say: "Tell Sam we'll be looking for him." Tickets for the famous Muny Opera were just a quick call away. The same was true for concerts, plays, and sports events. Waiters, parking attendants, ushers, secretaries, and hosts all had a fond regard for Muchnick and wrestling. Where appropriate, Sam was generous with a cash tip or a ticket to a card. He always had time for a smile and a story.

Sam and, by extension, both me and wrestling, were part of the fabric of the community. No promoter anywhere in the country enjoyed such an intimate relationship with his town. This was something other NWA partners and promoters, save perhaps Verne Gagne, failed to understand. The way Sam conducted a notorious endeavor like professional wrestling both in and out of the ring was unique — and all the little touches added up and mattered.

As the 1960s drew to a close, Sam handed me more and more responsibility. A couple projects took on lives of their own. I'd made connections with the weekly newspapers in the metropolitan area, and soon Sam had me writing news releases for them. At the time, this kind of grass-roots contact with wrestling fans was important. When the total circulation of *The Bugle*, the *Evening Whirl*, the *Millstadt Enterprise*, *The American*, and other publications came together, wrestling propaganda reached impressive numbers.

Sam had a great rapport with area radio stations, so he guided me through formalizing a mailing list of those outlets. I became the contact for information and complimentary tickets. Naturally, some stations would talk about wrestling more than others. Put together, though, all of the weeklies plus the radio stations, KMOX, the *Globe*, the *Post*, Sam's own mailing list for his pamphlet (an amazingly effective tool), and "Wrestling at the Chase" resulted in a huge marketing effort. It was never just a matter of throwing out a lonely card and hoping to draw enough paying customers to break even.

At the start of 1970, Sam offered me a golden opportunity: to write what he called the "Wrestling" news. It was actually the four-page pamphlet that the St. Louis Wrestling Club published and mailed to subscribers roughly ten days before every Kiel or Arena card. Various sportswriters, including Ray Gillespie, had done it over the years. I would be replacing Howard Kee, who was actually a distant cousin.

It was a huge step into the inner circle. I would go to Sam's office at the Claridge Hotel the day after every Kiel bill and he would give me the lineup for the next show. Sam would talk with me about the angles, but generally left me to my own devices. Usually, I'd have to wait to see him, and I must admit I'd lean close to his office door so I could hear scraps of what he and Pat O'Connor, who had just replaced Bobby Bruns as booker, were discussing. Hearing Sam ask, "Where are you going with this?" is a powerful memory.

Fortunately, Sam did not know how poorly my college classes had prepared me for the technical details of design and type layout. Thank goodness for Ray Gillespie, Pat — my wife-to-be at the time — and a patient typesetter named Al Steck: somehow I muddled through, creating a professional-looking pamphlet.

The content was a piece of cake — it was something I had been doing for years. My goal was to make it comparable to *The Sporting News* or the daily sports section. While the publication was obviously intended to help sell tickets, it was also a chance to exercise my imagination and knowledge. My first edition was for January 23, 1970, when Von Raschke tangled with Wilbur Snyder, and Pat O'Connor took on Waldo Von Erich in a double main event.

The material from which I wove that initial issue came from the Kiel card of January 9, 1970, when 11,434 packed the building to see Dory Funk, Jr. retain the NWA laurels by virtue of disqualification against Dick "The Bruiser." Wilbur Snyder and Dewey Robertson won a handicap match from Von Raschke, who grabbed the first fall from Robertson but dropped the second stanza to Snyder.

Consider the names in this preliminary — Waldo Von Erich, Bob Geigel, and "Black Jack" Lanza, with Bobby Heenan managing, won a six man tag scrap from Ernie Ladd, Lou Thesz, and Tommy Martin. Guess who lost the fall? (It was Martin, who was also known as Leo Burke in Canada.) Pat O'Connor whipped Luke Graham. The Crimson Knight (my best early interview subject — Bill Miller) topped Ronnie Etchison. Frank Hester downed Mike Rolinsky. Thor Hagen flattened The Viking.

It was a few years until my own name appeared in "Wrestling," but the sense of accomplishment was overwhelming when I saw the final, blue-inked product. I got to tell the story of what had happened and what would happen. Every single word was mine — as it would be for the next 13 years.

By the end of my tenure at Southern Illinois University-Edwardsville, in the fall of 1970, I was spending more time at Sam's office than I was at college. That was when Sam offered me a full-time position with him at the St. Louis Wrestling Club. I remember clearly, he said, "I don't know how it will work out for you, but it should be great experience and I think you have a future in promotion if that is what you want out of life. Just be sure you're happy."

Happy was a mild way of describing how I felt. It was, as the storybooks say, a dream come true.

My first event in my new and more responsible role was the famous title duel between champion Dory Funk, Jr. and Jack Brisco at Kiel on January 1, 1971. With a complete sellout and fans rushing the ticket windows after all seats were gone, I was running all over the building with messages from Sam and the box office crew.

To top things off, Dory Jr. and Brisco staged a remarkable one-hour stale-mate that began a worldwide rivalry. The rest of the lineup wasn't shabby either. Pat O'Connor and Rufus R. Jones defeated Hans Schmidt and "Black Jack" Lanza (with that pesky Heenan interfering). Von Raschke whipped Bob Windham (a former New York Jet football player who would become "Black Jack" Mulligan). Pak-Son edged Dewey Robertson. "Big Bill" Miller flattened Reggie Parks (who designed and crafted the first and only Missouri State title belt). Eddie Graham (who was Brisco's mentor and the Tampa promoter) topped Stan Pulaski. Luis Martinez and Guy Mitchell took the measure of Tom Andrews and "Moose" Cholak.

During my first week in the office, Sam had me type and mail the January 3 lineup for "Wrestling at the Chase" to George Abel, who was doing play-by-play, and ring announcer Mickey Garagiola. George was the third host of "Wrestling at the Chase," following in the footsteps of Joe Garagiola and Don Cunningham.

By then, of course, I had already come to know George and Mickey, who both eagerly and openly allowed me to visit with them as they discussed the upcoming action. To help them, I would gather background information on the feuds and wrestlers and type out 3x5 cards with facts about each performer.

As exciting as the wrestling was, however, my deepest satisfaction came inside the historic offices of Sam Muchnick. There, the history of the business — not just in St. Louis — was laid out for me. Photos from 1945 to 1969 lined the wall. Every file drawer was open to me, and Sam, over time, encouraged me to look and learn.

I would read letters from Iowa promoter Pinkie George or Minneapolis boss Tony Stecher or Ohio kingpin Al Haft from 1949, when the National Wrestling Alliance was being formed. I'd also browse and study files about the Dallas wrestling war Sam helped resolve. Loads of material from the federal investigation of wrestling in the 1950s was available. There was also correspondence between Sam and so many of the famous promotional names: "Toots" Mondt, Vince McMahon, Sr., Frank Tunney, Eddie Quinn, Eddie Graham, Paul Boesch, Jim Barnett, Fred Koehler, Leroy McGuirk, Cal Eaton, Salvador Lutteroth, Wally Karbo, Fritz Von Erich, Roy Shire, Don Owen, and Stu Hart were all there.

It's not that there was great intrigue in the correspondence — Sam eventually told me that the most serious decisions were made face-to-face or on the telephone, especially after the controversy which led to the consent decree. It was more that I got a sense of how wrestling worked, the nuances of various relationships. Some letters were angry and some were friendly; others sought advice or were pushy and demanding. The variety pretty much described the business of wrestling.

There were many letters and memos discussing schedules and detailing complaints and negotiations between Sam and various NWA champions. I even discovered a 1969 letter from Harley Race, who would become a partner years later but was then just starting to make his mark in the ring. Harley thanked Sam for the opportunity to headline at Kiel Auditorium and humbly asked for another chance to prove he could be a main event performer in St. Louis. Over time, it became obvious to me that wrestling was a unique enterprise — and that St. Louis was a town unlike any other.

In addition, I plowed through all of the monthly bulletins Sam had written to NWA members since the birth of what was described as "a cooperative of wrestling promoters around the world." Keep in mind that wrestling in 1971 was a territorial business with roughly thirty different promotions spread all over the globe. Sam kept in touch with those belonging to the NWA (most were members) by regularly composing a lengthy memo of developments, ideas, changes, and even warnings. Misuse of the champion drove poor Sam up the wall! At the same time, the NWA by-laws and a history of various amendments were all there for me to research.

Soon, Sam had me typing and mimeographing those bulletins for him. Often he would sit and explain why he was wording something in a certain way. Sam's precise memory attached a thousand stories to each promoter. He could explain exactly how a controversial issue developed and why a promoter or wrestler reacted as he did. There was always a lesson involved, and I came to understand that "History repeats itself" became a cliché because it happens to be true.

Perhaps the most important thing I learned was that today's enemy might be tomorrow's partner. In the history of almost every promoter, Sam knew of a time when someone was a bitter rival — a few years later, inevitably, the two were associates in another venture. "Don't burn bridges," he said.

Sam did not spare himself from criticism. As we became closer, he would occasionally admit to making mistakes — in how he handled a particular incident or person. He would explain how he tried to resolve the situation so all parties would benefit. When it came to business relationships, Sam advised me to pay attention to every nuance, to every word exchanged, in order to get a handle on how someone might react under pressure or to figure out what an unstated goal might be.

It was just as enchanting to hear Sam talk about famous St. Louis sports figures. His stories were amazing, often tinged with a softness that the wrestling business rarely allowed. Sam was no less fond of wrestling's characters, but the hard edge of double crosses, lies, and trickery got his guard up. It wasn't the same when he talked about Rogers Hornsby, Bob Broeg, Bob Hyland, "Bing" Devine, or Joe Mathes — the great Cardinal scout who was a regular lunch partner of Sam for decades.

Every bit as fascinating to me was a collection of four grey, narrow tin boxes that held even more treasures. Inside were typed 3x5 cards. One box was labeled "Kiel Auditorium Results" and held the results, attendance figures, and gross receipts of every card Sam had promoted at Kiel or The Arena since 1945. Another was labeled "Individual Wrestler Results from Kiel." In it, clipped together as needed, was the entire history of every wrestler in St. Louis. I could look up Lou Thesz and find a summary of all his local duels.

Yet another box was marked "Television Wrestling Results" and it had the taping dates, air dates, and results from every Channel 11 show beginning in 1959. Naturally, the fourth container was an individual breakdown of each wrestler and what he had done on St. Louis television.

After every Kiel or television session, I would update those incredible files, just as Sam had for years. I even started my own identical file system at home. It was not unusual to see Sam browse his files as booking decisions were made, just as I would in the future. At the start, however, I think my impossible mission was to try to memorize every result.

But that still wasn't all of Sam's riches. In beautifully bound leather covers were all of the "Wrestling" news pamphlets, in mint condition, from every single bill he had ever promoted. Since he had also been the 50% partner in the Thesz promotion during the mid-1950s, all of those programs were there as well. It's not surprising that once I started writing those pamphlets, I also had the material bound in volumes every three years, just like Sam.

It was wrestling heaven — I could pull out the 3x5 card that listed attendance and results, study pamphlets to understand angles and the development of the territory's booking, absorb the colorful writing and then look at a wrestler's record, to see how he earned his position and analyze where he went from there.

Jack Brisco said it best: "Nobody had records like Sam."

Unfortunately, years later, when the wrestling war that changed the game came to a head, with neither Sam nor I still actively involved, those tin boxes were apparently lost, never to be retrieved. Later, Sam would ask why I hadn't just taken the boxes with me — but I left them behind, feeling they belonged to the partners who remained. When the St. Louis Wrestling Club folded, the boxes must have been "misplaced" in the rubble.

Even worse, the bound office set of the "Wrestling" news also disappeared. Years later, I was told that someone had pulled off the binding, trying to remove pages to either sell or distribute. I still have two sets of my own work from 1970 through 1983 and Sam's children have another couple sets dating from 1945 — so, that part of wrestling history, at least, survives.

Sam had graciously given me access to this material from the start, but it could not be absorbed in a week. In fact, it probably took a few years to assimilate. Sam never actually sat down with me and said, "Larry, this is how wrestling works." To the contrary, on one quiet afternoon in the early 1970s, Sam spoke of his own indoctrination into the business. Like me, he had some knowledge from the outside and, having been close friends with the likes of Ray Steele, possessed an inkling of what truly took place. But when Sam worked for Tom Packs, nobody ever tried to describe every part of the incredibly complex operation.

"I think you'll be better off to learn wrestling like I did," Sam said. "I learned by osmosis. Just being around it, watching and listening and working, I figured out what was going on. Don't assume anything you hear is written in stone. Take it all in. Listen to the fans. See what works. See what draws. Try to understand why. Learn the politics.

"The wrestlers already like and respect you," he added. "Now the promoters are learning who you are and what you can do. Just let it all happen. That's the way I learned it, piece by piece."

And that's exactly what happened.

Bobby Shane with the original King's crown

TWO ST. LOUIS FAVORITES . . . JOE MILLICH AND BOBBY SHANE

From two very different generations, Joe Millich and Bobby Shane were both products of St. Louis wrestling. Another connection? Millich trained Shane to wrestle.

Joe Millich was the quiet result of local wrestling in the 1930s, and everyone who mattered knew him. Joe trained many a fine young grappler, none of whom made him more proud than Bobby. Though Millich never topped a program in St. Louis himself, by the time I was a regular on the scene I discovered the tremendous respect everyone had for him. Joe had wrestled almost everywhere, literally, in the world.

Lou Thesz called Joe Millich one of the toughest men he ever knew — no small praise, coming from Thesz. Millich understood that a part of wrestling was knowing how to hurt someone, and Thesz was the same way. Joe would sometimes roll himself up into a giant ball to ward off an attack. It was called the "turtle trick," and he would use it to lure a rival close so he could hook a leg or arm.

One later star who would come in early just to work out with Joe was "King Kong" Brody. Millich and Brody would go to the downtown YMCA and Joe would show Brody tricks of balance — or how to grab someone's hand or wrist and break a bone. To anyone who knew Joe personally, the capacity for such violence would come as a shock. He had a long relationship with Harry Cook's daughter Vernice, and they loved to take friends (including me and my wife) out to eat or to see St. Louis Blues hockey. Naturally, Joe liked the fights.

When Joe began wrestling, St. Louis was almost a factory for young talent. Sam truly liked him and knew very well what his background was. Whenever some young, self-important stud would call the office and demand a match, Sam would ask Millich to work out with the guy. Most were humbled quickly, as Joe loved to "pull necks." Since Joe essentially had none of his own — his skull seemed welded right on top of his burly shoulders — he had an advantage. Locking up, the newcomer would try to pull Joe's head. Nothing would happen. Eventually, Joe would push straight down on his opponent's head, mashing his chin into his chest. Soon the challenger would either throw up or pass out. Then Joe would begin the workout. Few came back, although Bobby Shane did — again and again — until he was ultimately just as tough as Joe.

Millich taught self-defense to the military during World War Two and was a close friend of boxing great Jack Dempsey. He had spent years wrestling in western Canada, where he became a believer in the famous Stu Hart "torture chamber." Many times I would go behind the giant steel curtain which led to the Opera House stage at Kiel just to have Joe show me some new hold or explain the leverage behind some move so I could discuss it intelligently on "Wrestling at the Chase." Early in my broadcasting career, Joe took me to the YMCA to demonstrate and describe almost every hold known to man. "I know you know what they're called, but you have to understand how they feel," he explained. Guess what? It hurt — even though Joe took it easy on me.

Joe, who never divulged his age, taught me another valuable lesson. "Don't ever call a wrestler a veteran," he said, smiling. "It means he's old. Why tell everyone that?" From that point on, ringwise and crafty became the words of choice for me.

Millich won millions in the Illinois State Lottery in the 1980s and wanted to back me, financially, to start a promotion to challenge what the WWF/WWE was becoming. But he was a friend. I just could not bring myself to let him do that.

When the business was in a terrible state, during the early 1990s, my opportunity had passed; Joe Millich collapsed and died while walking the track at the Missouri Athletic Club. His money didn't matter — we'd lost a friend who'd freely given his time and knowledge to those of us who cared about this wacky sport.

❄ ❄ ❄

A bright, exciting career was snuffed out in the tragic airplane crash that killed Bobby Shane in Tampa on February 20, 1975. Bobby's real name was Schoenberger — but he wasn't related to referee Joe. Bobby's parents Lee and Delores were longtime wrestling fans and two of the friendly folks I first met in the crew of regular ringside fans at Kiel during the mid-1960s.

At that time, Bobby was one of the seconds, taking wrestlers' ring garb back to the dressing room. He was a 1963 graduate of Southwest High School in St. Louis and had been a diehard wrestling fan almost from birth. Like me, he was a sponge for everything that happened in local rings. Plus, he was training with Millich and "Wild Bill" Longson to realize his fondest dream: becoming a professional wrestler.

Though he wasn't big — at best maybe 5-10 and 225 pounds — Bobby had the kind of instinct that can't be taught, honed to perfection by hours and hours of watching wrestling's greatest stars work in St. Louis. He quickly captured the attention of many promoters when he made his debut in 1967. I spent time with Bobby, preparing a big magazine story about him and getting pictures, and we shared our common backgrounds.

He had a terrific early run in St. Louis during the winter of 1968, with wins over Corsica Joe, Danny Dusek, Mike York, and The Viking. He also had the chance to pair with Edouard Carpentier and Pat O'Connor in tag bouts. His potential was obvious and limitless.

Shane's greatest success came later, in Florida and Georgia, where he gained a reputation as an inventive performer with great imagination. In what became a cliché by 1980, Bobby was one of the first to involve his lovely wife Sherry as a ringside valet.

Jack Brisco, in particular, was very high on his abilities and understanding of wrestling psychology. As many others would later emulate, Bobby came up with the idea of calling himself "The King" and wearing a crown to the ring in the early 1970s. When he left the country for a tour of Australia, he gave the idea — and his crown — to a young wrestler he liked. That matman was working prelims in Tennessee and Kentucky — his name was Jerry Lawler.

When Bobby came home to visit during the autumn of 1974, he quickly picked up on the local tension that always simmered between Sam and his Kansas City partners (who did not yet include Harley Race). The hard facts? St. Louis was the major league, in Bobby's eyes, while Kansas City was the farm system. He had promotional ideas of his own, by then, and we talked openly about someday working together in St. Louis.

"What will happen when Sam retires?" he asked. "What will you do if the partners try to turn this into Kansas City East? Things are going to happen here and you need to think about them."

He was a friend who anticipated the future. Who knows what might have happened had Bobby Shane survived?

"The Fabulous Flying Frenchman" Edouard Carpentier

*Gene Kiniski uses the back breaker on NWA World Champion
Jack Brisco, October 5, 1973*

CHAPTER 4

SAM & ME

Part II

A major part of my learning curve was understanding Sam Muchnick's booking philosophy. I soon realized that many other promoters looked at booking as a way to "swerve" the "marks" into buying tickets. In time, I became familiar with the little chuckle that said, "We fooled them with that match." Lou Thesz would certainly say it came from the old carnival mentality.

Promoters who would announce a main event they knew would never happen, in particular, made Sam irate. Sure, maybe some fans were fooled into buying a ticket, but to Muchnick, that was never cute, and never smart. Worse, in the long term it was bad for wrestling. The gambit characterized both dishonesty and incompetence — or at very least revealed a businessman who was too smart for his own good. If a promoter's own workers could not draw as headliners, it reflected badly on both the talent and on his booking. Even the best, most honest plans go awry in the real world, Muchnick reasoned, so why insult your bread and butter with unethical ploys?

When Thesz was called in to replace an injured Buddy Rogers in 1962, Sam had enough forewarning that he was able to place extra advertisements in both daily newspapers, in addition to having posters printed to announce the change at the box office. Similarly, when Johnny Valentine developed heart trouble and had to be replaced by Gene Kiniski the night before the show in 1973, Sam and I moved heaven and earth to notify everyone possible. And when Ric Flair dethroned "Dusty" Rhodes as champion in 1981 — which meant Flair and not Rhodes would risk the gold belt against Harley Race at a Checkerdome show fifteen days later — the "Wrestling" news was mailed the day of the title change. Of course, we knew what was coming. Nonetheless, Sam went to the extra expense of printing and mailing a separate notification to every "Wrestling" news subscriber *after* the switch actually happened. Further expense was incurred correcting and remastering the edition of "Wrestling at the Chase" for that weekend. Sam did all of this because that's what being honest and reliable to his audience required. In St. Louis, nothing happened in the world of wrestling until it actually happened — we never, ever let on what might be coming in the months ahead. We respected the fans — the goal was never to fool them, but to reward their loyalty.

Some promoters and bookers put so much time and thought into devising methods for getting out of an ongoing rivalry, especially when neither wrestler wanted to lose, that the actual feuds suffered, often to the point of becoming illogical. More and more, by the 1970s, this meant run-ins, ref bumps, and blown decisions. It led to a predictability, and fan dissatisfaction, that was also bad for business.

At the total opposite end of the spectrum as a promoter, Sam came from a pure sports background and operated accordingly. Everything needed to be logical and legit, just like a race for the National League pennant. A led to B — which resulted in C. Respect for the wrestlers' skill and the finish were paramount. In St. Louis, the "way out" was to have a winner and a loser. It was that simple.

From Sam, I learned that calling fans "marks" was disrespectful, a shameful way to refer to people who were helping to put food on your table. Of course, some people considered a "mark" a wrestling devotee or enthusiast. Most people in the business, though, spoke of "marks" with disdain.

To Sam's credit, I never once — not on a single occasion — heard him use the term. There were only fans, a crowd, or spectators. Because he respected the audience, he felt they deserved the kind of resolution that only comes with a clean finish.

Wrestling journalist Dave Meltzer once remarked, "Sam must have shuddered at the idea of a World Series ump taking a bump, or of the Dallas Cowboys interfering in a Super Bowl they hadn't reached. He understood how allowing this kind of thing cheapened his own product."

Because St. Louis treated championship matches with respect and care, they always meant something. Even the Missouri State Championship, right up to 1983, guaranteed a tremendous pop when it changed hands. When there was a respected title to shoot for — a real, meaningful championship — everything else fit together.

Sam also taught me to never make a big deal about one wrestler trying to cripple another. "Someone is going to win and someone is going to lose — the fans will be satisfied," he said. "Hopefully, nobody is going to be crippled, never wrestle again. If fans are led to expect that, they're set up to be disappointed. Don't lie to them."

Because of these basic booking principles, a single defeat did not mean the end for any one wrestler's main event potential. Obviously, a series of victories would lead to a crack at the crown. But losing to the champion was not the end of the road. In fact, a great performance in a losing effort could often make the disappointed challenger a bigger attraction. It was an ongoing battle, up and down the ladder that led to the penthouse.

"Hot shots" were extreme angles, often based on personal issues between wrestlers. Sam believed "hot shots" should be used with care. "Look at towns that always used the 'hot shot.' They burned out the fans and, pretty soon, their business was in the trash barrel," he explained. While personal issues were certainly part of the competition, Sam always insisted they occur within the context of chasing a championship as well.

Muchnick had complete confidence in his methods. One bad house did not change anything in the overall plan. Surprisingly, he was perfectly content with occasionally drawing only 5000 spectators. "Nobody can sell out 17 cards a year," he cautioned. "Sometimes you put new people in main events. Sometimes your partners believe a wrestler can draw money and — even if you disagree — you have to give them a chance to prove their point.

"The bottom line is that I'll give up a couple huge houses because I won't 'hot shot,' but that also means St. Louis won't have the terrible gates that usually come right after the 'hot shot.' By emphasizing wins and losses between top attractions, we'll get our sellouts without doing anything ridiculous. Some cities may draw more than us some years, but then they'll draw a lot less the next year. St. Louis is always steady and profitable, with plenty of sellouts."

The idea was: consistency mattered. Fans always needed to understand what was going on — we owed them that. Rocky Johnson and Dick Murdoch might meet because they had a brawl after being on opposite sides of a tag match. Maybe Ted DiBiase would clash with Ric Flair because they had both been winning and only one could challenge for the World Championship. There was a reason for every match he made, and it was spelled out for the fans.

Because St. Louis refused to impress and then ultimately numb audiences with "hot shots," when something out of the ordinary occurred, it was a big event. Sam was not impressed with the booker who fed his own ego by creating something bizarre. Accolades for spectacularly unique angles meant nothing; selling tickets was the goal. He emphasized the basics, done correctly, because those basics would draw crowds.

But of course this didn't rule out exploring new avenues. Then, as today, a common wrestling angle involves a tag team match where the popular team loses one partner due to injury, thus making it two-against-one. When another baby face runs in to help, and batters one of the heels, it sets the stage for a singles feud.

I suggested to Sam that we reverse the situation on the "Wrestling at the Chase" show for May 31, 1981. In this case, it was favorites Ted DiBiase and "Spike" Huber against J.J. Dillon and Benny Romeo. DiBiase used the figure four leglock to injure Romeo and put him out. Harley Race, who was then the World Champion and awaiting a challenge from DiBiase, came to ringside, wanting to take Romeo's place. This time the "bad guys" were getting the high-powered substitute.

Sam came from the control room and consulted with the referees. He checked his watch and, because there was time left in the limit, permitted the substitution. Eventually, Race and DiBiase were at it, hot-and-heavy. Sam loved the idea — because it made sense, because it was something different, and because it was also properly executed.

I'm sure bookers like Bobby Bruns and Pat O'Connor also came to Sam with ideas that he invariably loved, helped refine or, sometimes, simply refused. But there was always a context, a philosophy, that the action had to fit.

Long-term planning was vital. St. Louis dates at Kiel and The Arena were always contracted a year in advance. In addition, the champion's appearances were also inked nine months — or more — ahead. Sam taught me how to book in reverse. If Dick "The Bruiser" was the challenger we wanted for the April date, planning had to begin in January at the latest. Who would he meet in February and March? What angles could we pursue? Everything was planned backwards, from the inevitable conclusion to the very beginning of a rivalry, months in advance. By the time March rolled around, "The Bruiser" should be primed for some sort of showdown from which the winner could go after the title. But wrestling doesn't end in April — the champion would have another defense in June. Naturally, whoever was scheduled for that slot should be getting his own push by that same April card.

As I've said, a big match loss for "The Bruiser" in St. Louis didn't mean he'd be diminished or forgotten. To the contrary, there were many opponents he could and should meet after a championship defeat. A challenger's path to the top spot created many logical storyline branches — and in exploring them we'd create other strong challengers. This wasn't just practical booking; in Sam's eyes, it was wise resource management. We earned the trust and loyalty of the talent because they knew they wouldn't be tossed aside like yesterday's garbage. I remember many instances when Sam took the time to personally discuss the direction of a program with a key star months in advance, so he could understand he really was a part of the big picture.

How often do the Cardinals and Cubs play in any given season? Why should one defeat eliminate a wrestler from going after the title again? Because St. Louis fans saw prime talents winning and losing in exciting matches, they all continued to be strong drawing cards. Predicting a winner on one of our cards was seldom cut and dried — and because any outcome was plausible, because both heels and baby faces could win on any given night, there was always a very real tension.

Actually, it was so simple that it was difficult. Plan, plan, plan: as I got involved in booking, I learned to always use a pencil — because my eraser was going to get plenty of work.

The most important principle? Protect the World Championship — not the World Champion — at all costs. Okay, not every champ would be as charismatic as a Ric Flair or Lou Thesz, but if the title meant something special, the fans would come. This meant that the champion should not be overexposed. Each outing had to mean something. And cute finishes involving the gold belt had to be avoided at all costs. Because we treated it like the Holy Grail, everyone who had ever held the title would always be treated with respect.

Today, Sam's booking philosophy must seem alien. Unlike WWE, he believed in his long-term planning and felt that a solid product would always find its audience. Our fans wanted to believe in our little world for a couple of hours a week, so it was critical to respect them. Now, titles are regularly disrespected and former champions are easily relegated to mid-card status. Storyline directions are often changed in response to poor television ratings for a quarter-hour period.

When questioned by a skeptical reporter about how he decided who'd get a victory, Sam would always answer honestly. "The best man wins." What went unsaid was that Sam, like any good promoter, decided who the "best man" was. And that decision was based on ability, match quality, booking plots and, primarily, drawing power. It made for a very real and challenging situation for wrestlers.

A main eventer earned the most money — by far. And guys who had their hands raised got those positions. Talent had to both cooperate and compete. It is impossible to have a first-rate match alone and sharp observers can always spot someone who is failing to carry his share of the load.

Nick Bockwinkel explained his perspective on "doing a job" or losing: "I want my opponent to look great when he wins, and I want to look great. I want the crowd to get excited. That's my job, what I'm getting paid for. The trick is that, after the bell rings, you want the promoter to wonder if the right guy won."

In any major league promotion, the talent needs to believe that the promoter is giving everyone his fair crack at making money. Sam was one of the best at earning that trust from wrestlers. Jack Brisco said, "In St. Louis, everybody did jobs. If you didn't do jobs, you couldn't work for Sam."

Brisco himself, and Gene Kiniski, illustrate this. Jack won the NWA crown on July 20, 1973, in Houston. He had been a solid main event talent for a few years in St. Louis — but he had never beaten "Canada's greatest athlete."

When Brisco was scheduled to go over Kiniski on October 5 at Kiel, here's the record we were able to quote to fans: the challenger had defeated Brisco three times in excellent battles — September 19, 1969; September 8, 1972; June 15, 1973. Clearly, the new champ had become a terrific attraction without beating Kiniski, and those results helped draw a big crowd for his ultimate triumph. Something that had begun four years earlier, in the end, worked out just as it should because of Sam's long-term booking philosophy.

Muchnick always wanted a flexible core of six to eight matmen who could draw money against each other or the champion. Sam disliked the practice of focusing everything around a single superstar — feeding him one rival after another — although he would admit it had worked for several promoters. Sam believed that no single performer was indispensable. And because of this, in an extreme situation, no individual wrestler could ever hold the promotion hostage.

Besides, what's more fun? A run-away pennant race? Or a season where several teams can come out on top?

Generally, Sam wanted to build toward a showdown. Unlike contemporary "sports entertainment," where a match is announced and then the two combatants attack each other repeatedly prior to the actual event — in St. Louis a tag team affair or a special attraction would spark and tease a specific rivalry. The fans would get a taste of how thrilling the pairing might be, and they would eventually command a main event.

In addition, with this type of matchmaking, there was always room for a hungry young star to break in and be made. St. Louis was where the likes of John Paul Henning, Dory Funk, Jr., Jack Brisco, Ted DiBiase, David Von Erich, and Bob Backlund were all first established as big stars. Sam grasped the energy and fire a new personality brought to the promotion.

Muchnick particularly respected his most loyal fans. He knew St. Louis could depend on a minimum of 4000 customers per card, simply because it was the first town to have season ticket reservations for wrestling. He stressed how important it was to give season ticket holders their money's worth, even if a program had not drawn as well as everyone hoped. As Bill Longson once said, "The smaller the crowd, the harder you work."

And what do the following matches have in common, besides being famous St. Louis main events?

Gene Kiniski versus "Killer" Kowalski. Rip Hawk versus Buddy Rogers. Lou Thesz versus Pat O'Connor. Dick "The Bruiser" versus Fritz Von Erich. Dory Funk, Jr. versus Pat O'Connor. Jack Brisco versus Dory Funk, Jr. Ric Flair versus Harley Race.

Each battle was either heel versus heel or baby face versus baby face. There was no need to confuse the fans by concocting some bizarre plot to "turn" one wrestler for the sake of a particular outing. This happens all too frequently today, just as years ago it happened in many other towns. And with the proliferation, each character switch, of course, becomes less meaningful.

As well, those memorable duels were ultimately part of a quest for the championship, where one of the sport's best faced another. Sure, personal issues were exploited to heighten the drama, but for the most part, each of these stars was "himself" in the ring. Nobody was playing a cartoonish role.

Kurt Angle, an Olympic gold-medal winner and former WWE champion, would have been a huge star in St. Louis, much like Brisco was in his era. How much bigger could he be today if WWE writers had not flip-flopped his character a dozen times? Or if he had not been forced to wear a miniature cowboy hat in someone's idea of a comedic sketch? Could anyone imagine Brisco appearing like that on "Wrestling at the Chase"? Ironically, Jack maintains, "Of all the current wrestlers, the one I would most like to work with would be Angle. He's a tremendous talent."

Another thing those St. Louis classics had in common was that each rivalry eventually culminated in a clean decision in the middle of the ring. Still, the loser was not relegated to the lesser-paying preliminaries. To the contrary, everyone involved enjoyed countless big money features for years to come. Now, consider one other vital likeness: each main event drew a capacity crowd that was passionate and loud. Usually, the audience's support was split fairly evenly between the two combatants. The atmosphere was great: empty seats make no noise.

Then as now, wrestling was generally based on the idea of good versus bad — even in St. Louis. The concept of the very best competing, however, was much stronger in St. Louis than anywhere else. Four different individuals were involved in the booking over the long period I'm talking about — but the only real constant was the blueprint Sam Muchnick had established. It was simple, direct, and consistent.

The trick was getting the casual fans, whether they were lawyers, doctors, truck drivers, or teachers, to buy tickets. These folks might come out three or four times a year, but they were a big part of every sellout. To keep everyone of all interest levels involved, the "Why" behind each match had to make sense.

Naturally, the right characters had to be in place. Spotting legitimate stars is a skill, and Sam was one of the best. During my tenure, he was always open to suggestions from O'Connor, Race, other promoters, experienced hands — and even me. On numerous occasions, Sam would join me at the KPLR studio to check out a tape of someone he hadn't seen before — he was always that eager to get new blood on the undercard.

Nobody respected wrestlers more than Sam, either. He understood the rigors of being away from home and wrestling thirty nights in thirty different cities every month. Even though wrestlers were and are a tough breed, a body slam is a body slam: it jars internal organs and rearranges the spine. Making a match intense and exciting requires smart, snug, and physical action, particularly in St. Louis. There is always danger and most wrestlers compile long lists of injuries. Those who can "work" in this environment have truly mastered what Thesz called the "art form."

Sam was always a sucker for great performers. He saw Elvis Presley in Las Vegas and, though "the King" was not his thing, he was blown away by Presley's incredible mastery and effort. Muchnick, who had connections everywhere, met with the star after the show. "I told Elvis he was one of the very best I'd ever seen, and I'd seen Sinatra and many others," he gushed. Sam was also delighted to find that Elvis was a wrestling fan.

Some wrestlers believed that the way to "get over" with Sam was to take big bumps. To the extent that every promoter wants to see his audience screaming and excited, that was true. I'd be rich, however, if I had a dollar for every time Sam said, "I'm so tired of these guys doing the same thing, arm whip to the ropes and then a big back drop." Superior athletic ability was an obvious plus. For Sam, though, deciding who to put on top was based on even more demanding criteria — intangibles like charisma, psychology, and intensity. Based on attendance figures, St. Louis fans agreed with his assessments.

Gene Kiniski was a whirlwind, but how many big bumps did he take? What about "Killer" Kowalski, another relentless competitor? A big bump for Dick "The Bruiser" was dropping to one knee. The story behind a match was more important than high risk maneuvers.

Baron Von Raschke has his own take on big bumps. "Once I was partnered with Harley Race and Roger Kirby in a six-man tag bout," he recalled. "The baby faces made a comeback and Harley took a terrific bump. He tagged in Roger, who could really fly, and he went sailing.

"Roger tagged me in and said, 'There you go, big guy.' Whoever the opponent was whipped me to the ropes. I knew I couldn't fly like Harley and Roger had. So when he bent over to flip me, I kicked the guy in the head."

In 1975, Sam wrote in a special column for the "Wrestling" news, "You may be interested in knowing who my favorite wrestlers were during these years. Actually, I can honestly say I had no favorites. To me, the lowliest preliminary boy is as valuable as the biggest star and gate magnet. Before you get main eventers, you have to have the understudies and they, eventually, if they have the right kind of ability, graduate to the top rung. I have always appreciated the work of the men in the earlier matches as much as I did those who were in the features and received the big money."

Keep in mind, this came from a person who measured every single word he said or wrote, in addition to investigating every nuance of what someone said to him. Many times, in the office, I would get a call from some promoter while Sam was gone and we might chat a bit about what he wanted. Sam would always want to know *exactly* what was said, what the tone of voice was, what words were used. He was very sensitive to every personality and issue.

That really came into play when Dory Funk, Jr., then NWA champion, allegedly suffered a shoulder injury and face lacerations in a truck accident on February 28, 1973. Dory Jr. was scheduled to risk the laurels in St. Louis on April 6, but other political machinations were in motion. Funk had rung up a terrific record as champ since dethroning Kiniski on February 11, 1969, in Tampa. And though his drawing power had waned a bit and the range of plausible, exciting opponents was dwindling, he was still generating respectable gates. But after all, it had been four plus years.

It was time for Jack Brisco to become the new champion — he was scheduled to beat Funk in Houston on March 2, 1973. These kinds of decisions were typically made by the small Board of Directors of the NWA. Sam, of course, led the board and was highly influential — though the negotiations were serious, hardball, and often unsavory.

Before Dory Jr. was selected to replace Gene Kiniski in 1969, many NWA insiders anticipated that the prize would go to "Cowboy" Bill Watts, who had a terrific collegiate background in football and wrestling at Oklahoma. An intimidating powerhouse, Bill had drawn several big houses against Kiniski in St. Louis. Watts was also an established star in several territories. When it came to a vote, however, Sam recalled that Watts had only the support of Leroy McGuirk, the promoter in Tulsa. Dory Funk, Sr., Dory's father, had worked the politics beautifully and got the votes for his son. Sam himself was reluctant to go with the "Cowboy" because, he told me, "Watts is so big and powerful, I'm not sure anyone would believe he'd ever lose."

Sam understood that one of the reasons for Funk's initial box office success was that fans looked at him in a match and believed that the title would change hands. This kingpin just looked so young and vulnerable after the rugged dominance of Kiniski and Thesz. Dory Jr., however, matured into the role wonderfully.

At any rate, when he was finally asked to fall to Brisco in 1973 — and then became "injured" — many promoters assumed that Dory and his father were trying to delay the inevitable or pull some sort of power play. Dory Sr. had a reputation of being a tough manipulator, and he was reportedly unhappy about the idea of his son being dethroned. Sam was stuck in the middle of this, and for days our office phone never stopped ringing. The other promoters all had opinions, and most demanded some sort of official NWA action. A few wanted Dory Jr. unceremoniously ousted, saying he should simply forfeit the prize. Whether the "accident" which caused his injuries even occurred was eventually questioned. Sam broadly hinted that certain persons might well be trying to split the Alliance for personal gain, and he was clearly suspicious about what Dory Sr. was doing behind the scenes. If Funk's lobbying was successful and other promoters continued to recognize his son as champ, then they'd effectively control the world title.

In part, all of this suspicion and intrigue was simply the nature of professional wrestling. Trust was seldom the rule, and with good reason. As early as the 1920s, promoters had been matching their wrestler against someone else's star with the idea of stealing a decision, a championship, and maybe even a town. Similarly, for decades wrestlers had made excuses to avoid a situation where they would be bumped from a top spot.

Dory Jr. produced hospital photographs and a doctor's statement to verify his injuries. The powder keg still wasn't diffused. The NWA was a tense organization — and on top of that Sam also had to make sure his own town did not suffer. He himself sent subtle political signals in the way he booked the next few Kiel programs — if the NWA were to wobble or if other promoters were to leave to recognize their own champion, Sam wanted to demonstrate that he had the resources to survive and thrive on his own. Sam also wanted to let the wrestling world know that he was happy to do business with New York should the need arise. Bruno Sammartino, not the WWWF king at the time, but still solidly aligned with Vince McMahon, Sr., was brought in to headline the April 6 bill. He defeated Ivan Koloff, while Kiniski won by disqualification over the masked Invader in the co-feature. I listened as Sam called Vince Sr. and calmly and logically explained how important it was for Sam to have Bruno work in St. Louis. McMahon agreed immediately.

Sammartino, like Thesz, also fit the bill in terms of what Sam expected of a champion outside the ropes. A straightforward bear of a competitor inside the squared circle, Bruno was articulate and comfortable in a coat and tie. He was a welcome guest of Sam and Helen at dinner parties with, say, a sports editor at Ruggeri's.

On April 27, in front of 10,387 fans, Sammartino pinned and unmasked the Invader (who was Dick Murdoch) after a war waged inside a seven-foot high chain-link fence. Kiniski won the other main event, when special referee Joe Louis (that's right, one of the greatest boxers who ever lived was an official for Sam) disqualified Race for jumping off the top rope.

Finally, the NWA, through Sam, and with me furiously typing his words, announced their official position: Dory Jr. should not attempt to wrestle until his doctors had given him a clean bill of health. Still, the Funks were angry that Dory Jr.'s injuries were publicly questioned.

Kiniski and Race squared off in a no disqualification duel on May 18 with 8138 in attendance. The Canadian won. Sammartino continued his winning streak by topping Rip Hawk. Brisco fought to a 30-minute draw with Terry Funk in a special attraction.

Finally, Dory Jr. was able to compete. In Kansas City on May 24, only days after returning to action, his reign ended when he was defeated by none other than Race. Why Harley? Why Kansas City?

Sam told me about the switch on the afternoon of the 24th and I recall him saying, "Dory won't be leaving Kansas City as the champion." First, the date was the earliest the NWA felt they could do the switch. Second, the Funks had a long and close relation with Race and Kansas City promoters Bob Geigel and Gust Karras. Finally, the K.C. faction (at the time Geigel, Karras, and Pat O'Connor) were all minority partners in St. Louis with Sam.

Had there really been a problem with Dory, it is likely that a version of the WWF's notorious Montreal screwjob would have occurred. Instead, Dory was the consummate professional and the strap went to Harley — for a moment.

This, in turn, made it possible for Race to face Sammartino in St. Louis on June 15. Once more, Sam and KPLR went to the expense and headache of having me announce the change after a duel between Bruno and Dory had been promised on TV. Race and Sammartino battled to a fabulous one-hour stalemate, with Lou Thesz as the special referee. Kiel was jammed, with 10,043 fans.

The final chapter to this whole story came when Brisco flattened Race in Houston on July 20, 1973. Sam was on hand that night to present Brisco with a new, expensive, gold title belt that replaced the one that had been in use since 1959. Race's reign had lasted exactly 57 days — at the time, the third shortest tenure in NWA history.

When all was said and done, Sam had somehow guided the NWA through a tumultuous situation *and* emerged unscathed. One unfortunate consequence was the end of a longtime friendship between Dory Sr. and Eddie Graham. Graham was a strong backer of Brisco, who recalled that "Eddie and Dory Sr. became bitter enemies after what happened." Dory Sr. passed away, suddenly, not long after the controversy.

I can vouch for the fact that Sam was often skeptical and angry about the business. Never anyone's fool, he always knew the truth. Outside the office or on the telephone, however, he was a voice of calm and reason.

As it turned out, both Dory Jr. and his brother Terry (who also had a solid title run, which he began by beating Brisco on December 10, 1975, in Miami) were involved in many terrific championship matches with Brisco and Race over the next few years. In addition, Harley earned a lot of respect and thanks for the way he dealt with the tensions of 1973. This ultimately played a part in the decision for him to take the crown from Terry on February 6, 1977, in Toronto.

In '73, I was still a fringe player, intently observing Sam handle a tremendously stressful situation. Clearly, he'd sent a message to some unstable promoters by booking Sammartino. At the same time, he was indicating something to the wrestlers involved — at the very least, he had the resources to do superb business with or without the NWA champion. Somehow, when the dust settled, the Funk reputation was restored and the Alliance was intact.

There was always something going on in the early 1970s. At the suggestion of Ted Koplar (Harold's son) and Sam, I began my television career as a regular guest commentator on "Wrestling at the Chase" with George Abel on February 12, 1972. Eventually, George was bumped for Sam Menacker, and I became the "color" commentator. After paying my on-camera dues — just like a young wrestler inside the ring — on October 13, 1973, I was finally on my own. Mickey Garagiola became my sidekick.

The director's position, by the way, alternated between Ted and Jim Herd, who later became a part of World Championship Wrestling under Ted Turner and WTBS.

On August 18, 1972, Sam made me ring announcer for cards at Kiel Auditorium and The Arena. Standing in the middle of that ring at Kiel, I finally understood the adrenalin rush that every performer feels. Just the way the crowd would react to my every inflection was overwhelming. The response a star received as he stepped out of the dressing room and began the long walk to the squared circle was humbling.

On my first night out there was a double main event: Brisco pinned Race and Kiniski downed "Cowboy" Bob Ellis. When Kiniski got into the ring for his bout, he growled, "Having fun yet?" Von Raschke also acknowledged me when he entered for a tag match (Raschke and "Moose" Cholak lost to Rufus R. Jones and Pat O'Connor) — by bouncing off the ropes, lifting his claw hand to within a foot of my face, and winking. Dick "The Bruiser" welcomed me by chasing me out of the ring after he won by disqualification over "Black Jack" Mulligan (Bob Windham).

In those days fans also heard my voice on the 24-hour wrestling "hotline" we ran out of the office of the St. Louis Wrestling Club. I would update the message almost daily, usually by adding or describing bouts for the upcoming Kiel card. Ticket information was also provided. And reminders were made about the broadcast schedule of "Wrestling at the Chase." After every Kiel card, my wife and I would return to the office and record the results, with a more detailed description of what had happened in the features.

When the title changed hands, I would rush to the office as soon as Sam notified me. Remember, in wrestling something hasn't happened until it happens! Not only would I change the "hotline" message, but I'd make calls to our various media outlets. At the same time, Sam would notify NWA members and send telegrams to the national press services.

Even today folks come up to me and say, "I called 231-7487 on Friday nights. The line was always busy and it took forever to get through to find out what had happened at Kiel." The line eventually became so busy that the telephone company finally insisted we add an extra machine and line.

The wrestling office and "hotline" moved as hotels around St. Louis closed. The Claridge, once a beautiful place that relied heavily on the railroad business at Union Station a few blocks away, fell on hard times when I started working fulltime for Sam. He always liked the idea of a hotel office — the talent could stay close and someone was always on duty at the desk to take messages or receive video tape shipments, 24 hours a day. Also, I think because of his days traveling with the Cardinals, Sam just liked hanging out in fancy lobbies.

The office revolved around Sam, "Wild Bill," and me — O'Connor was only in town on wrestling weekends. Sam had been in the Claridge at 18th and Locust for 27 years, but it had become special to me too. It was the scene of my first meeting with Sam. It was also where I saw Sweet Daddy Siki carrying a purse, something unheard of in that era. And nobody at the hotel dared ask him about it.

The Claridge was where my wife Pat first met "Cowboy" Bob Ellis. Afterward, still shocked by the huge and numerous scars on Ellis' damaged forehead, she said, "If he even squints, he's going to bleed!"

"Wild Bill" Longson once hustled me out of the Claridge's restaurant so our regular day-of-card dining companion O'Connor, who had gone to the restroom, was left to finally pick up a tab. (Pat was notoriously tight with a dollar.) Of course, we peeked back in to watch O'Connor looking for us with dismay. Longson could not stop laughing.

Naturally, Sam did not want to leave the Claridge. But we eventually found an excellent spot in the Warwick Hotel at 15th and Locust, only a couple blocks from Kiel. We were the second last to leave: the only remaining resident was a dancer from a club on DeBalivere strip! The Claridge was boarded up within a week and eventually flattened.

The Warwick was our home from February 1973 until September 1980, when it was wrecked for the construction of a new bank. The office was actually a small, three-room apartment overlooking the corner. But oh, the memories.

Off the lobby was a lounge where many wrestlers and fans congregated after the cards. One night we met Andre the Giant coming out of the elevator as we were about to go up to our second floor space. Andre was drinking two beers, one in each hand — he had a large capacity. Suddenly, an excited fan ran into the lobby and yelled, "Some guys are trying to start a fight with the wrestlers!"

I decided to try to diffuse the situation, but Andre rumbled, "Let me go, boss."

Andre waved his beer bottles and I followed. "The Giant" was roughly seven feet tall and at the time weighed more than 400 pounds — everybody turned to look when he entered the lounge, including the rednecks who were stirring the trouble.

Andre slammed his beer bottles on the bar. It sounded like a rifle had been fired. "Who wants to fight?" he roared.

Dead silence.

The door to the lounge opened, three guys left, and everyone went back to socializing like nothing had happened. Andre smiled at me and chuckled, "See, boss. No problem."

On January 27, 1978, Ric Flair had his first ever St. Louis main event; he beat Dory Jr. It was a brutal night, only twelve degrees outside after a nine-inch snowfall. On top of that, Flair had taken a tumble over the top rope and cracked his head on the sturdy wooden steps. A chunk had been carved from his scalp and blood poured down his face.

Flair, Dick Murdoch, my wife, and I walked back to the Warwick together. We were all bundled to the hilt, except for Flair, who did not even wear a coat, because he thought it kept him from looking sharp. We were trudging through snow up to our shins and leaning forward against a stiff north wind. Murdoch never let up on Flair: "You duffus, you're from Minnesota. Didn't you learn to wear a coat in a blizzard?

"When you cracked your head open, I thought it would knock some sense into you!" Dick shouted. Flair just laughed.

Back at the hotel, Ric refused to go for stitches despite the recommendation of the doctor, who just happened to be Sam's son, Dick Muchnick. "They'd have to shave my hair," he said, shaking his long, blond locks. "Can't have that happen to the 'Nature Boy.' It'll heal." There was no messing with the man's image.

On another journey back to the Warwick from Kiel, on May 27, 1977, my wife and I were escorting The Fabulous Moolah (Lillian Ellison), possibly the most famous of all lady grapplers. One block north of the auditorium was a grassy, tree-laden area. We heard some noise and there was Jack Brisco, ready to annihilate some drunken fan who, apparently, had said the magic word, because Jack was always composed, professional, and friendly.

I rushed over, because it really was a no-win situation for any wrestler.

"Jack, it's okay. He's an idiot. Let him go. Relax," I urged. But Jack was steaming and had the guy by the throat.

Suddenly, there was The Fabulous Moolah. She reached out, softly stroked Jack's arm, and cooed, "Jack, honey. It's fine. Moolah loves you, baby."

Brisco burst out laughing, released the fool, picked up his bag, and walked with us to the Warwick. Somewhere in St. Louis, there's a drunk who owes his well-being to The Fabulous Moolah.

When the Warwick went down, in September 1980, the wrestling office moved to the Lennox at 9th and Washington. By then, I'd also lost the companionship of "Wild Bill" Longson. With his health failing, he sold his stock in the St. Louis Wrestling Club to Verne Gagne, with Sam's approval. Bill passed away that December.

Once more, we proved to be a jinx. The Lennox closed suddenly, in February 1981. And again, we were the last to leave. In fact, the Lennox was officially locked up before our departure. I became good buddies with the security guard — we were the only ones around for weeks.

Our final move was, surprisingly, to the Chase Hotel. (Why didn't we go there sooner?) The "hotline" got a new number (361-6870) which caused no little confusion among loyal followers. We actually had two rooms (one for Sam, one for me) this time, though they weren't connected. Still, we turned both those offices into wrestling showcases. Sam had the older stars and photos of his sellouts on his wall. I had the more current standouts in action shots, mostly taken by a young Roger Deem from Jacksonville, Illinois — with many more snapped by Mike Gratchner and Wayne St. Wayne.

It was not long after wrestling had left the Chase that the hotel itself was nailed by our jinx. It closed for several years, until finally being renovated and reopened in spectacular fashion in 2000. Actually, when the promotional war of 1983 broke out, my office was one floor above the old St. Louis Wrestling Club.

Mickey Garagiola and I were just as engrossed as the fans

HE'S ONE OF A KIND . . .
MICKEY GARAGIOLA

Everybody remembers Mickey. He was a big part of the public face of wrestling in St. Louis.

And what a genuine character! His younger brother Joe was Sam's first announcer on "Wrestling at the Chase," while Mickey was the ringleader of a hyper group of waiters at the legendary Ruggeri's restaurant on the Hill. Every evening Mickey joked, needled, teased, and generally entertained the patrons, which usually included the upper echelon of the sports community, and often Muchnick.

Mickey took care of the wrestlers who came in. To this day he remembers how "Johnny Valentine always had us put extra garlic on his steaks. Usually, he'd ask for even more garlic. He had to stink of garlic in that ring! How could anyone wrestle him?"

Another of Mickey's favorites was Longson: "I grew up with 'Wild Bill' and Ray Steele as my favorite wrestlers. It was a thrill to meet Bill, because he was a great guy and liked cigars as much as me!"

In 1969, Sam invited Mickey to visit a taping of "Wrestling at the Chase." Then, Sam handed Mickey a set of 3x5 cards with wrestlers' names and weights written on them. "You're my ring announcer," Sam told him. I got the job for Kiel and Arena cards, following in the footsteps of Johnny Curley and Eddie Gromacki, because Mickey couldn't take the time off from Ruggeri's or, later, Pietro's, on Friday evenings.

Mickey left with me in the wrestling rebellion of 1983. I started my own St. Louis promotion when the St. Louis Wrestling Club fell into disarray after Sam's retirement. Mickey had become a true friend, loyal and honest. I remember advising him to stay with the established company, since there was certainly no guarantee mine would survive. Mickey said, "Where you go, I go."

Mickey became renowned for fleeing the announcer's table whenever someone like Dick "The Bruiser," "King Kong" Brody, or Dick Murdoch zeroed in. He'd catch sight of one of the combatants taking a glimpse at the table and that was it. As I was broadcasting, I could see Mickey's right foot slip off the platform, just moments before mayhem descended upon the table. Mickey looked like a sprinter ready to leave the blocks for a 100-yard dash toward Lindell Boulevard.

Someone once asked him why he didn't take the ring bell with him. "The bell isn't mine. Let somebody else save it," Mickey responded.

"The Bruiser" took joy in feinting at and threatening Mickey. Once Dick made a hasty stop, just inches in front of Mickey's face: an audible "Don't hurt me!" was broadcast through his mic. Another time, as "The Bruiser" was being introduced before tackling a particularly annoying foe, Dick grabbed Mickey's glasses.

"Dick, I can't read the cards!" Mickey yelped.

"Don't worry," barked "The Bruiser," carefully putting on Mickey's glasses and then attacking his surprised foe. After tossing the chap from the ring, "The Bruiser" brought the glasses back and placed them on Mickey's nose.

"See," Dick said, "I told you not to worry."

Once Mickey took Murdoch and Gene Kiniski out to eat after a Kiel show. On the way back to the hotel, a rowdy group of maybe twenty delinquents flipped rather unflattering hand gestures at the crew in Mickey's car. Murdoch, angrily trying to open the door, yelled, "We'll get out and whip your butts" — with a few more "specific" adjectives thrown in.

Mickey put the pedal to the metal. Kiniski said, "Oh, hell, Dickie and I would've handled it. You could have stayed in the car."

I remember fondly a time when Mickey thought he had gotten himself fired. A red-hot tag team duel pitting Ted DiBiase and Paul Orndorff against then-World Champion Harley Race and "Bulldog" Bob Brown had just ended with a stunning turn of events as DiBiase pinned Race. But of course, the champion cannot lose his title in a tag team match. Mickey, though, was so caught up in all the hysteria in the studio that he announced: "The *new* World Heavyweight Champion . . . Ted DiBiase." Race was on his knees, screaming, "No, Mickey, no!"

I quickly asked the director to switch directly to me, rather than cutting to a commercial break. I explained that Race was still the champion and remarked on Mickey's excitability. At that moment, none other than Sam Muchnick came running to our table; he tried to crawl across me to yell at Mickey about the mistake.

Mickey was totally distraught, but Sam calmed down and forgave him. The truth became pretty clear after the show was telecast — St. Louis knew Mickey was honest. Once in awhile he garbled a name or announced the wrong hometown. He's human. It's part of what has always endeared him to fans. What happened in the Race-DiBiase situation was completely, totally unrehearsed and unexpected. Mickey had done what most of the fans would have done themselves in the same predicament. And it made DiBiase's pin of Race much more than just another result.

To this day, when DiBiase comes to St. Louis and sees Mickey, he says, "Thanks for making me the World Champion, Mickey!"

Even Race later laughed, "It made for a hell of an hour of television."

What probably made Mickey happiest about "Wrestling at the Chase" was the effect it had on viewers who were elderly or ill and watching from hospitals or homes. They jeered, cheered, laughed, and momentarily forgot their plight. Few people ever knew how much Mickey cared about the disabled and handicapped, or how much time and effort he gave to helping them. He sought no reward or recognition. It was just the right thing to do.

The celebrity "Wrestling at the Chase" brought was something Mickey truly enjoyed: "Even today people come up to me and remember what I did on 'Wrestling at the Chase.' That makes you appreciate the impact wrestling had on this town. Anyhow, everybody's got a little ham in them — and I got a big one."

He still enjoys nothing more than a giant cigar and the chance to gab about baseball, politics, and wrestling with his buddies on the Hill. For my money, and I mean every penny, there is not a better human being in the St. Louis community than Mickey Garagiola.

Pre-blond, future Governor Jesse Ventura arm locks Don Diamond during a Kiel tag bout on August 11, 1978

Sharing a laugh with "Giant" Baba in the Checkerdome dressing room, February 11, 1983

CHAPTER 5

SAM & ME

PART III

No matter where the office was, Sam Muchnick had one routine he never altered. When a bill came in the morning mail, Sam had the payment sent out by lunch. If Sam was out of town, he left me signed checks and explicit instructions: pay immediately or sooner. It's a telling indicator — Sam did simple things to earn respect. He wanted to be sure that the businessmen who looked down on wrestling in general could not feel the same way about his operation.

Similarly, every canceled check and check stub was rushed to our meticulously honest accountant, Richard Kawanishi, for the end of each month. Every bill was also turned over, so a detailed monthly statement could be given to all of the partners. Not a penny of what passed through the wrestling office went unaccounted.

Joe Failoni, once the manager of Kiel, teased Sam because guarantees for dates were always sent in three or four shows ahead of schedule.

"Sam, you can wait until one show is over before sending the guarantee for the next date. It's not necessary to have money here three cards in advance. I trust you," Failoni, a jovial character, would say.

Muchnick would shake his head and answer, "I don't do business that way." It's part of the reason no one had more respect in St. Louis — and why that respect eventually transferred to wrestling itself.

As time passed, I also continued to learn valuable lessons about booking; one that really stuck came when the Missouri State Championship was created. After the Kansas City group, specifically Gust Karras, Bob Geigel, and Pat O'Connor, got stock in the St. Louis Wrestling Club, Sam agreed to recognize a regional title for the first time, and Harley Race was announced as the Central States Champion.

The first time Race defended the prize was in a special attraction against Ronnie Etchison at The Arena on April 2, 1971. The main event that evening was a fence match between NWA king Dory Funk, Jr. and "Black Jack" Lanza.

Harley successfully defended the Central States belt throughout 1971, though it was obvious to me that Sam was very uncomfortable with how the situation was being handled. What really put Sam over the edge was when O'Connor defeated Race for the title on "Wrestling at the Chase" on January 15, 1972, and then bested him again in a rematch at Kiel on February 4.

The problem was this: in the Kansas City territory, Race was still defending the championship. Sam hit the roof and instructed me to write an article for the "Wrestling" news that explained he was withdrawing recognition of the Central States title and considering the creation of a Missouri State Championship.

Sam instructed O'Connor to put together a tournament which could be televised and climax with the first Missouri State king being crowned. Unfortunately, this led to even more frustration. The tourney began fine on March 18, as Jerry Brisco (Jack's younger brother), Johnny Valentine, and "Cowboy" Bill Watts all won matches.

Then things fell apart — mostly because of poor planning. Pak-Son won tournament bouts two straight weeks. Then, over the next month, Race was the victor in four more contests. Only Jerry Brisco, of the original winners, was involved in a loss. Finally, a few shows went by where no tourney matches took place. Sam told O'Connor to get things moving. A match was thrown together in which Race pounded poor, unknown Tom Demarco. Valentine was given a reason to drop out of the competition; he was getting ready to face Dory Jr. for the NWA honor.

By September 1972, a Missouri State Champion still had not emerged.

The title belt, beautifully crafted by Reggie Parks, was ready and waiting. Sam gave the order: that's it! Finish it on September 16. Watts had become more involved with his own promotion in Oklahoma-Louisiana and simply had no time to appear. A forfeit was announced so Race and Pak-Son could clash in the final. Race won and became the first Missouri State Champion.

To his credit, Race was involved in a string of excellent battles and important victories that put the Missouri State Championship on the map as something legitimate. Harley was a fantastic worker — at that point in his career doing moves that were often copied and which are wrestling staples even to this day. Harley was one of the first to popularize the diving head butt (remember Harley when Chris Benoit does it) and the delayed suplex (which today everyone seems to use in some form).

Sam was protective of the Missouri championship belt. No wrestler ever kept the strap with him. It was always in the office and brought to the card by either me or Bill Longson. The champion gave us the belt back at the end of the show.

Why? Sam was afraid that a grappler might literally lose or misplace the belt. Or, far worse, he might be convinced to use the Missouri crown in some crazy angle in another territory.

This system did lead to a night of crisis on March 3, 1978. Dick Murdoch was defending the Missouri laurels against Dick "The Bruiser." Somehow Bill and I crossed signals and the belt never made it to Kiel. At the start of the 15-minute intermission before the main event, Dick came to me searching for the belt.

Panic! Ray Lauer, then the sergeant who handled our police contingent, came to my rescue. Luckily, since it was a cold and snowy night, Ray had parked his squad car by the stage door entry. With red lights blazing, we rushed to the Warwick Hotel. I ran up the steps to grab the belt. Ray hurried me back to Kiel and nobody knew a thing when Murdoch, the belt secure on his waist, strutted to the ring.

Maybe the loudest crowd I ever heard was gathered on January 19, 1973, to witness Johnny Valentine defeat Race and become the second Missouri State Champion. Valentine had a long-standing feud with Harley, and over the years had come close to taking the NWA title from the likes of Thesz and Rogers. At the time, I'm sure most fans believed Valentine would never win a major championship.

But when Johnny dropped the brainbuster on Race for the victory, 10,750 fans blew the roof off Kiel. I could not even hear my own dramatic announcement about the title switch. But when I yelled the words, "The new Missouri State Champion . . . Johnny Valentine," the roar somehow became even louder. Valentine, a master showman, stood and stared at the throng. For almost five minutes, the din built towards an unbelievable crescendo.

No fireworks. No confetti. No music. Just raw emotion. Every fan standing, screaming! I was deaf for hours.

Understandably, after the entire Missouri championship headache and with what occurred just a few months later between Valentine and Terry Funk, Sam was beginning to lose faith in Pat's ability to "color within the lines." It certainly made it easier for me to carefully, tentatively go to Sam with a two or three show program of bouts. He'd smile, then relate how he had done something similar 25 years earlier or make a small but vital suggestion. Eventually he said, "Show this to Pat. Talk to him about some of these ideas."

For me, it was another part of paying my dues. And obviously I was the beneficiary of Sam's grooming as I got my feet wet as a booker. But for O'Connor, it had to be unsettling. Pride was involved; that's simple human nature.

Pat was on the downside of a remarkable in-ring career. His future — booking and promoting — was in the office. Getting input from a non-wrestler, particularly one as young as I was (even though we got along well), must have rankled. It was probably difficult for him to accept that someone who had not been in the ring could evaluate talent — although it had certainly been done before, by Sam and a few others.

When it comes to identifying star power, a grappler's experience alone is not enough. A gifted wrestler like O'Connor can assist a young talent with many aspects of his performance, but only enough to make it smooth and workmanlike. That's certainly crucial, but. . . .

To become the kind of magnet that draws money and establishes an emotional tie with the audience, a wrestler needs an almost indefinable mixture of charisma, ability, timing, and intensity. No gimmick, and no instruction, can make someone potent enough to lure fans, especially the casual followers who are only hooked by someone truly special.

Suppose it were left up to a panel of wrestlers, with no other background or scouting ability, to spot star quality. They'd be hard-pressed to find enough great attractions to sell out even a medium-sized hall. Discovering the next hot headliner takes more than just in-ring experience (although it certainly can help).

In fact, it's the fans — men and women who never ever step into a ring — who make stars. The best promoters and bookers are like the general managers of championship teams, architects with a gift for unearthing and fitting together unique performers. In wrestling, that architect might have mat experience, or he might just be someone who has immersed himself in the intricacies of the game. Sam Muchnick never took a bump in his life, but he was among the best of the best at spotting performers with that rare, almost mysterious "it" factor. Because of his success, I got my opportunity.

Pat O'Connor must have felt additional pressure. He was tied, financially, to Kansas City, and he wanted to give talent from that office as much of a boost as possible. While I recognized the benefits of having that cluster of talent on hand, my only goal was to put the best on top — regardless of where they were from. That was the St. Louis way.

O'Connor also at times struggled with scheduling. Putting together television tapings and juggling air dates and house shows was complex, and details did not always come easy for him. Ultimately, watching Terry Funk batter Johnny Valentine with a chair in front of the referee made Sam doubt Pat's judgment. Nonetheless, O'Connor put on a good face, and we talked regularly. More and more, I saw ideas I'd proposed creep into the final product. And by 1979, I was officially working with Pat on the booking. Harley Race became a partner at that time, buying up the late Gust Karras' stock. Sam had no foreknowledge of what the Kansas City group planned, and he was perturbed by the ownership change. The partnership agreement should have given him veto power over any stock sale. He was not angry that the new partner was Harley, *per se*, but rather that the deal opened the door for more input from Kansas City. Karras had been a quiet partner; Race would push for more K.C. involvement.

Since Sam never employed a St. Louis stable, a central crew of wrestlers, he always felt it was wise to have partners with ties to different promotions. Kansas City made sense, originally, because it was close geographically and could economically help fill an undercard. And while he believed he could have gone to court to block the transfer of stock to Race, Sam did not want to inundate the business with more legal wrangling. He also didn't want to squeeze the Karras family financially — he'd liked Gust. Still, what happened convinced Muchnick to keep a much tighter reign on the sale of "Wild Bill" Longson's stock in the St. Louis Wrestling Club.

Harley eventually exerted a general influence, but his own travel schedule meant that he did not sway card-to-card developments. Naturally, he was most concerned about his own matches and finishes.

Pat liked to make the calls to promoters when we were booking dates for various wrestlers, but everyone knew of the role I now played. Later, when O'Connor ran into some personal problems, I had the honor of booking St. Louis solo. "Bulldog" Bob Brown became our dressing room representative while I was occupied with television commentary or Kiel ring announcing.

At the time, I also began doing some traveling, getting a first-hand look at how other promotions conducted business in the process. I even helped Geigel and O'Connor in Kansas City, doing some TV work when their regular commentator, Bill Kersten, was unavailable. I soon realized K.C. ran a hard-working, if unimaginative ship. It was a good place to get experience, but they simply did not generate the gates to pay superstars like St. Louis. Again, it was clear, as Bobby Shane said, "Kansas City is minor league and St. Louis is major league." Still, this always bothered Sam, who believed Kansas City was a good town, and that it could do comparable business if it were promoted correctly.

Similarly, when Gene Okerlund was unavailable, I traveled to Minneapolis and Winnipeg, Canada, to do play-by-play and interviews for Verne Gagne and his partner, Wally Karbo. Those trips were great fun; Karbo was a dear friend of Sam's, and he had a whole new catalogue of wrestling stories for me. I was Wally's seat mate for one long flight, and the trip resulted in some serious abdominal pain — his tales were absolutely hilarious and I laughed for two hours straight. Wally also introduced me to some interesting variations on the booking patterns I had learned from Muchnick. He was a very smart and entertaining personality.

One trip to the Twin Cities was distinguished by some interesting behavior from none other than Jesse Ventura, who years later would become the Governor of Minnesota. I'd become pals with Ventura when he was doing prelims in St. Louis and breaking into the sport on the Kansas City circuit. In fact, one of Jesse's earliest television interviews came on "Wrestling at the Chase" on August 30, 1975. Somehow the pace of the show had been messed up, leaving a couple extra minutes at the end of the final bout. I suggested grabbing the outspoken Ventura for an interview, promising Sam that if Jesse froze I'd ask a 90-second question.

So, did he freeze? No way! Jesse was sensational. He was a natural on the mic. Three years later, when "The Body" was starting to click as an attraction, he passed through St. Louis again; the interview we did on August 26,

1978, proved Jesse Ventura had become one of wrestling's most colorful and charismatic characters.

Traveling to help Gagne in 1981, I was seated next to Jesse, waiting for a flight from Minneapolis to Winnipeg to depart. Ventura had developed into one of Verne's top attractions but took a moment away from playing "air guitar" to complain to me about being underpaid. His anger built as our departure neared. When Verne finally boarded the plane, Jesse suddenly rose.

"Verne, you been f---ing me on the payoffs," he snapped. "That's it. I quit!"

Ventura grabbed his bags. Imagine the reaction of other passengers as this 6-4, 275-pound muscular blond giant stormed off the flight.

Shaking his head, Verne plopped in the now vacant seat next to me.

"That's Jesse," he shrugged. "He'll be back."

And in a couple of days he was.

Gagne was another fascinating personality. He had been one of the finest amateur wrestlers ever and a Hall of Fame professional. Among those who made the sleeper hold famous, Verne was a star on nationally televised cards in the early 1950s. He was always hunting for successful athletes, preferably wrestlers, to lure into the professional game, and he helped train many superb talents, including Ric Flair, Ken Patera, Jim Brunzell, Baron Von Raschke, and his own son Greg.

Gagne, too, presented a classy image. Like Sam and Wally, he was at ease with all segments of society. A trip to Minneapolis always meant sharing the best seats at hockey games and dinner at a swank country club. And when Verne was engaged in other business, it was Wally who'd make sure I ate at the best steak house in Winnipeg. The day's top stars liked working for Verne and Wally because the money was good, the travel was tolerable, and their shows packed houses in major cities like Chicago, Omaha, Milwaukee, and Denver. Some grapplers apparently clashed with Verne in the kind of battle of egos typical of the sport, but those problems seldom outweighed the benefits of being associated with his promotion.

In the end, Sam lived with the fact that Gagne and Karbo had created the American Wrestling Association and recognized their own World Champion. The truth was, it made the incredible travel schedule of the NWA titleholder a bit more bearable. Still, when they broke away in the late 1950s, it was an emotional, heated time. As usual, Sam found a way to finesse the situation and keep everyone satisfied, if not happy. Over time, AWA talent became a regular feature of the St. Louis lineup.

Sam was quite satisfied when Verne bought out Bill Longson's stock in the St. Louis Wrestling Club in 1979. In fact, he engineered the deal. Sam had considered talking to Fritz Von Erich or, believe it or not, Vince McMahon, Sr., before concluding that Verne was the best fit. Verne had occasionally stepped into what were perceived as other promoter's towns — most notably San Francisco and Los Angeles — but somehow peace had always been restored. And while the Kansas City faction was unhappy, Sam correctly believed that having Verne as a partner would make top-notch talent even more available to St. Louis. Ironically, when Vince McMahon, Jr. began his drive to create a national promotion, one of his rationalizations was that if he didn't, Gagne would. Vince Jr. lobbed an early bomb in the war by raiding Verne's talent — not only in the ring, but also among his television staff.

Naturally, another notable trip for me was to New York, for a visit with Vince McMahon, Sr. himself. It was standard practice for us to trade programs with other promotions, which often led to new ideas or twists on storylines someone else had successfully explored. Paul Boesch in Houston and Eddie Graham in Tampa were influential, and so was McMahon. I had explained our method of taking season ticket reservations and sending the "Wrestling" news to our fans in many conversations with Vince Jr. and Howard Finkel (who eventually became Vince Jr.'s right hand man). Vince Jr. was, in fact, doing play-by-play for the then-WWWF television, the same role I played on "Wrestling at the Chase." We were two of the youngest, if not the youngest, announcers in the country. Vince and Howard had an idea or two that I adopted for St. Louis as well.

In 1982, I flew to New York to see a Madison Square Garden show and the WWWF taping sessions in Allentown, Pennsylvania. I was also there to do an interview with Andre the Giant that would air in St. Louis. The entire trip was educational. Vince Sr. explained that he maintained a solid line between office and talent, and that he expected both factions to respect each other. He also talked openly about his booking philosophy for New York, Boston, Philadelphia, and his other towns.

McMahon was another class operator, and he picked up my hotel bill, made sure I knew where to eat, and had Howard chauffeur me to the television tapings. It was a major league operation and New York was clearly home to all the major media. It would not be long before the entire wrestling business found out how important this was.

Actually, it was Sam who sent a very successful future WWWF champion to New York. Bob Backlund had been earning early praise for his potential while he wrestled in Florida. Like me, Sam loved what he saw of Backlund's personality and ability. We got an early glimpse on December 5, 1975, when Backlund was defeated by "Bulldog" Bob Brown. Pat O'Connor, too, was high on Backlund, and Harley Race simply raved about him. Soon, I was talking about Bob's potential on "Wrestling at the Chase," while putting small plugs about him in the "Wrestling" news as well. On March 26, 1976, he returned to St. Louis and won a surprise victory, via disqualification, from Race, who was once again the Missouri State Champion. For the curious, in the main event that evening, Terry Funk successfully defended the NWA title by winning two-of-three falls from Jack Brisco. Next, Backlund went on a long winning streak, and he eventually whipped Harley for the Missouri honor at Kiel on April 23, 1976. He then had an excellent one-hour battle with Terry Funk for the gold belt on October 8. Since Funk won the only fall within the sixty-minute time limit, Terry's hand was raised — but Backlund was "made" as a major national player.

Everyone was amazed at how serious Backlund was. He regularly put in sixty minutes, working out and running the steps, before he even stepped into the Kiel ring. He wanted to learn and valued constructive criticism. After the Funk match, Sam and I were both laughing at how Bob had grabbed each of us, separately, to ask: "Was I okay? Was the match any good?"

All I could say was, "Relax. It was great."

Even as Vince Sr. tapped flamboyant "Superstar" Billy Graham to be the WWWF champion, he was already looking for someone to follow his reign. Sam suggested Backlund; he'd be the "All American Boy," following the bleached blond, muscle-bound hippie. Backlund eventually lost the Missouri title to Jack Brisco, while Graham himself went on a hot run in St. Louis during early 1977. "Superstar" dethroned Bruno as WWWF king on April 30 in Baltimore.

On May 27, 1977, Graham actually defended the WWWF championship against Backlund at Kiel. The chemistry was right and the battle exciting. "Superstar" won when Backlund missed a flying head scissors, sailed over the top rope, and was counted out.

By the time Bob returned to St. Louis on January 4, 1980, he was the WWWF champion, having whipped Graham on February 20, 1978, in New York. Sam was no longer the president of the NWA and he'd become, in fact, unhappy with some changes within the organization he'd been so instrumental in creating. Down deep, Sam did not mind causing a little scare and announcing his displeasure. Backlund quickly racked up several victories (including one over "Bulldog" Bob Brown, to even the score) in St. Louis as the WWWF titleholder.

It all culminated with Race defending the NWA title against Backlund, the WWWF champion, on November 7, 1980. They split two falls before Backlund was disqualified for tossing Harley over the top rope. It was considered an historic *and* political match. We were disappointed, however, when the showdown drew just 7896 spectators. It was clear that business had peaked and receded in the month since a duel between Race and David Von Erich drew record receipts and 15,464 fans to The Checkerdome on October 3rd. To make matters worse, Backlund was unable to clear dates for live appearances on "Wrestling at the Chase." Sam's theory, that no promotion can sell out all the time, again proved correct.

Ironically, another youngster who was to become a major player for Vince McMahon, Jr.'s WWF got an early taste of wrestling in St. Louis in 1974, when a young "Rowdy" Roddy Piper came to "Wrestling at the Chase." Piper, of course, became the key heel in a confrontation with Hulk Hogan on the first WrestleMania. He also stirred hot controversy as a wrestler/announcer on the WTBS wrestling shows on early cable television.

Unfortunately, in St. Louis, Pat O'Connor sometimes mixed up names and we called Piper "Ronnie" for his seven losing appearances! On St. Louis TV on November 9, 1974, Piper was defeated by Lord Alfred Hayes. Poor "Ronnie" followed up with losses to "Bulldog" Bob Brown, teamed with Joe Blanchard (Tully's father) in a losing six-man tag match, and was on the losing side in two consecutive four-man tag affairs. Finally, Piper again lost to Hayes and Brown.

Despite Piper's lack of early success in the won-loss column, Sam Muchnick really liked him. So did I. And O'Connor spoke highly of his aptitude and attitude. In those days, Sam often talked about a wrestler needing "face." He meant charisma and expressions that showed emotion. Roddy Piper had it all. He also had fire; his hunger was obvious to everyone.

Sam called Fritz Von Erich on Piper's behalf, and Fritz brought him to Texas. Fritz then recommended Roddy to Don Owen, who invited him to Oregon, a strong developmental territory at the time. Piper clicked, tackling the likes of rising star Rick Martel and seasoned scrapper "Killer" Brooks. History tells the rest of the story.

Cooperation in scouting and training new talent was not at all unusual in those days. Being exposed to different philosophies and ideas about wrestling was a great learning experience. Up-and-coming grapplers got to become proficient in many different styles. Therefore, they weren't just one-dimensional in the ring. They'd also polish their interview style. Mistakes could be made, and they didn't have to worry about getting fired.

Over time, the likes of a Piper or a Backlund could create their own personality and repertoire. And once they were ready to move on to larger markets, they were prepared to draw sellout crowds. The territories so important to their early development benefited from the steady supply of fresh and eager talent to augment salty, experienced hands. Many cut their teeth on supporting bouts in big towns and then topped shows in smaller locations.

When Jim Raschke, for instance, was breaking into the business and evolving into the Baron, he had the opportunity to do everything — from setting up rings to sitting in the television control room. He was able to work preliminaries in the Twin Cities and Canada against seasoned, smart professionals. Although he was a superb amateur wrestler and football star at the University of Nebraska, the young Raschke had much to learn.

"Making the long trips with guys who understood the business turned a car ride into a classroom," he remembered. Early on, Raschke got to work with the likes of Johnny Kace, Billy Red Cloud, Gino Brito, and the Rougeau brothers. "You hadn't lived until you made a car trip from Winnipeg, Canada, to Pekin, Illinois," he said.

By the time Raschke was headlining St. Louis, he saw other youngsters receiving their own education in matches with men like Roger Kirby, Ronnie Etchison, Angelo Poffo, Tom Andrews, and Luis Martinez. The loss of this proving ground was one of the major tragedies of the death of territorial wrestling. Vince McMahon, Jr.'s WWE now faces real difficulties in finding and developing new stars, for the simple reason that there essentially is nowhere to learn anything but the WWE way of doing business.

Another young man who would make a huge impact on the world of professional wrestling made a visit to St. Louis in 1972. Shohei "Giant" Baba, at that point headlining for his own promotion in a war with Antonio Inoki, paid homage to Sam and paved the way for his inclusion into the NWA. At the time, Mexico had long been a part of the NWA, but there were no Japanese Alliance members. Nonetheless, a select few stars had earned lucrative paydays wrestling in Japan. Thesz, for one, had often — on his own — defended the title in Japan. His collisions with Japanese icon Rikidozan were legendary. Lou was like Babe Ruth to the Japanese fans, who believed the NWA championship was wrestling's ultimate prize. And Sam himself was already a personal friend of Toru Shiriki, the owner of both Channel 4 television and the Tokyo Giants baseball team.

Baba formalized relations with the NWA through delicate diplomacy with Muchnick, who was more than impressed. He brought presents for Sam, his wife, and even me and my wife. He also brought a gift for "Wild Bill" Longson, who he called "a huge, famous star." I still have Baba's good luck charm hanging from my front door.

Baba took time to understand Sam's concerns, and vice versa. All Japan Pro Wrestling eventually became a full member of the NWA, and Inoki's promotion was, for all intents and purposes, blocked. The Funk brothers, "King Kong" Brody, Dick Murdoch, and Harley Race became marquee idols in Japan. The deal with Baba opened up a tremendous market for American wrestlers, who also benefited by being exposed to new wrestling styles. Sam visited Japan on several occasions and was treated like nothing less than royalty. To Japanese fans, St. Louis was a shrine.

Sam initially hesitated over the deal, however, fearing Japan would put even more pressure on the NWA for championship dates — but this did not prove to be the case. And ultimately, the upside in terms of exposure and public recognition was well worth the trouble. For the champ, Japanese dates were definitely better than working small towns in Kansas or Alabama — this kind of small-time local travel always annoyed Sam because the title-holder was exhausted for little return.

In all of this, Sam reluctantly gave his blessing for one thing he may have eventually regretted — a quick title change. On December 2, 1974, Baba unseated Jack Brisco in Kagoshimi, Japan. For one week, Baba was the NWA kingpin — until Brisco regained the laurels on December 9, in a Tokyo rematch.

Since Baba had made several appearances in St. Louis during the early 1970s (including a big victory over Dick Murdoch on June 14, 1974), Sam felt it would make sense to stage a "rubber match" between Brisco and Baba at Kiel. On August 8, 1975, the Japanese media, including daily newspapers and television crews, jammed Kiel's ringside as Brisco captured two-out-of-three falls to keep the NWA title.

And while Sam never approved of such a bang-bang title exchange again, once he had retired as NWA president the practice became relatively common. In the process, some of the championship's credibility eroded.

Talking with Sam years later, he still expressed displeasure about making the decision, even though Brisco versus Baba was a major event in Asia.

And though handing the gold belt to Baba for a week was something that Brisco himself really wanted to do, it unfortunately may also have set a bad precedent, giving other champions a way to rationalize going into business for themselves.

In 2001, I produced several editions of a historical "Wrestling at the Chase" for the Samurai Network in Japan. The response, I've been told, was magnificent. A television reporter was even sent from Japan to interview me for a network show on "famous" sites like Kiel, the empty Arena grounds, and the Chase.

Whatever Sam believed, I wish he had realized how special his decision had made St. Louis in the eyes of the Japanese. Still, he was right; the rapid title switch let the genie out of the championship bottle. In the long run, that hurt the NWA.

After Muchnick gave up the Alliance presidency, the business began to change in subtle ways. Our Kansas City partners tried harder than ever to maneuver their talent into higher spots. Sam generally resisted, although he relented on occasion — allowing "Bulldog" Bob Brown and Bob Sweetan (solid performers, but not headliners), for example, into main events.

When crowds were poor, Sam knew he'd proven his point. "St. Louis has never been a territory town," he explained. "The guys in Kansas City don't understand that."

Verne Gagne entering the mix provided another source of first-rate talent, but the push-and-pull over booking was always there. The partners wanted their talent to get the paydays; I didn't care where a wrestler was from as long as he could draw. That usually meant I wanted to use someone from the AWA (or elsewhere!) for main events, which always aggravated the K.C. guys.

Ric Flair's St. Louis debut is a case in point. The strutting blond bomber had been on fire in the Carolinas, where he was breaking box office records. I had mentioned Flair to Sam several times, and he eventually spoke with Carolina promoter Jim Crockett, Jr. about booking "The Nature Boy."

Pat O'Connor, however, dragged his feet. On one occasion Pat actually told Sam and me that, "Flair is a terrific worker, but he's too small for St. Louis." I was flabbergasted. Ric was the same size as Jack Brisco — and O'Connor himself.

Sam attributed Pat's reluctance to Kansas City pressuring him to give its performers work.

"If Flair comes in, he eats up another major spot on the card. Business isn't that good in Kansas City. The guys don't make much money, so it's hard for them to get really top hands. They want to tie in St. Louis to give their regular guys more work," Muchnick explained. "I don't mind that in preliminaries, but they have to understand that St. Louis has always stood alone. Our main eventers are the best from around the world."

Gagne, too, strongly recommended Ric for St. Louis. Finally, I got some tape of Carolina matches featuring Flair. He was simply amazing, oozing charisma and athleticism. Sam joined me one afternoon in the control room at KPLR, and we watched Flair in action. Within five minutes, the decision was made. "I'll call Pat and tell him to book Flair," Sam said. "The guy looks better than Gorgeous George and Buddy Rogers combined."

To O'Connor's credit, once Sam made the call, he accepted our assessment of Flair. But securing him for dates was not easy — Ric was already becoming a hot attraction across the country. Nonetheless, with his debut victory over Omar Atlas at Kiel on January 6, 1978, Flair became a solid main event star in St. Louis. And by October of that year he was already challenging for the NWA title.

Sam was clearly the final authority on all things wrestling. He was also a realist, though, and began selling off tiny pieces of his stock to his partners as he laid out a plan that would allow his wife Helen to be set for life when he eventually passed away. I wanted to purchase stock, and had been urged to get a piece of the action by O'Connor and Geigel — who even considered trying to get Ted Koplar to buy in so that KPLR would still have a vested interest in the business when Muchnick finally stepped out.

Sam counseled differently: "Never use your own money. They need you. Let things develop and, sooner or later, one of the ways they can compensate you is to give you stock, paid for out of the profits."

When Helen passed away, suddenly, in 1981, Sam's careful plans were rocked. More importantly, his heart was broken. Although he was always a hardened realist, Helen's death robbed him of a certain hunger. It still mattered, and always would, but wrestling was no longer truly important. Sam accelerated the process of removing himself from the business.

His retirement card at The Checkerdome (as the Arena was called at the time) on January 1, 1982, stands as St. Louis' greatest one-night promotion. In fact, an argument can be made that it is among the most significant in wrestling history, factoring in the outpouring of public and professional respect.

With the help of his daughter Kathy and sons Dick and Dan, Sam adjusted to life without Helen. In wrestling, he became a wise counselor who could anticipate every angle of a situation. When I broke away from the St. Louis Wrestling Club in 1983, Sam gave his approval and even said he felt it was inevitable. "You're used to how I did business, and that's not how they operate," he said. Quietly, behind the scenes, Muchnick helped me.

But even Sam was surprised when Vince McMahon, Jr. launched his takeover of the wrestling world. When the dust had settled in St. Louis, and I had reluctantly become involved with the WWF, Sam asked me one question: "If I hadn't retired, do you think Vince would have tried to take St. Louis?"

Here was this giant of the wrestling world — clearly the most influential promoter of his time — asking his protégé something critical. With all the esteem and devotion I had for the man, I answered, "I think Vince would have respected you so much that he would have tried to do the right thing and work out a deal with you. He would never have tried to push you out."

Sam nodded.

Perhaps he even believed me.

The truth is, Vince Jr. would have gone after St. Louis just as ruthlessly as he went after everything else. Maybe Sam's local contacts would have kept Vince at bay — for a while. As the other promotions fell, however, Muchnick's St. Louis would have become a lonely island. I could never have said this to Sam.

The questions I would love to have asked Sam can never be answered. What if Sam Muchnick had been younger, hungrier, and at the height of his power — not just in wrestling, but in the world of politics and the media? My own experience tells me that he would have eagerly utilized the new technologies of television and promotion at his disposal.

What would have happened if a younger Sam Muchnick and Vince McMahon, Jr. had gone to war?

Well, it would have been a helluva fight. And everyone knows whose side I would have been on.

Wrestling

Saturday, December 26, 1970   ST. LOUIS WRESTLING CLUB — Subscription $1 for Entire Year — Single Copy 15¢   Page One

JACK BRISCO

Will New Year's Day Bring New Champion?

If Dory Funk, Jr. believes in omens, he has to be apprehensive about his Jan. 1 championship scrap with Jack Brisco at Kiel Auditorium.

Brisco today and Funk two years ago were at practically the same spot in their careers. Many mat experts felt that Funk lacked the ring polish to become an immediate title threat. But then Dory set wrestling on its ear by knocking off tough Gene Kiniski on Feb. 11, 1969.

The record of Brisco indicates that he has been a consistent winner for several months. Jack really peaked when he overwhelmed "Big Bill" Miller in the finale of a "Wrestle Royal" on Dec. 4 at Kiel.

Moreover, both Funk and Brisco have superb wrestling backgrounds. Dory was trained by his father, while Brisco began his career on the high school mats of Oklahoma. Jack lost only one match during his high school and college career. Upon turning professional, Brisco came under the wings of Eddie Graham and Lou Thesz.

This New Year's battle could be just a preview to one of the great rivalries of the next decade.

Brisco Gets Chance of Lifetime Against World Champion at Kiel Jan. 1

Jack Brisco has waited a lifetime for the chance he'll get in the main event of the outstanding Kiel Auditorium wrestling bill for New Year's Day — Friday, January 1. Brisco will challenge titleholder Dory Funk, Jr. for the World Heavyweight Championship in a best-of-three-falls duel with a one-hour time limit.

The sensational Oklahoma "Wildcat" jumped into the title picture with a thrilling triumph in a sixteen-man "Wrestle Royal" at Kiel on Dec. 4. After thirteen matmen had been eliminated by being thrown over the top rope, Brisco was left in the ring with the dangerous duo of Hans Schmidt and "Big Bill" Miller.

But Brisco quickly dispatched Schmidt over the top strand with a kangaroo kick. That left Brisco and Miller to clash in a regular one-fall bout to determine the winner. Brisco, however, made short work of "Big Bill" and polished off the former Crimson Knight with the figure four grapevine in a mere 3:05.

The victory netted Brisco $9600, and Jack felt that the title shot he earned made the triumph even more valuable. "This is something I've worked for all my life," explained Brisco. "It is a dream come true."

Brisco, of course, realizes that he has his work cut out for him in the battle that St. Louis fans are eagerly anticipating as a sparkling, scientific struggle. Although both grapplers have shown an ability to take and dish out the rough stuff, they have made their reputations on fast-paced scientific wrestling.

Funk, who has held the crown since Feb. 11, 1969, when he whipped Gene Kiniski in Tampa, Fla., is rapidly

DORY FUNK, JR.

developing into one of sport's greatest champions. Dory has drawn the largest crowds of any titlist in the past twenty years. His successful defense of the laurels has taken Funk across the United States, Puerto Rico, Canada and Japan.

Brisco and Funk both boast a crippling leg hold—Jack, the figure four grapevine, and Dory, the spinning toehold. One advantage that might lie with Brisco is that the grapevine is virtually impossible to break once applied. However, a truly knowledgable scientific wrestler might be able to escape the spinning toehold.

Jack Brisco hopes that is an edge which helps him to realize a lifelong dream — the World Heavyweight Championship.

RING THE BELL FOR . . .

JACK BRISCO VERSUS DORY FUNK, JR.

It was one of the greatest series of matches in the long and storied history of St. Louis wrestling. And the rivalry proved, once again, that two fan favorites can face each other and draw serious — very serious — money. The crowd was split pretty much in half, with each man having his share of support. Unlike today's WWE bookers, who manipulate everything into a heel versus baby face confrontation, Sam Muchnick did not care. He understood the basic premise of sports, that people want to see the best against the best. The name of the game is simple: draw big crowds and give the people what they want. And that's precisely what Funk and Brisco did.

Consider their long and amazing list of collisions. Anyone who was there remembers, to this day, the entire crowd — every single person — coming out of their seats and screaming when Brisco countered the spinning toehold or Funk reversed the figure four leglock.

January 1, 1971: Dory Jr. retained the NWA crown by going to a one-hour draw, where each combatant took one fall. Kiel was sold out to the tune of 11,587, and more than 4000 others were turned away. Police had to restore order in the lobby when portable ticket booths were nearly overturned.

November 19, 1971: Once again Dory Jr. kept the title, capturing the only fall of the one-hour time limit match. Brisco had him in the figure four when the clock ran out. Nearly 13,000 witnessed this epic confrontation at The Arena, and everyone — not just the grapplers, but the fans (and the ring announcer) as well — was absolutely exhausted after the struggle.

April 19, 1974: By now the NWA title was with Brisco, having passed to him from Harley Race. But Dory Jr. could not retake the gold belt; Jack captured the lone fall in 60 minutes.

June 14, 1974: Another sellout of 10,669 at Kiel, and their fourth consecutive one-hour war. Each man won a single fall so the verdict was a draw.

November 15, 1974: For the *fifth* time, Dory Jr. and Jack battled for a full hour. Lou Thesz was the referee, and he disqualified Brisco for the only fall of the match. Funk was bleeding at 51:30 when Thesz ruled that Brisco had intentionally thrown Dory over the top rope. The final bell sounded with Brisco, who would not submit, in Funk's spinning toehold. Since NWA rules said that the challenger had to win two of three falls, and that the deciding fall could not be by disqualification, Jack remained champ.

February 7, 1975: Over 10,000 on hand again at Kiel as Sam abolished the time limit and made the conditions two-of-three-falls to a finish. Brisco captured the decision, winning the first and third stanzas in a barn-burner of a duel that lasted roughly forty minutes.

February 27, 1976: Neither man was champion for this one — Dory Jr.'s brother Terry wore the gold belt. Brisco was hot on Terry's trail and scored a huge triumph by pinning his old foe.

May 21, 1976: The kind of tag team pairing that could only happen in St. Louis. Brisco joined forces with Gene Kiniski to take two-of-three falls from the Funk brothers in a wild affair. Dory Jr. forced Brisco to submit to an abdominal stretch for the first fall. Brisco made Terry give up with the figure four for the second. Kiniski clinched the victory by pinning Dory Jr. in the final stanza.

August 25, 1978: The classic rivalry was on display for the final time. Pat O'Connor was the referee as Brisco surprised Dory Jr. with a reverse full nelson.

"St. Louis will always have a special place in my life," said Brisco. "Those were great times. My matches with Dory were athletic contests. We never cheated the fans."

Two of the best talkers ever, Bobby Heenan and Lord Alfred Hayes, February 23, 1974

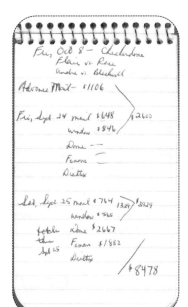
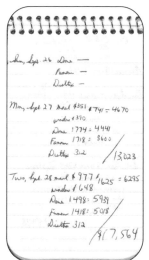

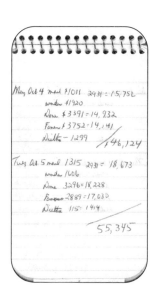

The advance and final sales from October 8, 1982: as always, kept in the style Sam Muchnick taught me

 # FRIDAY NIGHT

When a weekend of wrestling began with a bang on Friday evening, what was going on behind the scenes, in the hidden dressing room? What developments influenced the hypnotizing spectacle of athleticism and drama that entertained thousands?

When I was fifteen, that's what I wanted to know, just like every other rabid fan. Fortune was with me; I got to live my dream and discover the answers.

Once I was working for Sam Muchnick, I would arrive around 6 p.m., when the guts of Kiel Auditorium were still empty. The Convention Hall, as it was called, was dim except for the glare of the lights over the gleaming white wrestling ring. The ghosts of wrestlers, the NBA's St. Louis Hawks, and politicians floated through the vaguely haunted space.

Activity, though, was beginning. The smell of popcorn began to mingle with the scent of fresh ink from copies of the "Wrestling" news being unpackaged at the concession stands. I remember the rush of movement, voices, laughter.

In the lobby, at both 14th and 15th Street, tickets were being sold. The crowd lined up at the windows. Outside, at the 15th Street stage door, loyal wrestling devotees were gathered, hoping to catch a glimpse of a star or maybe even get an autograph or photo.

My first stop, after strolling through the spooky auditorium, was Committee Room A, where the Essers were coordinating box office sales. A scrupulously honest husband-and-wife combination, Dick and Arline Esser had been with Sam Muchnick from the very beginning — the duo also handled ticket sales for the St. Louis Hawks. In the days before computers simplified box office life, the Essers and their crew had to hand count every dollar and every ticket stub, just to make sure the correct taxes were being paid.

Sam (fresh from a radio interview with Bob Burnes on KMOX) would not be far behind me, because serious business had to be conducted before the doors were thrown open. Everybody had to ante up his dollar for "The jackpot!" Looking at the advance sale, a dollar wager gave everyone who participated a chance to predict what the final gross sale for the event would be. Though the jackpot generally was not much more than ten dollars, Sam seemed to get more enjoyment from his occasional wins than from a sellout! It was spirited competition, because all of us had become pretty adept at what to expect from our walk-in crowd. Having three people predict the gate within $20 was not unusual.

That serious bit of business behind us, action moved to the dressing room. At Kiel, the rooms were a level up from the venue's actual floor. "Wild Bill" Longson set up shop at the top of the stairs so he could direct wrestlers to Sam's room, the athletic commission officials (where "Dutch" Schneider and Tom Behan held court in more than cooperative fashion), or the doctor for an examination. Four hallways with small cubicles wound away from Bill's location. It was a maze for the uninitiated.

The Arena (Checkerdome) was simpler — just a round, wide hallway with perhaps four large dressing rooms, set up for teams. Kiel had more mystery with its private, hidden nooks.

Sam always presided in the corner room, near where "Wild Bill" directed traffic. At some point in the evening, every wrestler would stop to pay respects to the boss. General decisions about finishes were finalized earlier in the day at the office, so Pat O'Connor, or whoever was booking, could carry out his duties and give instructions quickly in the dressing rooms. When the door to Sam's room was shut, everyone knew serious negotiations were taking place.

Every matman at one time or another heard Sam's favorite story. It featured Ali Baba, a Turkish tough guy who had held what was recognized as the World Championship in 1936. Ali Baba claimed he had the hardest head in wrestling when he came to St. Louis to work for Tom Packs and his assistant, Sam Muchnick.

"Right in this very room, Packs challenged Ali Baba to prove how hard his head was," Sam would recall with a smile. "Ali Baba was insulted and said he could prove it easily. He offered to ram his head into the concrete wall. Packs told him to show us. Ali Baba lowered his head like a bull. Then he charged, right into this very wall, head first, and knocked himself silly. It took us an hour to revive him so he could wrestle that night!"

But the story did not end there.

"Ali Baba was embarrassed," Sam continued. "Two weeks later, he was back for our card and complaining he must have hit the wall wrong. I suggested he try it again. Sure enough, like a wild bull, Ali Baba lowered his head and charged even harder at the concrete wall."

Here, Sam chuckled. "Bang! He rammed the wall and knocked himself completely unconscious. He never talked about it again — but I have to admit Ali Baba had a hard head."

The St. Louis dressing room was unlike most others, primarily because Sam brought in talent from many different territories. On May 2, 1975, he added the miles his talent had traveled to be there — the incredible total was 9176! Of the, say, 18 wrestlers we used on any given night, maybe four or five worked out of Kansas City. The rest came from territories scattered throughout North America. There were no cliques in the room, and few jealousies or personal issues had time to build. A St. Louis card often felt like a reunion for stars who rarely saw each other. And always, we were considered a serious promotion. Arguments about finishes were brief, almost nonexistent, and took place behind closed doors. The "ribs" for which wrestling and wrestlers were famous were not as prevalent.

I was fortunate. I never really had to deal with the cruel pranks that were often played on younger wrestlers. Okay, I wasn't a wrestler. But other guys in similar positions elsewhere weren't immune. My relationship with Sam, however, gave me immediate respect and probably caused no little uncertainty about how I should be treated. Perhaps some guys feared I would tell the boss about their escapades. But in time, as the wrestlers began to trust me, I heard all the inside stories. Still, it was always clear that St. Louis wasn't the place for the usual capers.

Like I said, St. Louis was all business. And though plenty of wrestlers got wild and crazy when they came to town, almost all of them took Bill Longson's "Close the door" to heart. It's ironic, two who had reputations for being among the most untamed, Dick Murdoch and "King Kong" Brody, sought me out. I developed sturdy friendships and business relations with both over many plates of pasta at Bartolino's.

Every one of the guys who came up those steps to the dressing room had a fascinating tale of his own. Wilbur Snyder, "Moose" Cholak, and Ronnie Etchison were three of the most captivating old school pros. By the time I was really involved, the trio were on the downside of excellent careers. Their knowledge and experience, however, still made them valuable performers. They were always among the first to arrive, and never, ever caused a problem.

Snyder was a fabulous athlete who had played college ball before joining the Edmonton Eskimos of the Canadian Football League. His teammates included Gene Kiniski and Joe Blanchard. They all ended up wrestling, primarily because of the influence of famous Canadian promoter Stu Hart. (Stu's sons, of course, included the late Owen Hart and Bret "the Hitman" Hart of WWF fame.) In the 1950s, many expected Snyder to become the NWA champion. Often compared to Verne Gagne, Wilbur's pure athleticism was top notch. He was like a giant cat, landing drop kicks and leap-frogging over charging rivals. His abdominal stretch set the standard for the hold.

Snyder had epic battles with Lou Thesz, including a 90-minute (that's right, 90 minutes!) draw in 1956. But the politics were never quite right and the title ended up around O'Connor's waist in 1959. Still, Snyder was a first-rate drawing card throughout the Midwest and particularly in St. Louis, where he collided with Fritz Von Erich, Dick "The Bruiser," and Kiniski during the 1960s. Eventually, he partnered with "The Bruiser" in operating the Indianapolis promotion. This cut down his travel, but also probably guaranteed him a slot just below the main event. Eventually, wrestling became more a job than a passion for him, but Snyder was a great influence on rising stars.

"Let the match come to you," I heard Wilbur say when he was asked for advice. "One drop kick at the right time is worth more than ten drop kicks that don't mean anything. Relax and take your time."

Edward Cholak was a true tough guy who had been a boxer in the Navy. About 6-4, and somewhere between 300 and 365 pounds, "Moose" used to wear antler headgear into the ring for bouts in his native Chicago. Sam nixed the idea for St. Louis, but had a lot of respect for "Moose." When Cholak hit his giant splash, somebody was getting turned into a pancake.

Once, Cholak broke the nose of "Bulldog" Bob Brown in five places. And even though Jerry Brisco, Jack's younger brother, scored a win over "Moose" in Jerry's debut at Kiel on October 15, 1971, he walked out with a bloody nose, a bloody lip, and blood coming from his ear. "Cholak didn't realize how strong and rough he was," Jack said.

"Moose" did well against former world champions in the mid-60s, going to time limit draws against both Bobby Managoff and Pat O'Connor. Cholak was also in an unusual handicap match, with Waldo Von Erich, against none other than Lou Thesz on November 11, 1965. Thesz pinned "Moose" and then went the remainder of the 30-minute curfew without a fall against Waldo.

In the 1970s, Cholak owned and operated a well-known bar in Chicago while still wrestling. He would time his drive to St. Louis to coincide with Sam's interview on KMOX Radio. "I should be listening to Sam saying whether there are any tickets left about the time I cross the bridge into St. Louis," Cholak explained.

Classy Ron Etchison got nowhere near the respect he deserved as his career waned. Ronnie actually wrestled in six decades — from the 30s to the 80s. By the late 1970s, he was like a popular and respected uncle who always got a warm welcome in Kiel openers.

But how many remember that Etchison challenged Buddy Rogers for the NWA crown on August 11, 1961? And who recalls that he was a foe to the young and hungry "Giant" Baba, when the 6-9, 310-pound Japanese star (who was billed as seven-foot-tall!) was making one of his first American outings on February 7, 1964, at Kiel? The two battled to a rousing time-limit stalemate.

Ronnie headlined plenty of cards, particularly in California. It amazes me that his spectacular finish is not being performed today — although the giant swing is tougher to pull off than it appears. After knocking an opponent down, Etchison would hook the foe's ankles under his arms and swing the poor guy around in ever widening circles.

Think of the strength and balance required, as Etchison made those fast, hard steps to get his victim airborne. After five or six rotations, he'd let go; his opponent crashed, and then Ronnie would cover him for the pin.

Hiroshi Hase used the same maneuver in Japan; in fact, he used to try to establish new records for number of rotations. He once went for more than forty. Kiniski tried the giant swing in one St. Louis battle, whirled his foe around maybe a dozen times, and then staggered and stumbled dizzily until he himself fell through the ropes and out of the ring.

Like "Wild Bill," Etchison loved big, pungent cigars. Once, when Ronnie and "Wild Bill" were puffing away, the smoke was so thick that Dick Murdoch, who never found a dressing room he could not make noisy, went running down the narrow Kiel hallway, screaming, "Call the fire department! The old farts did it! They're burning down Kiel Auditorium!"

What was Mary Ann Kostecki feeling when she went to those dressing rooms to prepare for her first St. Louis match in 1957? Mat fans know her as Penny Banner, one of the greatest lady wrestlers ever, a star amongst the likes of June Byers and Mildred Burke. Her family and friends knew her as an athletic young lady from south St. Louis's Soulard neighborhood.

"I guess I was thrilled, but mostly I was scared!" Penny remembered. As a teenager in the mid-1950s, she was working as a governess for three children. In the basement of the home was a weight room. Penny started using it while the children were in school. Soon she was taking judo lessons and also working at the Arabian Lounge.

Boxing folks hung out at the Arabian, and somehow stories about the beautiful but tough young gal got back to Sam Muchnick. Lady wrestling was just starting to click, so Sam had "Killer" Kowalski call Penny to see if she had any interest.

"I hung up on him," said Penny. "And when 'Cyclone' Anaya called me, I hung up on him too. I thought it was a big joke someone was playing on me."

Finally Sam himself called and convinced Penny to give wrestling a try.

"I agreed to train with Billy Wolfe, the promoter in Columbus, Ohio. And I never looked back!"

For female athletes of that time, there were precious few options. "I wish I could have tried basketball or volleyball, but I loved wrestling," Penny explained. In time, she also got to work on "Wrestling at the Chase," where she battled Kay Noble and was interviewed by Joe Garagiola.

"Oh, my, that was great!" Penny remembered. "I can honestly say, though, that as thrilled as I was to be in that big hall at Kiel, I was scared to death I'd mess up."

She didn't.

"Superstar" Billy Graham was something entirely different when he entered the dressing room. In the doctor's cubicle on November 5, 1976, I did a brief interview with Billy, just to get some background info for the television show and the "Wrestling" news. Throughout the chat, all "Superstar" did was flex and look at his bulging biceps. He was not "working" me — every time I saw Graham near a mirror in the weeks to come, he was doing the same thing.

Graham's plight (today he's virtually crippled) is well-known. In the mid-1970s, some wrestlers, football players, and body builders used performance enhancing drugs openly. Billy was one of them. Those were naïve times. Unable to anticipate the physical horrors to which steroid abuse could lead, no one even stopped to consider the risks.

Sam was leery about booking Graham because he had a reputation for blowing dates and refusing to cooperate on finishes. For the most part, though, "Superstar" was reliable in St. Louis. Of course, his only true defeat came at the hands of Jack Brisco on March 25, 1977, though he also suffered a disqualification loss to Harley Race a month earlier on February 11. He fought to a double count-out with Harley on March 4 and to another with Dick "The Bruiser" on May 6. On November 3, 1978, he also fought to a double disqualification with Rocky Johnson.

By booking only that one loss in two years, Sam clearly felt that he had been more than fair with Graham. Then, without warning or notification, on December 8, 1978, "Superstar" failed to show up to meet Bobo Brazil. Let's say Sam was "irritated" in the dressing room that night. He made a few calls to other promoters and tried to reach "Superstar" over the weekend, but got no satisfaction about what had transpired.

When Sam arrived at the office the following Monday, he took a hard look at Graham's photograph on the wall. "You might as well take that down," he told me. "Graham just died as far as St. Louis is concerned." He was never invited back.

Guys like Bobby Heenan made a dressing room fun. As with Graham, Sam was at first reluctant about using the man who would soon be known as both "the Brain" and "the Weasel" because he was not a big fan of managers or their outside interference. So, it was a big deal when Sam allowed Heenan to manage "Black Jack" Lanza on "Wrestling at the Chase" on April 6, 1968.

The act clicked. Lanza was a reliable if unspectacular performer, but "Pretty Boy" Bobby Heenan added a jolt of electricity. Bobby could talk, and he was more than willing to accept Sam's guidelines about what he could do around the ring. Naturally, on those special occasions when Sam loosened Bobby's chain, it was even more exciting.

In interviews, Heenan was nothing short of brilliant. He was always sure to get the fans' blood boiling, but at the same time he could turn a phrase that would make them laugh despite their anger. Bobby also understood how important the "chase" was. Nick Bockwinkel, managed by Heenan in St. Louis in 1976, said, "Bobby knew how to leave them screaming for more."

A perfect example came when O'Connor faced Lanza at Kiel on April 25, 1969. Five minutes alone with Heenan loomed as Pat's reward for a victory. But "Black Jack" bested O'Connor, and after the bout both villains put the boots to him. Edouard Carpentier, coming to the ring for his match (in which he defeated none other than Harley Race in Harley's first St. Louis main event), saved Pat by knocking Heenan from the ring.

Spectators always wanted to see Bobby get the beating of his life, so there was plenty of excitement when someone like Dick "The Bruiser" was hot on his heels. Heenan was definitely a big part of what made the feud between Lanza and "The Bruiser" so successful at the box office.

Bobby was why Sam first surrounded the ring with a seven-foot-high chain-link fence (an early version of a cage match). When Lanza challenged titleholder Dory Funk, Jr. at The Arena on April 2, 1971, the structure was erected specifically to keep Heenan from interfering during the contest.

By the time I got to know Bobby, he and Sam apparently had solved their one big problem. On Heenan's first few payoffs at Kiel, Sam had given him opening match money even when he handled Lanza for a main event. Heenan was respectful, used diplomacy, and finally prevailed upon Minneapolis promoter Wally Karbo to convince Sam how important Heenan was to Lanza's draw. Sam upped the money and Bobby appeared satisfied — even though he probably wanted more.

Heenan and "Wild Bill" were always jawing at each other. One evening the debate was about who had the best leap over the top rope and out of the ring — a move Heenan had mastered as part of the "chase." My vote? Heenan went a little higher, but Longson definitely went farther.

In 1974, Bobby began managing Lord Alfred Hayes. It didn't quite click as well, since Heenan was about Hayes' size and both parties could certainly handle themselves on the mic. Eventually, he moved on to manage Nick Bockwinkel, becoming an integral part of Verne Gagne's AWA. When I visited that territory, it became clear that Bobby was taking as many bumps as the wrestlers.

He returned to St. Louis to try to breathe life into the team of Lanza and

Bobby Duncum for a few tag team bouts, including a loss to Jack and Jerry Brisco on April 28, 1978. Heenan also wrestled many of the higher prelims in St. Louis, because, after all, he really was an excellent worker. And again, the crowd always enjoyed seeing him get smacked around.

Bobby was a treat in the dressing room. Jack Brisco remembered that Heenan was invaluable to the Sunday tapings at KPLR: "We did three shows in one day and it was tough. Thank goodness when Bobby was there. He kept everybody up and laughing."

Completely professional, with little ego and a great sense of humor, Bobby would always make sure to visit with Sam at Kiel. The proof was in the record — Sam never had another manager in St. Louis. That role was reserved for Bobby Heenan.

Of course, over the years, there were a few harsh moments in the back. One came on November 1, 1974, when I ran into Lars Anderson (Larry Heinimi) *leaving* at 7:45 p.m. Lars had been a successful amateur grappler who many expected to make a big impact on the pro game. But it hadn't really happened; he seemed to stall just short of big market main events.

His hopes were probably high when he was booked for a bout with Bobo Brazil, but as he carried his bags out that night, Anderson looked stunned. I asked "Wild Bill" what had happened. He said, "Anderson thought he was more important than he was. Sam knows what's best for St. Louis, and tonight it was Bobo getting his hand raised. Sam said to give Anderson his 'trans' and tell him good-bye."

Forever.

No scene. No argument. The message, though, was clear. Wrestling is a hard business.

It can also be unfair. Bruce Reed had everything he needed, save experience, to become a star. It was obvious from his very first appearance on "Wrestling at the Chase" in 1979. Despite his athletic ability and natural appeal, Reed seemed humble and quiet to the point of being shy. We booked him to appear at Kiel on November 2, 1979; he arrived just in time, rushing and puffing up the steps.

Apparently, some other wrestlers from the Kansas City territory had promised him a ride, but instead left him behind, with no way to St. Louis. Using his head, Bruce grabbed a Greyhound bus. Supposedly, the same thing happened before a few of his television shots. Like most young wrestlers, Reed was strapped for money and had to rely on other performers for support.

Was it because he was black? Was it because some of the cynical wrestlers who would never rise above their current status were jealous of the youngster? Was it just some cruel "rib"?

"Bulldog" Brown shrugged it off, calling it, "Just one of those things."

Reed got an offer to work in Florida; he clicked and was quickly bumped into main events. When he returned to St. Louis, I gave him a push — but I was still constantly butting heads just to get "Butch" (the nickname he had picked up in Florida) the victories he needed.

By 1982, though, it was no longer a problem. He'd gained self-confidence and caught fire. After Kiel triumphs, by disqualification over Race on November 5, and by pin over Ivan Koloff on November 19, it was time for the big push. Developing the finish for an epic tag team duel featuring Reed on December 3 confirmed how easy it was to work with true professionals.

No matter what town it was, the dressing room was where finishes were devised. There was no choreography, just a decision about who would win and, in general terms, how. This was another reason Lou Thesz called wrestling "an art form." The talent put the action together — on the spot — in the ring.

O'Connor taught me an early lesson by looking back upon one of the first finishes he put together for Sam. On October 4, 1968, "Cowboy" Bill Watts faced Gene Kiniski for the NWA crown. Pat had an action-packed scenario laid out.

"I explained it to them and neither man responded," he said. "So I asked what was wrong. Watts said, 'That's a great finish for you, but I can't do that stuff.' Kiniski said the same thing."

According to O'Connor, all three then worked out a finish that had the crowd roaring and fit in with both Watts' and Kiniski's repertoire. "You gotta remember," Pat stressed, "that the finish has to fit the style of the guys in the ring. They couldn't do what I did, but then I couldn't do what Kiniski and Watts did."

In the end, Watts went for a giant splash, but Kiniski jammed his knees up into "The Cowboy's" stomach, stunning him long enough to earn the victory.

History buffs will want to know that this was a rematch. On May 3, 1968, "Dr. Scarlet" was scheduled to face the champion when Sam Muchnick ruled that a masked wrestler could not compete for the title. So, before the bout began, "Dr. Scarlet" removed his disguise, revealing himself as "The Cowboy." With that, the crowd immediately anticipated a title change. Kiniski, however, thwarted their expectations. After the loss, Watts got into a squabble with the special guest referee, who just happened to be "Whipper" Billy Watson. This led to the main event for September 7, where "The Cowboy" bested Watson to earn another title shot.

But back to "Butch" Reed. On December 3, 1982, I had Reed and Dick "The Bruiser" going against "Crusher" Blackwell and Ric Flair — who was the NWA champion at the time. Retired, but still a consultant, Sam agreed that it would be a perfect chance to boost Reed to a title shot — but not in the obvious way, by having "Butch" pin "the Nature Boy." Flair and I had plans to help fire the rivalry on TV. If anything in wrestling could be subtle, this had to be it.

First fall, Blackwell pins "The Bruiser." Second fall, "The Bruiser" pins Flair. Deciding fall, Reed pins Blackwell. Everybody but Flair was getting something, and Reed was getting the most because he needed it to earn the championship match. I was so respectful of the stars in that room that I felt the need to thank "The Bruiser" and Blackwell, while also pointing out that even though Flair was the champion he wasn't even winning a fall.

"The Bruiser" looked at me, grinned, and said, "No problem. It sounds good."

Blackwell, a great guy, just laughed, "It'll be a blast. Helluva match!" Flair, the champion, pointed out, "I got it to give, so let's give it to 'Butch' Reed!"

No wonder Sam found dealing with true professionals so satisfying. Flair, Blackwell, and "The Bruiser" realized that the goal of the match, besides giving the fans a huge bang for their buck, was to establish Reed as a legitimate contender. The quartet put together the finishes for all three falls and had a dynamite battle, perfectly manipulating the crowd and moving with their emotions. The deciding stanza was inventive, setting up a spot for Reed to knock Flair out of the ring and catch Blackwell with a flying cross body block for the pin.

For Butch, it had to be a rush. And by the way, his showdown with Flair, on New Year's night 1983, drew a capacity crowd of 11,029. Flair won the only fall within the hour they battled, but Reed did not have to ride a bus to get to Kiel that night.

Another thing that was always evident in the dressing room was how much physical punishment the wrestlers took. It left an impression, hearing "King Kong" Brody tell a newcomer: "I'm going to blast you so hard that the guy in the top row of the balcony can hear it."

George Wettach, one of our doctors, was a cardiac specialist who would often take the pulse of wrestlers fresh from the ring. "Some of their hearts should have exploded, the rate was so high," George said in amazement. "Of course, there was also a guy like O'Connor who was always sixty, no matter what he did!"

Often I would come to the dressing room at intermission and find a wrestler collapsed on the steps, gasping for air or in serious pain. On the other hand, there were some athletes blessed with incredible genetics (like Thesz, Flair, Brody, Race, O'Connor, and Kiniski) who could take any bump and go forever.

The bruises, the blood, the twisted ligaments, and the aching backs were all part of the price wrestlers paid. "Cowboy" Bob Orton, son of Bob Sr. and father of current WWE standout Randy, explained, "Your body gets used to the punishment night after night. It hurts to get whipped into a corner or slammed. Taking a big chop in the chest knocks the wind out of you. It's after you retire that you really start to feel all the punishment you took."

Harley Race, who has had neck surgery and can hardly turn his head, said, "I feel for Chris Benoit. This is what years of doing the diving head butt did to me. He has the same problem in his future."

Terry Funk, a great storyteller, once told me a terrific tale as he sat in his cubicle before a card. "There's this old star who's been around forever," Terry began. "He's limping and hobbling so bad nobody can tell whether his back or his knees hurt more. In the dressing room, all night, he's telling the young guys how beat up he is, who he was wrestling when he got which injury, and that he doesn't think he can go one more time. Moaning, groaning — the ole boy is a wreck and everybody is afraid he's going to collapse right there. Then the promoter sticks his head in and says, 'You're on in three minutes.' Man, the old star jumps right up and runs out of the room. As soon as he gets out in the crowd, he pumps up and sprints to the ring. He has the best match on the card by a mile, comes back to the dressing room, drops on the bench, and says he'll never be able to do that again. . . . Until he does it the next night. Now, that's what wrestling is all about!"

Funk might well have been talking about himself.

Wrestling, in the Kiel dressing room, was also about hearing Bobby Jaggers, hard-working and ambitious, good-naturedly complaining about how everything in his life was confused, how he never got any breaks, and wondering when he was going to get a chance at main events. "Wild Bill" would respond, "I know when you're coming, Bobby. I can see that big, black cloud that always hangs over your head coming up the steps first."

That room was also where Kiniski found an unusual distraction while getting ready for his final crack at the NWA prize on April 30, 1982. Almost 10,000 were on hand to see if "Big Thunder" had one last rumble in him — the kind of storm needed to unseat Ric Flair. Gene, though, was more concerned about his son, Kelly, who was making his debut in a preliminary. "St. Louis has been so good to me. I hope Kelly does the town proud," he said. Kelly did, beating Jerry Brown and looking sharp.

And so did dad, who at the end of a sensational fracas was disabled by Ric Flair's legendary figure four leglock. Later, when I approached Gene's cubicle to thank him, I found "Big Thunder" putting a small pebble into his shoe.

"Don't want to disappoint the people waiting outside," he growled when he saw my quizzical expression. "This will make me limp."

In the best "old school" tradition, with the grand illusion maintained for a hundred fans, Gene Kiniski hobbled out of the 15th Street stage door and waited until I could get my car to drive him back to the hotel.

Perhaps the most nervous wrestler I ever saw was none other than Wendi Richter. On February 8, 1980, it was only her fifth outing as a professional, and it was the capital of wrestling — St. Louis. Worse, she was in a mixed tag bout, joining Tom Andrews against "Bulldog" Brown and none other than the legendary Fabulous Moolah. She ultimately survived, and even got the decisive pin over Moolah. A sweet kid, she went on to become one of the hottest celebrities in the early days of the expansion of the World Wrestling Federation. Obviously, she conquered her anxiety that night at Kiel.

The lady wrestlers added something to the atmosphere and the action. "Wild Bill" and I always knew where we could find referee Chuck Riley — he would be trying to prevent the gals from getting bored, teasing and joking with them. Still, the likes of Debbie Combs, Joyce Grable, and Betty Nicoli were just as professional, athletic, and dependable as any guy.

When ladies were featured, they always dressed downstairs in small rooms right next to the Opera House entry. If there was a concert on the other side of the giant steel curtain at the same time as wrestling, it was not surprising to see grapplers — both male and female — peeking out at the performers. Likewise, those same singers and musicians often drifted over to our side to watch the wrestling. Many a friendship was made between those on opposite sides of that divider — but then again, each and every one of them were entertainers. I can recall seeing both Eddie Money and Luther Vandross hob-knobbing with the wrestlers in the area between the Opera House and the Convention Hall during our intermissions.

Kiel was unique in that events could take place simultaneously on either side of its huge steel curtain. The Convention Hall was shaped like an enormous "U" and patrons at one event were not aware of the noise from the other. And in fact, the basement was actually an exposition hall. It was possible to host 10,000 for wrestling in the big Convention Hall, an opera entertaining 3000 in the intimate Opera House, and a car show for who knows how many in the Exposition Hall — all on the same night!

With the Savvis Center replacing much of Kiel a few years ago, all that is left now is the deserted Opera House. Amazingly, the dressing rooms the wrestlers used are still intact, lonely and dark. The stage door sign is unlit and dirty. But on May 11, 2005, at the request of Lou Thesz' widow Charlie and Lou's biographer Kit Bauman, I joined wrestling collector Mitch Hartsey at that very spot to spread some of Lou's ashes. How many times had Lou Thesz greeted fans right there as he entered Kiel for a classic main event?

On Friday nights, the pace always quickened as the clock struck eight. The tension built. Sam was a stickler for punctuality, so at 8:25 I would head for the ring. Going into the main hall past the giant American flag, I could feel the rush of anticipation — as though I personally had given 10,000 people a special signal. Walking down the aisle and hearing the excited fans shout made my pulse quicken.

"Who's going to win, Larry?"

"Is David okay?"

"Tell those referees to watch that damn Heenan!"

"When is Brody coming back?"

"I hope Bruiser hits Murdoch with a chair."

"Ted is finally winning that title tonight!"

I hopped into the ring under lights that were now hot and glaring. I watched the contestants for the opening bout follow the same long, winding path to the squared circle. At exactly 8:30, it was show time.

"On behalf of promoter Sam Muchnick and the St. Louis Wrestling Club, welcome to tonight's event! Would everyone please rise and face the flag for the playing of our National Anthem."

And then the fun would begin.

What I first noticed stepping between the ropes in 1972 was how solid and hard the ring at Kiel was. Most have some give, a little life. At Kiel, however, the ring was huge and as solid as a rock. If I noticed it, think what the wrestlers felt. Unfortunately, there was nothing we could do about it — the ring belonged to Kiel and was part of the building rental package.

David Von Erich claimed taking a body slam on it was like falling on concrete. Harley Race once said, "I might as well take a back body drop outside on Market Street, the damn thing is so hard." After first unleashing his giant flying knee drop, "King Kong" Brody declared he could have landed on the runway at Lambert Airport and it would have hurt less. Baron Von Raschke maintained, "The softest part of that ring was the concrete floor it was sitting on!" Yet for all the griping, not one single wrestler ever cut back on his or her effort; they recognized that fans in St. Louis were knowledgeable, sophisticated, and demanding.

The ring's size, approximately 24 feet by 24 feet — instead of the usual 18 by 18 — also surprised newcomers. After bouncing off the ropes for a flying tackle for the first time, "Spike" Huber said, "I felt like I was on the suicide team for a kick-off at a football game. I had to run fifty yards just to hit my opponent!"

Johnny Valiant, who had a wild sense of humor when he teamed with his supposed "brother" Jimmy, devised a spot that had the wrestlers watching him work laughing. (Many of the guys on the lineup would quietly sneak onto the stage and watch the action from behind the huge flag.) John always complained that the Kiel ring was just too big for him to do flying tackles. One evening, Valiant and his rival both hit the ropes and began criss-crossing — but not colliding. The opponent stopped, but John kept chugging along from side to side...slower and slower and reallllly slooooooooooow.

Finally, gasping, Valiant doubled up and tumbled through the ropes and out onto the floor. The crowd got a kick out of his antics, but not for the same reasons as the hidden wrestlers who laughed so hard they were nearing tears.

When Von Raschke made his St. Louis debut on October 4, 1968, he tried to watch the earlier bouts from that same hiding spot. He had a problem, though. "Without my glasses, I couldn't see two feet in front of me," Raschke, one of the nicest guys ever to pull on tights, explained. "Nobody told me where the wrestlers came in from. When it was my turn I thought I was in the wrong place and stumbled clear across the stage to the other side. I was lost! Thrashing around between the fans and trying to find my way to the ring, the crowd really got into it. When I stormed into the ring after going down about three wrong aisles, everybody was in an uproar so I just went along with it. I was wrestling Pat O'Connor, and he had to be laughing at me. I don't know, because I couldn't see him."

It was during that battle when Raschke's claw was born. "We were going pretty good and Pat whispered to me, 'Put on the claw.' I didn't know what it was so I whispered back, 'What the hell is it?' Somehow I got on something that looked like the claw and the fans really screamed," he said.

Soon after, Von Raschke went to Texas and watched Fritz Von Erich use the move. "I really learned how to use the claw then," he recalled. "But Pat was a super worker and really got me started doing something that enhanced my career." (Even if he got lost while going to the ring!)

Occasionally, the famous ringside press table came into play. It wasn't a gimmicked, plywood, WWE table that cracked if someone accidentally bumped it. This baby was made with two-by-fours, with heavy legs and sturdy braces underneath its flat surface. Fans loved when someone like Dick "The Bruiser" slammed a foe's head onto its solid surface.

In one match, Race took what is called a "dead man's fall" onto the table. His opponent smacked him, and Harley fell, backwards, across the narrow aisle from the ring apron. He hit the table so hard that he crashed through the surface, sending huge splinters everywhere. Race suffered numerous lacerations over his back and side.

The most horrifying tumble I remember, though, came when Ivan Koloff missed a flying tackle and sailed like a rocket over the top rope and onto that unyielding wooden surface. Ivan hit like a cannonball, and the table seemed to explode. Huge chunks of wood landed three rows back. That Koloff survived was nothing less than a miracle. The wrestlers were still buzzing about the bump when we taped "Wrestling at the Chase" two days later.

Things could get rough ringside, and occasionally even I got smacked. On April 18, 1975, Johnny Valentine lost a terrible decision to Race when referee Frank Diamond from K.C. counted a pinfall against him while his leg was clearly draped over the bottom rope. Johnny always had a powerful emotional attachment with the crowd and the building erupted angrily. It was definitely "bad heat."

I'd never seen such a reaction — Race and Diamond bailed out immediately, sensing things might get ugly. As I announced the winner, I spotted something flying toward the ring. Luckily, I ducked. The beer bottle projectile struck the ring light and shattered, most of it raining down on top of my head. Had I been looking up, the shattered glass would have hit my eyes.

Valentine scampered out of the ring. I did, too! Blood streamed down my face from the cuts in my scalp — a couple nicks colored my cheeks and chin. Another bottle hit, skidded across the mat, and struck Ray Gillespie at the press table. Irate spectators rushed the ring, trying to find the referee. Only great work by the police on hand prevented a full-fledged riot.

After things had settled, there was still a tag team match to announce. Stan Stasiak, who was teamed with "Big Bill" Miller against Bobo Brazil and Edouard Carpentier, came up shaking his head at my bloody face. "Helluva bump, kid," he said, praising either my stupidity or courage as I headed back into the ring.

Miller wasted no time, saying, "Make it fast, Larry!" and then jumping Carpentier to divert the crowd from its anger. Like the police, "Big Bill" and the other seasoned pros did a superb job. In no time everyone was happy and cheering.

It was a rare instance of St. Louis fans reacting poorly. It was also an example of how a finish didn't fit the town — something a good booker always takes into account. After all, what works in Dallas might not succeed in New York. Even now, it's worth noting that a St. Louis-based referee was not asked to be part of that finish. When I left the building that night, numerous fans offered apologies for the actions of those one or two idiots, and walked me all the way back to the Warwick Hotel. Our audience was the best, bar none. The incident would never change my mind.

Sam was angry with himself for allowing another situation to get out of hand and turn nasty on the night of August 9, 1974. Eddie Farhat, who was known as "The Sheik," owned the Detroit promotion and was an NWA member. The long, bitter promotional war between him and Dick "The Bruiser" had just ended and there was pressure from a few of the NWA regulars for Sam to book him in a gesture of good faith. Sam agreed.

The Sheik had done impressive business in Toronto and Detroit. He had a reputation, however, for creating violent mayhem, and for drawing some big houses with matches that had no real finish. Ultimately, these kinds of things killed the towns he worked — enraging the fans to the point where they just stayed home.

Sam was skeptical, but O'Connor wanted to give him a shot: Farhat's style was unlike anything St. Louis had ever accepted. When Sam asked about an opponent and a finish, Pat said he would wrestle The Sheik and win by disqualification, "To see how it goes."

It was an unmitigated disaster. Before I could even announce a word, The Sheik attacked O'Connor in the aisle among the fans. Unknown to Sam, The Sheik's manager, Eddie Creachman, was also on hand to storm the ring. This, too, was seriously "bad heat." No bell ever sounded. There was no match. And once more fans erupted into a near riot. Somehow, again, the police kept things civil.

Muchnick was livid. He kept his word, and had The Sheik back for another date, but he made his anger known in the Kiel dressing room. "This is how you kill a great town," Sam barked at O'Connor. The old carnival philosophy that sometimes held sway in wrestling argued that provoking a riot would draw fans. Sam disagreed, and this was the proof.

The following Monday, Farhat called the office looking for Sam, who had gone to lunch. "I guess the old man didn't like my thing," Farhat said with a hint of a chuckle. Having learned diplomacy from the best, I did not disagree, but I also refrained from adding fuel to the fire. When The Sheik beat Devoy Brunson in the third bout on August 24, Creachman was nowhere to be found. (Where was Heenan when you needed him?) Farhat was on his best behavior for the dull, two-minute affair.

And that was the end of The Sheik in St. Louis.

Nick Bockwinkel saved my life during a near disaster of my own making on January 2, 1976. A scrap between Bockwinkel and Joe Blanchard ended in a double DQ, with both combatants battering each other. Where my brain was that night is a mystery to this day — I found myself climbing through the ropes just as Blanchard launched Nick from the opposite corner.

When I looked up, I had just enough time to realize that the 245-pound Bockwinkel was going to staple my skinny body to the turnbuckles. At that point, Nick executed the kind of change of direction that would've made Michael Jordan or Marshall Faulk proud. Just three steps away from crushing me, Bockwinkel slid over a few feet and launched himself over the top rope. I have thanked him many times since — and I'm doing it again here.

"King Kong" Brody and Dick Murdoch could have mashed me in major league style on March 6, 1981. The two were in the midst of a wild donnybrook that had spilled onto the floor when Brody was counted out. As I tried to maneuver toward the ring steps, Murdoch hooked my arms and used me as a shield.

Brody was so fired up that his eyes seemed as big as Andre the Giant's head. He yelled, "I had an argument with O'Connor and I'm leaving! Find me after the show." In the din of the crowd's pandemonium, nobody had a clue about what he'd said. Then, he began jockeying to throw a punch — Murdoch was still hiding behind me, and the fans were still going crazy.

"Okay!" I yelled back.

Brody shouted again. "Now, duck!"

I did and "King Kong" smashed Dick's head. The pair continued their brawl while I escaped into the relative safety of the ring.

This 1960 meeting of NWA powerbrokers brought together some of the most storied names in wrestling, including Leroy McGuirk (front, center), Toots Mondt (back, left), Frank Tunney (back, 2nd from left), "Whipper" Billy Watson (back, 3rd from left), Bobby Bruns (back, 5th from left), and NWA Champion Pat O'Connor (back, far right)—perhaps ironically, Vince McMahon, Sr. (back, 6th from left) and Sam Muchnick (front, far right) are pictured close together

The famous one-hour duel between Lou Thesz and Pat O'Connor, February 5, 1965

Lou Thesz: the meaning of the word "Champion"

Gene Kiniski abuses Pat O'Connor, April 17, 1970 (Photo by Wayne St. Wayne)

Dory Funk, Jr. prepares to wallop Dick "The Bruiser" while his dad and
Bobby "Hercules" Graham recover, June 18, 1965

Dory Funk, Jr. with the toe hold on Harley Race, October 19, 1973
(Photo by Wayne St. Wayne)

Pat O'Connor with the leg split on Lord Alfred Hayes, August 24, 1974
(Photo by Wayne St. Wayne)

St. Louis favorites, Johnny Valentine and "Cowboy" Bob Ellis

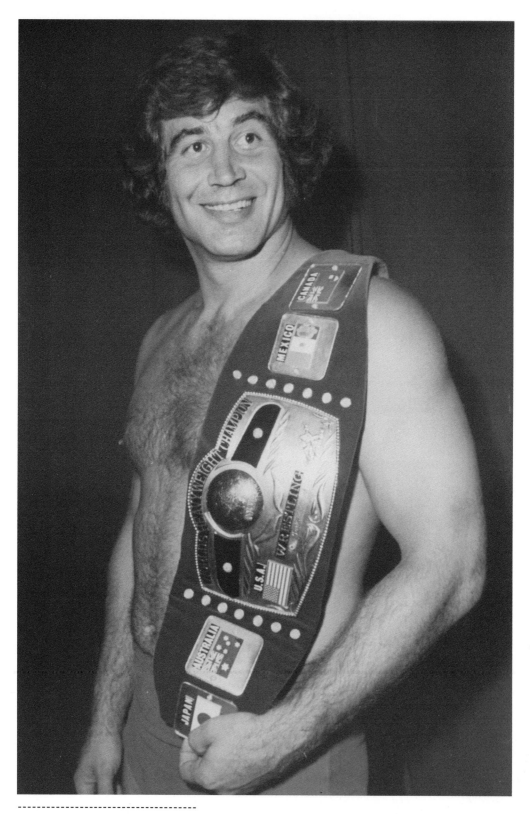

A class act: NWA World Champion Jack Brisco

The Invader (Dick Murdoch)
puts the bow and arrow on Jim
Padoruski in the Khorassan Room,
December 10, 1972
(Photo by Wayne St. Wayne)

Dick Murdoch compliments
my choice of slacks
(Photo by Mike Gratchner)

Turbulent Terry Funk with the gold

Me, Mickey, and wrestling's biggest prize

Interviewing a true professional: Ted DiBiase

Fritz Von Erich's advice was invaluable

Eddie Smith raises David Von Erich's hand, with his father, the inventor of the Iron Claw, by his side, September 21, 1980

AWA kingpin Verne Gagne, with referee Larry Lisowski, Milwaukee AWA promoter
Dennis Hilgart, a visiting German promoter, Nick Bockwinkel, and Bobby Heenan

Bruno Sammartino has his hand raised by
Johnny Ramirez on "Wrestling at the Chase,"
May 26, 1973

"The Nature Boy" Ric Flair

Butch Reed prepares to pummel Baron Von Raschke, February 20, 1981

Talking with Kevin Von Erich, November 18, 1979

The 1981 Police Relief Celebrity Softball game at Washington University:
Mickey Garagiola shows how a wrestler "looks" to "Bulldog" Bob Brown,
Kerry Von Erich, me, and Pat O'Connor

Sam uses the "big stick" to keep Dick "The Bruiser" in line

The Champions: Kiniski, Rhodes, O'Connor, Flair, and Race,
January 1, 1982

Gene Kiniski entertains Joe Garagiola, Sam Muchnick, and me

Pat and I celebrate Kelly's college graduation at Fat Matt's Rib Shack
in Atlanta, Georgia

Joe Schoenberger, until his knees betrayed him, was one of the finest referees in the country. He was the third man in the ring when Kiniski beat Thesz for the title in 1966. Later, after Lou Dietrich and Bob Hoffman, he became the timekeeper at Kiel.

A successful insurance salesman, Schoenberger was also the heart and soul of the exceedingly popular amateur Lemay Baseball Association at Heine Meine Field in south St. Louis. Two of his best baseball products, the Warren brothers, also became top-notch wrestling referees under Joe's tutelage. Lee and Ed recalled that Joe would meet with them in the LBA clubhouse after a card to critique their work.

Joe had worked at Cook's Gym, and had first met Sam when Muchnick was employed by Tom Packs. He learned the business from the ground up. "As a kid, Lou Thesz would work out with George Tragos, and even Olympic wrestlers, every single day," Joe recalled. "Sam would come in to play handball. I was a second when Sam asked me to referee back around 1950. What a thrill! My first match was Joe Millich against Warren Bockwinkel."

The Warrens say Schoenberger taught them to stay out of the line of fire — but he himself learned the hard way how important that was. "You have to anticipate, because the wrestlers have their own thing going on and they aren't looking out for the referee. If you get in the way, you get flattened. It's happened to all of us."

The key, Joe pointed out, was to work with professionals. "The top guys never put you in a spot. They don't take advantage of you or pin you in a corner. Dick 'The Bruiser' would scare you, put you in a spot, but then he'd take you out of it."

Working in St. Louis made things a bit easier on a ref. In the dressing room, Sam would always stress the same thing: a wrestler did not touch his referees. "Sam would say, 'I want these guys protected,' and we were," Joe said. Lee Warren added, "Thanks to Sam, the respect was there both ways, for the wrestlers and the referees. What happened in the ring, happened in the ring."

Still, a referee had to be in shape. "Belly down" is how Lee and Ed remember it. The referee was expected to dive to his stomach and slide a hand under a wrestler's shoulders. Joe thought his toughest match, physically, was when Thesz and O'Connor went an hour on February 5, 1965. Thesz took the only fall within the time limit. "Up and down, up and down!" Joe laughed. "I lost some weight that night."

Likewise, Lee recalled officiating a one-hour draw between Ric Flair and "King Kong" Brody on February 11, 1983, at The Checkerdome. "Flair and

Brody never spent more than a minute in any one hold," he said. "They punished each other. If I was exhausted, they really had to be drained."

Lee had reason to respect St. Louis fans as well, saying, "Generally, you would block the crowd out, but one night I made a call most fans didn't like. People were calling me every name in the book. When I left Kiel, a bunch came up to me and asked why I did what I did. I explained as best I could, but one drunk kept carrying on and started cussing me. The other fans stuck up for me and shut him up. One big fellow told the guy, 'He explained it, so leave him alone.' Everyone agreed. Away from the ring, all our fans were just terrific. They even treated the referees like celebrities."

Joe Schoenberger was the referee at the St. Louis House when Joe Millich tackled "Killer" Kowalski in the early 1950s. "Kowalski was a brute of a man back then," Joe Schoenberger chuckled. "At one point, his leg was under the ropes and I spotted some lady fan run up and stick a hat pin into his calf. Kowalski yelped, jumped up, saw the pin sticking out, and cussed. He pulled out the pin, saw some blood, threw the pin into the crowd, and kept on wrestling! Now that was one tough guy."

But even Schoenberger, who had seen his share of nasty bumps and bruises, had to agree that Ted DiBiase proved how tough he was when Ted squared off with "Big John" Studd at Kiel on March 6, 1981. Studd was huge, a bit clumsy, and a punishing opponent. Even "King Kong" Brody admitted that, "When John clubs you, it's like a baseball bat slamming into your chest." DiBiase said, "John never realized how strong he was. He hurt you when he just touched you!"

During the match, Studd used a bearhug to lift and ram DiBiase into the turnbuckles. Since Studd was 6-8, and because Ted was a very flexible 6-5, DiBiase's head snapped back, cracking against the ring post. DiBiase went down, stunned, and blood began to pour from the back of his skull. A hunk of flesh had been torn from his scalp by the unforgiving steel.

When Ted got back up, it was like he'd been showering in blood. Red streamed down his chest and back. When they locked up, DiBiase's blood got all over Studd. It was scary. Somehow Ted gutted out a victory. Stepping into the ring to make the announcement, I felt like I was in a slaughterhouse.

Pat O'Connor often talked to me about having "an ear" for the crowd. "Listen," he'd say, "and they'll tell you what they want." Ring psychology, especially of the top wrestlers, drew us into another world. When the unexpected developed, the best wrestlers knew how to deal with it.

In and out of the ring, I enjoyed the excitement of all those great duels: the remarkable athleticism of Edouard Carpentier doing a back flip off the top rope and sticking his landing so he could unleash a perfect drop kick; the artistry of Jack Brisco and Pat O'Connor rolling around the mat with incredible skill and precision; the intensity of "King Kong" Brody, determined to make everyone understand how devastating he could be; the fear that only Dick "The Bruiser" could instill as he was on the edge of a volcanic eruption. Doing the ring announcing, I finally realized why nobody ever voluntarily retires from wrestling. Energy flows back and forth between performer and spectator. Even the mic man feels the rush and becomes a tiny cog in this machine. It's a shared emotional zenith, nearly impossible to replicate. Saying good night and departing through the excited throng was like leaving a world of pure magic.

"Thank you for your attendance this evening. Be careful on your way home. Good night."

"Bulldog" Bob Brown clobbers WWWF champ Bob Backlund, April 25, 1980 (Photo by Mike Gratchner)

HERE HE IS . . .
"BULLDOG" BOB BROWN

How many St. Louis cards had him in the opening or second bout? And how many got off to a blazing start thanks to his tirades? His pushed-in nose made him look just like a "Bulldog." The fans loved to bark at Bob Brown.

Brown had reputedly been a pretty tough hockey player, with more than his share of penalty minutes. Then he supposedly spent a year or so as a Winnipeg policeman while he worked his way into the wrestling business. In western Canada, "Bulldog" often formed a main event tag team with Gene Kiniski.

He settled in the Kansas City area, where he became a regular main event performer, and St. Louis, where he perhaps had only one main event ever. A close ally of Bob Geigel, "Bulldog" worked in the K.C. office. Many of the wrestlers were careful around him, fearing Brown was a "stooge" who would carry gossip back to Geigel and Pat O'Connor.

Bob and I became good friends, especially after spending many Friday afternoons in my office before Kiel cards. I would lay out ideas for the sequence of matches, while Bob commiserated with me about how

Pat often had problems making all the television air dates and Kiel dates fit together smoothly. Eventually, Brown became the guy who carried instructions to the dressing room for me when I was booking, particularly when O'Connor was no longer around.

Married once for a brief period and with a son he deeply loved and missed, Brown's life was wrestling. In the ring, he was loud and obnoxious. In the office, he sincerely wanted to help make things run well. But down deep, "Bulldog" seemed a very lonely person. He passed away of a sudden heart attack while working in a casino in Kansas City years after the business had changed.

Jack Brisco said, "Brown was such a sad guy."

Nick Bockwinkel added, "Every time I saw him, Bob looked like a lost little boy."

"Bulldog" best stated his personal philosophy during a bout on "Wrestling at the Chase." Brown was making life miserable for some youngster by pulling his hair and strangling him, which enraged an older female fan in the first row. She blistered Brown for being such a nasty person. Brown leaned forward, yanked the kid's nose sideways, and growled, "Lady, it's a hard life!"

It was my wife Pat who caused "Bulldog" his biggest embarrassment. We were giving him a ride to the Lennox Hotel after a show, because there was a downpour just as we left Kiel. Cautiously, because he wasn't sure how much she knew about the business, Brown began asking what I thought of the show and, finally, his own performance.

Pat perked up and said, "I sure didn't like when you were trying to scrape the guy's eyes with your boot. There was two feet between it and his face!"

Knowing how tight the action was expected to be in St. Louis, and having been called to task in a pleasant manner, "Bulldog" was completely deflated. "Was it really that bad?" he asked sorrowfully.

Pat recognized immediately that he was hurt. Obviously, she felt terrible, but she still didn't want to lie. So she softly, almost gently, answered, "Well, yes."

"Bulldog" Bob Brown never did the move again.

IT'S THE HIGH FLYING . . . ROCKY JOHNSON

There's no better time to bring your wife and young son to a wrestling card than when you are challenging for the National Wrestling Alliance heavyweight title.

And that's just what dynamic Rocky Johnson did when he took a crack at titleholder Harley Race on February 17, 1978, at Kiel. Over 10,000 fans braved the elements on that snowy night to watch Johnson and Race battle to a scintillating one-hour draw. Neither man captured a fall, even though it was a best-of-three match.

Rocky remembers two things in particular: "I took so many suplexes from Harley that night that my head was spinning. That hard ring at Kiel made sure I felt every one of those suplexes for the next week. And it was the biggest payday I had in wrestling! Sam Muchnick was the greatest payoff man in the business, right down to the last three pennies."

In the dressing room that night, Rocky's young son was the real charmer. "He wouldn't let go of my leg," Johnson laughed about his youngster, who was five at the time. The kid had charisma, though, smiling shyly as he clung to his pop.

Yes, the boy grew up to become The Rock, action movie hero and World Wrestling Entertainment superstar. It might have been difficult to spot athletic ability in someone so young, but Dwayne Johnson's sparkling personality was already evident.

His genes, after all, were good; his father could always generate ooohs and aaahs. Once a boxer, who sparred with heavyweight king George Foreman, Rocky had stunning agility for a guy who was a block of muscle and weighed in at 250 pounds. Johnson's drop kick was poetry in motion; he could launch three or four in a row and leave a foe stumbling.

In his prime, Rocky was at the top of the heap and earned four cracks at the gold belt. He dropped a razor-close best-of-three falls duel to Jack Brisco on October 3, 1975. Sam was so impressed that he gave Rocky a rematch for November 21 of that year. That titanic struggle went the full sixty minutes, with Brisco and Johnson each winning one fall.

His first title bout with Race, in 1978, was actually the second time Rocky and Harley had butted heads in a grueling time limit match. Back on August 22, 1975, when Rocky challenged Race for the Missouri State Championship, the result was also a one-hour stalemate.

Harley again managed to fend off Rocky's bid for the NWA crown on June 13, 1980. Each man had one fall to his credit when the champion managed to sidestep Rocky's high-flying drop kick. Johnson ended up straddling the top rope, nearly cutting himself in two. Doubled up and obviously injured, he could not even stand. The referee awarded the decision to Race, who in a surprise show of respect helped Rocky leave the ring. Only in St. Louis would something like that happen.

"St. Louis was the best town anywhere for wrestling," Rocky said. "And I know, because I think I wrestled in them all." Indeed, Rocky headlined cards from California to Florida. In St. Louis, he was a favorite tag team partner of both Dick "The Bruiser" and Andre the Giant.

So tell that Dwayne kid, shy and smiling in the dressing room at Kiel a few years back, not to get too cocky. His old man was a stud, too!

Rocky Johnson main-evented before 10,800 at Kiel, February 2, 1979

WRESTLING

Saturday, November 18, 1978   ST. LOUIS WRESTLING CLUB — Single Copy 50¢   Page One

To Capture World Laurels, DiBiase Must Subdue Race

Champ Launches Reprisal Against DiBiase Nov. 24

TED DiBIASE

Thanks to a bitter challenge from Harley Race, Ted DiBiase may be on the verge of becoming the World Heavyweight Champion.

Wrestling's biggest prize, symbolized by the sparkling gold belt, is up for grabs when titleholder Race opposes DiBiase at Kiel Auditorium Friday, Nov. 24.

Since Race bumped Terry Funk off the National Wrestling Alliance throne in Toronto on Feb. 6, 1977, the crafty kingpin has been intent upon demonstrating himself to be one of the best champions ever.

Naturally, Race's record speaks for itself. Harley has been around the globe and kept the crown from many dangerous contenders.

But DiBiase is part of a new and fast-rising breed which means even more trouble for Race. And DiBiase showed just how much trouble when the exciting youngster pinned Race to end a tag fracas on "Wrestling at the Chase" Oct. 28-29.

When DiBiase used a driving back suplex to smash Race into the mat, the champion had irrefutable proof that still another threat was hot on Race's trail.

Fuming and shocked, Race demanded a showdown with DiBiase, who has made no secret that his goal is to win the World Championship.

Is DiBiase ready to take the crown? Ask Dick Slater, Bob Brown, Jerry Brisco, "Buck" Robley and the many other victims of DiBiase.

And ask Race, who may always regret the angry request which gives DiBiase his chance Nov. 24.

HARLEY RACE

DiBiase Adds Polish From Funks

Ted DiBiase has plenty going for him in his bid to snatch the World Heavyweight Championship from Harley Race Friday, Nov. 24.

One of the most important factors in DiBiase's favor is the training of the Funk brothers, Terry and Dory Jr., both of whom have held the title and gold belt.

Of more significance, the Funks were both dethroned by Race. What went wrong is something the Funks have analyzed and graciously passed along to the talented DiBiase.

Actually, DiBiase has been a protege of the Funks ever since Ted's father, "Iron Mike" DiBiase, passed away after a tough match.

A serious and skilled student of wrestling, DiBiase has incorporated what the Funks have taught into Ted's own style. The mixture must be good, because DiBiase has burst into brilliant stardom.

CHAPTER 7

SATURDAY

While the finishing touches were put on matchmaking for Kiel and "Wrestling at the Chase" early every Saturday, my biggest task was designing and writing the "Wrestling" news.

As time went on, a significant portion of the upcoming cards was booked so far in advance that it was only necessary to fill one or two preliminary slots, with talent from Kansas City or sometimes Indianapolis. Featured performers had such heavy schedules that it was imperative to confirm dates and details weeks in advance.

The "Wrestling" news, however, could not be written until one story (the card from the night before) had happened, and the next (the upcoming lineup) could be prepared. As I've mentioned, Sam was fond of saying, "In wrestling, it hasn't happened until it happens." And even the best-laid plans had to be flexible enough to incorporate unexpected developments.

Creating the "Wrestling" news was always a personal challenge. Every word, from story to headline, was mine, save for the occasional column by Sam or the headlines my wife wrote to help me get everything finished before sunrise.

I was so obsessive about making every edition different that I kept a record of the verbs used in every headline on page one and on the mailing label side of page four. I would never allow the same words to appear more than once in every four or five programs. In the 1970s, printing was still done with "hot type," which was very specific as to size; it did not allow for simple alterations like offset or computerized printing would later. Determining headline and story length required meticulous calculation, as did laying out the photos, which were actually mounted on wooden blocks and could not be resized.

The joy, for me, was in the writing. It was always factual, but a healthy dose of pizzazz crept in to help elaborate on the stories the boys told in the ring. While the "Wrestling" news was obviously designed to help sell tickets, we believed the objective could best be met with an attractive, journalistically-sound publication.

Writing about upcoming main events only reinforced what I'd already learned about booking — everything had to make sense. Explaining why someone was getting a title match meant describing how he had earned that privilege. When two stars squared off in a main event, it was necessary to detail what had created their rivalry and what their reward would be for winning. Top preliminaries got exactly the same treatment. Add it all together, and hopefully the demand to see the confrontations would be stronger.

Consider these excerpts from page one on April 3, 1970:

Funk, Jr. Faces Biggest Challenge as Titlist;
Meets O'Connor April 3rd

One of the most sensational scientific battles of this, or any, decade is on tap in the main event of the St. Louis Wrestling Club program Friday, April 3.

The National Wrestling Alliance heavyweight championship will be at stake when kingpin Dory Funk, Jr. squares off with former world champion Pat O'Connor. A one-hour curfew has been set on the best-of-three falls struggle.

This could prove to be Funk's sternest test . . . many mat experts rate Funk a serious threat to the all-time greats of the game . . . Pat O'Connor has been there before . . .

The likable Irishman has proven his skill in recent weeks. He has beaten Waldo Von Erich, Von Raschke, Luke Graham, Joe Blanchard and Dick Murdoch. The 235-pounder also was the lone survivor and winner of a six-man tag team elimination bout, gaining falls over "Black Jack" Lanza and Bobby Heenan to take that victory.

The icing on the cake, however, came on (Channel 11) March 7–8, when O'Connor held Funk to a blistering 30-minute draw. O'Connor's sleeper hold took the opening fall, while Funk used a reverse rolling cradle to even the bout with less than three minutes remaining.

Funk was able to apply the cradle only because O'Connor had mistakenly assumed that he was the winner. A ring-shaking body slam had stunned Funk, but Dory managed to drape his leg across the bottom rope as the referee counted two. O'Connor did not realize this and turned his back to the wily Funk, allowing Dory to get the cradle . . .

And with the world title hanging in the balance, fans can expect a battle that will receive a prominent place in mat annals.

❈ ❈ ❈

Seamless booking and marketing were still just as evident in the edition for November 20, 1981:

David Opposes Flair

With a full head of steam, David Von Erich is taking dead aim at the World Heavyweight Championship and gold belt on the Kiel Auditorium slate Friday, November 20.

To reach his goal, Von Erich must remove none other than "Nature Boy" Ric Flair from the throne.

The flamboyant Flair and the aggressive David have tangled twice. Flair won once; David won once. Things are different, though, since those two great battles. Flair is now the champion, thanks to a victory over "Dusty" Rhodes in Kansas City on September 17 . . .

On October 2 at The Checkerdome before 18,055 fans, Flair retained the crown by going to a gruelling one-hour stalemate with former kingpin Harley Race.

David has been riding high himself. He beat Race by disqualification August 23 and flattened Sgt. Slaughter October 23 to go along with several other important triumphs. Maybe the biggest change for David, however, is that the sleeper hold has become a trusted part of his repertoire . . . trying to protect against the sleeper AND the Iron Claw could force unexpected openings for other moves with which David can score . . .

This is something extra to worry Flair, who intends to avoid change in the ownership of the gold belt Friday, November 20.

❈ ❈ ❈

I had the most fun producing the features which fleshed out a wrestler's personality or background. They could also be used to explain some aspect of the business. Sometimes this material would come in my column, "Rolling Around the Mats"; on other occasions it would appear as a stand-alone piece.

Here's a typical feature, from February 20, 1970:

Thesz, Graham Aided Brisco

There is a high school football coach in Oklahoma who wouldn't rate very high in a popularity poll taken of professional wrestlers. That coach is the guy who caused fiery Jack Brisco to go into wrestling. Now Brisco is threatening the upper echelon of grappling.

Brisco lettered in football as a high school sophomore and seemed to have a great future on the gridiron. Then that coach told Brisco to get into some other sport during the off-season to stay in shape for football.

So Brisco began to wrestle — and wrestle and wrestle. Soon he had won the Oklahoma State high school mat title, which belonged to Jack for the next two years. Football — well, there just wasn't time for that.

Brisco then grappled for Oklahoma State University under the tutelage of Myron Rodrick. In three years, Joltin' Jack lost only one match — in the finals of the N.C.A.A. tourney. Within one week of that defeat, Brisco was active in the pro ranks.

"Without that amateur background, I'd be nowhere," Brisco admitted. "I learned timing and balance. The pro game is different, but nobody could succeed without a good amateur background."

Originally, Brisco had trouble getting his weight up to pro standards, but that's hard to believe looking at his powerful 230-pound body today.

"Eddie Graham and Lou Thesz gave me the most help," Brisco said. "Eddie taught me the figure four grapevine, while Lou showed me the airplane spin."

Brisco has a clearly defined goal. "I want to be the world champion. I hope that I'm on the right track."

He is. And all because of that high school football coach.

❄ ❄ ❄

Here's another interesting piece, from September 8, 1972:

Kiniski Merges Philosophy,
Self-Discipline for Success

Gene Kiniski, a philosopher?

To many wrestling fans who know the former world champion as a rampaging force on today's mat scene, this may seem more than a little incongruous. It is a fact, though, that Kiniski has a clearly established philosophy of life.

"If a man cheats you once," says the proud Canadian, "you should be ashamed of him. If a man cheats you twice, you should be ashamed of yourself.

"And when you are in the ring, do unto others before they do unto you," nods Gene knowingly.

Without a breath of hesitation, Kiniski declares that his philosophy is successful. "You measure someone's success by his accomplishments in a chosen field," pointed out Gene. "I chose wrestling and I made it to the very top."

Indeed he did. Kiniski held the World Heavyweight Championship as recognized by the National Wrestling Alliance from January 7, 1966, until February 11, 1969. If he had any fear of any opponent, it wasn't apparent. He took them all on and beat every single one until Dory Funk, Jr. was able to stop Kiniski.

"I never abused the championship," insisted Gene. "I met every challenge placed before me. If there is one type of person I can't stand, it is the one who abuses high honors and political power. This is simply repulsive to me."

Kiniski is quick to admit that he owes a debt to many people for his rise to fame and fortune. "Leo Magrill was the finest there was. He taught me wrestling at the Edmonton YMCA and never got a single penny for his efforts. I couldn't begin to total the number of youngsters he has helped."

Complete happiness in his profession is one gift Kiniski claims. He calls his body "my factory — with all the mental and physical parts in perfect condition."

Self-discipline, along with a workable personal philosophy, is the key Kiniski has used to open the door to life's riches. "How can people get hung up on alcohol and drugs? How can they destroy God's most perfect invention?

"Develop whatever talents you have to their fullest extent — that is the way to get to the pinnacle in this world," states Gene Kiniski.

He knows. He's there and he intends to stay a long, long time.

❉ ❉ ❉

And here's another of my favorites, from March 1, 1974:

Japanese Prove Marvelous Hosts

Sam Muchnick touched all bases, including a press conference at 2:15 a.m., during a recent tour of Japan in his capacity as President of the National Wrestling Alliance.

"Jack Brisco, the World Champion, and I had just stepped off the airplane at 2:15 in the morning and there was the press waiting to talk to us," a smiling Muchnick related.

This was Muchnick's third trip to Japan and "it was the best," according to the popu-lar St. Louis promoter. Despite a hectic schedule, there was time for Sam to visit the horse races, a Turkish bath, the Sumo-wrestling training center and the Imperial Palace.

Muchnick talked to the wrestling fans at cards held in Tokyo, Nagasaki, Hiroshima, Osaka and Nagoya. He also videotaped segments for the mat show on the Nippon Television Network, Channel 4.

"Japanese fans are very sportsmanlike," Muchnick stated. "Not once was there a jeer or catcall for me or any of the American wrestlers.

"In fact, the Japanese are very sophisticated. They think nothing of seeing two grap-plers together having a meal," explained an impressed promoter. "It's realized that what happens between athletes on the battleground is not necessarily connected with their private lives."

Shohei "Giant" Baba holds the Pacific Championship and is regarded as a "true super-star" by Muchnick. The N.W.A. chief also spoke highly of Tommy Tsuruta, "a youngster, built like Dory Funk, Jr., who could become an all-time great."

Muchnick renewed a friendship with Toru Shoriki, the owner of Channel 4, the Yomiuri newspaper and the Tokyo Giants baseball team. Sam was also reunited with Hideaki Miyagi, a youngster who once visited Muchnick in St. Louis.

"I'd lost Hideaki's address, but the TV stations and newspapers mentioned this," Muchnick recalled. "And there was Hideaki waiting for me in Osaka. That's just another example of the tremendous reception everyone in Japan gave us."

❊ ❊ ❊

In another typical piece, from June 17, 1977, we once again printed the tale of the World Heavyweight Championship. It was actually none other than Ray Gillespie, another of my mentors and a longtime baseball writer friend of Sam, who came up with that original research. Gillespie was an editor for *The Sporting News*, then the highly-influential "bible of baseball." In fact, it was Ray who composed most of the publication's eye-catching alliterative head-lines. Ray also wrote the "Wrestling" news for Sam, from the 1950s into the early 1960s. He was the first to undertake the challenge of putting together a definitive list of wrestling's champions.

"What a mess it was figuring it all out!" I remember him telling me. "There were double crosses in the ring and between promoters, plus a lot of claimants in the 1930s, especially." Sam, of course, knew most of the stories, and delighted in recounting all the subterfuge for Gillespie. Unfortunately,

Ray still had the problem of trying to sort out the frustrating, tangled mess.

In the end, Sam told Ray to do his best — find a lineage that made sense. Gillespie simply dropped reference to the more confusing incidents and traced the developments as best he could. Muchnick gave the final account his seal of approval. He told Ray that it was important for average fans to be able to follow something that was, essentially, accurate. Gillespie's history was eventually reprinted, over and over again, in wrestling publications around the world.

Ray's work has stood the test of time — it's still the most widely-used version of "the tale of the title."

St. Louis Haunts Champions

Of all the places in which the World Heavyweight Champion must defend his laurels, probably none is greeted with more mixed emotions than St. Louis.

Fourteen times the title has changed hands in St. Louis. No other city is even close. The fact causes a tingle of apprehension for any kingpin, despite his appreciation of the lucrative paydays and classic battles generated in St. Louis.

It was a duel in St. Louis, for instance, which led to an important rule regarding title matches. To become the champion in a best-of-three falls tussle, the challenger must win two falls (the last not by disqualification) within the time limit.

Naturally, the champion retains his honors and gets a triumph if he earns the lone fall within the curfew. If, though, the challenger grabs the only fall before time expires, he is declared the victor but does NOT get the crown and gold belt.

This rule was initiated after a confrontation between Lou Thesz, then the champ, and Pat O'Connor on February 5, 1965 in St. Louis. Thesz took the sole fall within one hour, but the question arose about what would have happened if O'Connor had that solitary pin.

A special meeting of the National Wrestling Alliance convened and a ruling emerged that the CHALLENGER could become champion by winning the only fall. But this created such a furor that the edict was changed into present form. The general feeling is that a champion should be shorn of his crown only if he is clearly beaten at the conclusion of the bout.

And that has happened more often in St. Louis than anywhere else in the world.

❊ ❊ ❊

In the September 14, 1979, issue, a new tactic was revealed in the "Wrestling" news.

Kevin Develops Crushing Body Scissors

Although his father's influence has obviously been huge, Kevin Von Erich has not learned everything he uses from Fritz.

In fact, a famous grappler Kevin never met has provided a crushing hold which could be one of the keys as Kevin establishes himself among wrestling's finest.

Actually, it was promoter Sam Muchnick who tipped Kevin to study the moves of the late Joe Stecher, who held the World Heavyweight Championship three times.

Muchnick noticed that Kevin has tremendously powerful legs, as did Stecher. And Stecher, of course, developed the body scissors into a feared submission grip.

Stecher, whose third reign began in 1925 when he beat Stanislaus Zbyszko in St. Louis, spent hours honing his leg strength. Eventually, Stecher was able to actually smash bags of wheat and sand simply by applying the body scissors.

Kevin studied Stecher's training methods and, with the help of his brother David and Fritz, began special exercises to gain even more leg power and extension.

Now Kevin, like Stecher, has progressed to the point that he too can literally crush large sacks of wheat and sand with the body scissors. Imagine the pressure of that hold clamped on a foe's stomach!

"I hope my body scissors can become even more effective than the one Stecher invented," Kevin divulged. "This makes me more versatile. Because I can go for a concession or roll into a pin position with the same hold — the body scissors."

With all of the weapons already at Kevin's command, the body scissors might do for Kevin Von Erich just what it did for Joe Stecher.

❄ ❄ ❄

Even business matters occasionally made the "Wrestling" news, as in this item for June 16, 1978:

Fans Find Great Buy in Wrestling

Many reasons exist why professional wrestling is such a durable and popular sport . . . another aspect which must be considered is the fact that wrestling has not priced itself out of the market . . . for instance, since 1948 rental costs have increased SEVEN times that rate. Of course, expenses for advertising, insurance, ticket sellers and transportation have jumped dramatically.

Now check the ticket prices. In 1948, seats cost $1.00, $1.50, $2.00 and $2.75. In 1968, tickets were $1.50, $2.00 and $3.00 with $4.00 added for championship cards.

Today the prices are $2.00, $3.00, $4.00 and $5.00 regularly, with $3.00 through $6.00 on title bills. Plus, in 1948 most slates had ten wrestlers in four or five bouts. Now most lineups have 16 to 18 grapplers in more matches.

❄ ❄ ❄

Sam talked about the economics of wrestling in my column for October 19, 1979:

Rolling Around the Mats

When Sam Muchnick rented Kiel Auditorium in 1945, the price was $350. In 1975, the rate was $1950 guaranteed. Today, Muchnick must pay almost $3000, plus a percentage increase as the crowd grows.

"Our transportation for wrestlers used to run around $500," Muchnick added. "Now we normally pay something like $2000 per night." . . .

"Our (ticket) prices will still be comparable to or less than in other cities and a much better bargain than the tickets in other sports," pointed out Muchnick.

❄ ❄ ❄

On April 25, 1980, a story about "Fashion," of all things, made the cut:

Private Designers Help Flamboyant Flair Shine

When it comes to producing dazzle and glitter, "Nature Boy" Ric Flair has a little help from two nice, quiet ladies in Atlanta.

Olivia Walker and her sister, June Scribner, are the designers and makers of Flair's extensive ring wardrobe. According to Mrs. Walker, it takes about two months of daily work to make one of Flair's robes. "Every stone is put on individually," she noted.

Mrs. Scribner added that "sometimes we even have to wear sunglasses, because we get dizzy from the glare of the rhinestones."

Perhaps the favorite creation of Mrs. Walker is a white robe with lavender butterflies and sleeves cut like butterfly wings. Close behind is a magnificent robe covered with 500 feather tips from peacocks.

When Mrs. Walker finishes an effort, Flair flies her to wherever Ric is, gives her a check, and flies her back home. The price? "Oh, it has been anywhere from $5000 to $8000 each," Mrs. Walker said.

Her worst moment came when Flair lost a deep red robe with rhinestone swirls and crowns embroidered into it. "We cried," admitted Mrs. Walker, "but Ric just had us make another new one."

❄ ❄ ❄

Wrestling historians will want to know that, yes, Mrs. Walker was the wife of matman Johnny Walker, known as the masked Mr. Wrestling II in the South.

In each issue, I'd also throw in results from the previous program, along with mentions of what old favorites were doing. Similarly, I'd introduce new names and speculate about who might be squaring off in future collisions. Finally, after adding the basics about ticket sales, future dates, and television time slots, the "Wrestling" news was complete — a true clearinghouse of information for St. Louis fans.

Typesetter Al Steck would pick up the copy from the front desk of whatever hotel we were in early Monday morning. Proofs were ready later that night and printing took place on Tuesday.

Yearly subscribers generally accounted for 4000 copies, but deciding on the print run, I'd also have to factor in sales at the Arcade Building box office and at Kiel or The Arena on the night of the card. Subscribers' copies were mailed out, roughly ten days prior to an upcoming event. Different colored inks were used for every issue. Purple was the royal color; it was always reserved for issues covering World Championship programs!

After putting the entire package together and making sure everything connected clearly and cleanly, my adrenalin was already freely flowing for Sunday's television taping.

Late at night, after a show, in the Warwick Hotel office

Dick Murdoch never met a microphone he didn't like

THERE IS NOBODY LIKE . . . DICK MURDOCH

Was there ever a more rambunctious character?

The truth is, Dick Murdoch never realized how good he was. Bobby Heenan once claimed, "Based on talent, Murdoch should have been the NWA champion. But he really wanted to be 'Killer' Karl Kox." Like Kox, Dick was just as well known for getting crowds to laugh as he was for inciting their hatred.

Ted DiBiase declared, "Dick should have been the champion. He was maybe the most colorful ever. I guess the problem was that nobody knew if Dick could stay serious long enough to be champion!"

And "King Kong" Brody once said, "I used to think Murdoch was all blow and no go. Turned out he could go. Dickie is one tough guy."

What the fans saw was exactly who Dick Murdoch was. Whatever a viewer felt Dick could have done, he probably had. Dick's father had been a wrestler, so he'd been hanging around wrestling rings since the age of five. His connection to a crowd was almost spooky.

He certainly did not look like the chiseled, steroid-pumped athlete of 2005. In fact, over the course of his career he would be needled about looking like a big grape perched on two toothpicks. Dick was, however, both as strong as a bull and a completely natural athlete. Though he never actually played football, Dick once talked himself into an alumni game in Amarillo and spent the entire contest beating up on the other players.

Joining me for a late dinner at Bartolino's on Hampton Avenue, relaxed, open, and for once not telling an unbelievably tall tale, Dick once spoke about breaking into the pro ranks.

"I was just a baby, maybe 1967 or so, and I went to work for Kansas City. I must have wrestled Pat O'Connor, and once in a while Bob Geigel, for six straight months," Dick said. "I spent a helluva lot of time looking at ceilings. Damn, I didn't have any skin on my back when I left Kansas City. But, man, I knew how to work and take care of myself."

Murdoch gleefully schooled other youngsters in the same manner. Ron Powers, a potentially outstanding talent who was buried by wrestling's contraction in the early 90s, bumped heads with Murdoch on one of my cards in Belleville on March 28, 1993. "Dick hit me so hard and so often my face looked like a pizza," Ron said. "But I got the idea about working stiff. No wonder Murdoch could stir up the fans!"

Kevin Von Erich was a fabulous athlete, sure, but early in his career he had a reputation for losing control as he threw his body around the ring. He was an injury waiting to happen, both to himself and his opponent. On November 2, 1979, at Kiel, Kevin was pumped before his clash with Murdoch even began. After a long buildup and grooming period, it was Kevin's first St. Louis main event. I watched Dick getting angrier as the battle went on. Finally, he'd had enough. Dick nearly yanked Kevin's hair out of his head as he pitched him from ring.

Then Murdoch deposited Von Erich on top of the small table where I was seated with timekeeper Joe Schoenberger. With the crowd howling, Dick cracked Kevin with a shot to the bridge of the nose, hooked his head, and twisted his neck. Distinctly and slowly, so only Joe and I could hear what he said, Murdoch snarled, "Settle down or I'll rip your head off and stuff it up your ass!" Then, before shoving Kevin back under the ropes, he rolled his eyes at us.

Kevin, of course, calmed himself, and the two had the kind of sizzling match that kept fans on a thrilling roller coaster ride. In the end, Murdoch put Kevin over. It was the performance of a true master.

Murdoch was able to headline anywhere and the Kansas City office always wanted him back. "Geigel would dangle pushing me to be the NWA champion if I'd come in," Dick said. "I knew he didn't mean it, though, 'cause they'd never put the belt on someone like me. I'd have loved it, but I knew it wasn't going to happen."

It would have been interesting to see how Dick might have evolved as champion. He was known as a star everywhere, including Japan, where he had been the object of a bidding war between the promotion run by Shohei "Giant" Baba and the one led by Antonio Inoki. There was respect, tinged with a bit of fear, for how truly tough Murdoch was.

While Dick's reputation in St. Louis was as a heel brawler, in other territories he occasionally played the baby face. I saw tapes of Murdoch working in the Carolinas and was stunned at how well he could drop kick, and even score with a flying head scissors. When an opponent bounced off the ropes and charged, Dick leap-frogged over him and looked like Wilbur Snyder. Clearly, he could get down on the mat and trade hammer-locks and toeholds with the best.

Once I suggested he incorporate some of those moves into what he did in St. Louis. "It would be so different for a heel to do those things. Look how drop kicks helped get Brody and Fritz Von Erich over," I said.

Dick laughed. "Damn, Larry, I don't need that cute stuff. Why steal it from guys who need it? I can get people excited without doing a drop kick."

And oh, could Dick Murdoch get fans excited! The police who worked Kiel cards got a big kick out of him because he handled his own problems, quickly and decisively. Before a packed house of 11,055 on January 4, 1980, Murdoch was in a wild double DQ donnybrook against Kevin Von Erich. When I made the announcement, Dick came charging up to yell about how he had been cheated, yet again, by Sam Muchnick's referees.

As Murdoch got in my face and began poking a long finger at me, someone hurled a cup of beer. It bounced off my chest and splattered both of us. There was a second of hesitation, and then we both became enraged. The difference was that Dick leaped out of the ring; he'd spotted the guy, in his early 20s, who had tossed the beer.

The police, terrific as always, quickly nabbed the perpetrator and dragged him (with Murdoch in hot pursuit) to the hallway that led to the dressing rooms. Since it was also the last match before intermission, I was close behind. When I got there the police sergeant, Ken Gabel, told me, "Dick wants to handle this guy and it sounds good to us. If you want him charged, though, we'll do it."

I spoke with Dick and he told me his idea. It beat a $100 fine, hands down. The police were waiting with the "perp" in a cubicle when Dick and I appeared. The kid was big, maybe 6-2 and possibly 190 pounds. By now, though, he was scared.

He was even more afraid when Murdoch charged, grabbed him by the throat, lifted him to his tiptoes, and then off the floor itself. Dick then pushed him back against the concrete wall as he was in mid-air. Finally, Murdoch called him a couple of less than polite names and finished with, "I oughta tear you limb from limb, right here!"

At this point, our attacker was almost in tears. "I was stupid. I've been drinking. I'll never do it again," he whined. "Please, please."

Ken Gabel, officer Joe Walsh, and I grabbed Dick's arms and urged him to be calm and give the kid a break. Slowly, working the errant youth as well as he ever worked a sellout crowd, Dick reigned in his rage and released his hold. Ken asked if I wanted to press charges; I refused, as long as our new friend had learned his lesson. "Yes, sir," he glanced at the red-faced Murdoch. "I'll never do it again. No way, Mr. Murdoch."

I told the police to let the guy go. Suddenly, though, Dick reached out and grabbed the kid's shoulder. "If I ever see you do something like that again to anyone in that ring, I'll come down and beat your ass," he solemnly warned.

The guy, shaking, again said, "Yes, sir." Murdoch winked at me, stormed out of the room, yelling, "Bunch of sissy cops. . . . And you! He can fight. Let me kick his ass!" It must be added that I spotted the perpetrator during the main event. He looked just like a choirboy.

No wonder the police loved Murdoch. Gabel, Walsh, and all the other men in blue still enjoy telling stories about him. Ken explained that police called what Dick did that evening at Kiel "a chicken choke." He continued, "When you grab a chicken by the throat and choke it, the legs just dangle. That's what Dick did to that goofy guy.

"It was please, yes sir, no sir, Mr. Murdoch after that!" the officer laughed. Dick was so used to working rowdy crowds in smaller buildings early in his career that he told police, "Don't worry about what's in front of me. I can see that. Just watch my back."

Accounts of Murdoch's brawls, both in and out of the ring, are legendary. His first actual St. Louis push came when he donned a mask as The Invader in 1973. Dick had been on "Wrestling at the Chase," as Dusty

Rhodes' tag partner in 1968, and had worked a couple of prelims at Kiel in 1969 and 1970.

The Invader was clearly main event talent, which was what Sam wanted in a masked wrestler. It was St. Louis policy that if a masked wrestler were pinned or forced to submit, he had to unmask and reveal his identity. Sam maintained, "It only matters if the fans recognize the guy as a star when the mask comes off, or when it's a young guy who is going to the top." Murdoch was the latter.

Before he was unmasked by Bruno Sammartino inside the fence on April 27, 1973, The Invader had, not surprisingly, caused his share of controversy. While facing Johnny Valentine on "Wrestling at the Chase" on January 13, he got into trouble. Valentine ripped off the mask! And underneath there was — another mask! The Invader had doubled-up.

In St. Louis, there was no big star Dick hadn't battled. He was the Missouri State Champion three times. His back-alley brawls against Dick "The Bruiser" were brutal. "The Bruiser" was never going to waste time with leap-frogs and fancy mat wrestling, so Murdoch gave as good as he got, punching, kicking, and slamming all the way.

Murdoch generated a different kind of excitement against the likes of a DiBiase or O'Connor. There, the surprising back-and-forth of holds would catch the fans' attention, as would the superb display of agility from, of all people, Dick Murdoch. Together, those men could build a match to gut-wrenching intensity.

There were still more tricks in Murdoch's repertoire when he tackled Harley Race, Dory Funk, Jr., Andre the Giant, or the Von Erichs. Whether it was toe-to-toe brawling with another tough guy, a hearty dose of wrestling with a former world champion, flat-out comedy turned suddenly vicious against a behemoth, or the hardcore heel making the All-American boys seem like even bigger baby faces, there was no end to Dick's versatility. He'd control an audience, or an opponent, as though they were marionettes. He'd adapt his style to his foe to excite the crowd. Whenever we needed an exciting confrontation, Dick was there. It's the mark of a great "worker." As they said in dressing rooms everywhere, "Murdoch could wrestle a broom stick."

When Vince McMahon, Jr. and the World Wrestling Federation began to roll in the mid-80s, ABC television produced a program designed to show how "fake" wrestling was. One tactic they used was to slow down the tape of a bout. They chose a tag team war pitting Murdoch and Adrian Adonis against Jack and Jerry Brisco at New York's Madison Square Garden.

That was their first mistake. Their second was slowing down a spot where Murdoch was banging home a shot to Jack Brisco's face. It did not look fake at all. Wrestlers call a punch that really lands and really hurts a "potato." About 1:30 a.m. the next morning, my telephone rang and there was Dick Murdoch, guffawing and cackling: "Did you see that crap, Larry? Those morons showed when I potatoed Brisco! I damn near broke his nose with that punch!" Knowing Dick, it probably wasn't the only stiff shot. And, knowing Brisco, he probably loved it and got in a few blasts of his own!

In 1990 I ran a small show in Marion, Illinois, where Murdoch squared off with "Spike" Huber. Joe Zakibe, a young 300-pounder who wrestled as The Assassin and, like many recent talents never got the break he deserved, was watching Dick maneuver.

Joe was simply fascinated. "I learned more watching Dick Murdoch work for ten minutes then I did training for five years," he noted. "All he did was different variations of a headlock and he got the crowd ready to explode."

Dick, of course, loved to party. Von Raschke shared an apartment with him when both men were working in Florida. "Dick nearly killed me," the Baron said. "He was a great guy and a terrific talent inside the square. But I liked to get to sleep while it was dark and Dick kept going until after sunrise. He was never quiet!"

As mean and wild as Murdoch could be, there was another side to the man. When Bill Watts, then promoting the Mid-South territory, fired Kelly Kiniski, it was Murdoch who made the argument on Kelly's behalf. Murdoch deeply respected Kelly's father Gene, and thought Watts had treated his boy unfairly. Nobody else had the courage to confront the intimidating Watts.

Bill and Dick had a true love-hate relationship. As a booker, Watts gave Murdoch the room to make the most of his range of talent; he even created the "Captain Redneck" character for him. (Incidentally, a gimmick nickname like that would never have found favor with Sam Muchnick.) Inevitably, however, Murdoch and Watts would argue, and eventually verge on coming to blows over money or booking. Then, Murdoch would quit, storm out, and book himself somewhere else. But a few months later, Dick was always back with Watts. He grudgingly admitted that Watts was both a tough cookie and a smart booker.

At some point, the "Cowboy" found religion. And after yet another argument, he asked Murdoch to pray with him.

I asked Dick what he did.

"Are you kidding? If I ever was going to pray, it sure as hell wouldn't be with Watts!" he roared. "As soon as I would have closed my eyes, he'd have stolen my wallet!"

After a Kiel card one evening, Murdoch joined my wife and me for dinner with Dave Kraus (a childhood friend), Dave's wife Sandy, and their eight-year-old daughter, Kathy. Earlier that night, 10,000 people wanted to string him up by his toes. Now, Dick Murdoch was the hit of the party, telling tales, joking, and making everyone feel great. He play-wrestled Kathy and kept her giggling, flirted with every woman in the place, and showed off the bottomless pit of his belly with all the food he ate. He had the bartender laughing, and made the waitress feel like a million bucks.

No wonder that Dick's off-the-cuff interviews were the highlight of any television broadcast. Once, he carried a broom into the ring. "That old bat over there," he said, pointing to an older, redheaded lady who howled at the attention, "flew in on this broom. But I need it, Larry. . . ."

Like a good straight man, I asked, "What do you need a broom for, Dick?"

Swinging it over our heads, he snapped, "I'm going to sweep out all this riff-raff you got calling themselves wrestlers!"

Dick Murdoch was never riff-raff; he could have been the champ.

Randy Savage was always intense

HE IS THE MACHO MAN . . . RANDY SAVAGE

While the extravagant "Macho Man" achieved true fame in the World Wrestling Federation, his ties to St. Louis were strong.

When Randy graduated from high school, his father brought him to town for a tryout with baseball's Cardinals. Randy's father happened to be Angelo Poffo, one of the sturdy and solid wrestlers that populated the sport through the 1960s. He also happened to be a friend of Sam Muchnick, who was extremely pleased when Randy worked out at Busch Stadium for the Cards. Overlooking the youngster's effort was Sam's good friend and famous Redbird scout, Joe Mathes.

Sam said, "Randy hit some hot line drives. He was a terrific hitter."

The Cardinals signed Randy and he played in their minor league system from 1971 until 1973. He was released after suffering a serious injury to the shoulder of his throwing arm, a disaster for a catcher. Randy spent the next season with a Cincinnati Reds farm team before his weakened arm again cost him his spot.

With the determination mat fans would come to

know years later, Randy taught himself to throw left-handed so he could play first base. His powerful bat earned him a chance in the Chicago White Sox system, but it was all for naught. His baseball career was over.

Drifting into wrestling, he picked up the name Savage as he and his father started International Championship Wrestling (ICW) in the Tennessee-Kentucky area. ICW was an aggressive operation, and it turned out several good young wrestlers, including "Cowboy" Bob Orton and Bob Roop, a collegiate champion from Southern Illinois University.

ICW and Randy were in direct competition with the National Wrestling Alliance promoters based in Memphis and Nashville. Their war became very nasty, spilling out of the ring and into parking lots. There are many stories: Randy supposedly attacked a wrestler from the Alliance side, while that same grappler allegedly threatened Randy with a gun.

At one point, in 1981, Pat O'Connor and I were talking about young talent and who should be given a breakthrough shot in St. Louis. "The best one out there is Randy Savage," Pat said. "He can work like the devil and he's colorful." But then he added, "It doesn't matter, though. We can't use him."

After Sam Muchnick had retired and I had broken away to run independently in 1983, Savage was one of the first wrestlers I thought about for my own promotion. Fritz Von Erich also urged me to contact Randy. I drove to Lanphier High School in Springfield, Illinois, where Savage was topping an ICW card. His charisma was undeniable. Randy had "it."

Savage, Angelo Poffo, and I spoke after the action ended. He desperately wanted to crack into the big time by coming to St. Louis but was guarded because of the violent emotions his promotion had stirred. I promised him that I would be careful about how he was booked. Randy also asked to be announced as the ICW Champion, which was fine because it was clear to everyone that the NWA structure was already severely fractured.

The only person who was as stressed as I was on June 18, 1983, at The Checkerdome was Randy Savage. He was like a volcano, ready to blow, pacing endlessly through the building's catacombs. The opportunity obviously meant something to him, and he did not squander it. Savage was the surprise star of the night.

For a couple of cards, I used Randy only against wrestlers from ICW, which limited him. Eventually, though, as Randy began to trust me, I convinced him to do a tag team bout, with Tiger Conway, Jr., against Bob

Sweetan and Dick Murdoch. On August 19 the idea was that Savage, a natural "heel," would turn on Conway to create heat for a future bout. Conway was someone that Randy trusted would not try to double-cross or injure him.

Murdoch was a gem, putting everyone at ease and laying out some ideas to which Randy eagerly agreed. The plan worked and the crowd was hot when Conway and Savage, after arguing, finally came to blows. On September 17, Randy and Tiger Jr. staged a spectacular 20-minute draw that brought down the house. As Randy was gaining confidence in me, I was gaining confidence in him. My only regret is that we were unable to continue.

One sour note, about which I still feel responsible, involved none other than the ultimate outlaw, "King Kong" Brody. Randy and Brody had hit it off pretty quickly and Randy booked Brody in Cape Girardeau for October 30. The bout was to be against Savage, and Randy had decided to put the ICW belt on the big man.

The problem was that my new promotion was imploding. On October 29 I told Brody what was happening. Hard-core businessman that he was, Brody contacted Bob Geigel and negotiated a guaranteed money deal for a couple of St. Louis dates with him and O'Connor. The old partners believed that Brody was jumping ship. The truth was, he already knew how things were going to play out for me.

Sadly, as I discovered when Randy called the next day, it also meant that Brody was leaving Savage high and dry in Cape Girardeau. I can still recall the anguish in Randy's voice when he asked, "Where's Brody? Why is he doing this to me?"

Brody did what he did because it was what was best for himself — that was and still is the way the wrestling world operates. Unwittingly, though, I caused Randy pain and embarrassment, and I still feel guilty about it.

In some tiny way, perhaps, I helped make things right when Vince McMahon, Jr. a year later asked me what I thought Randy could do in the WWF. I told Vince that Randy was an untapped gold mine. By that time, Savage had also normalized relations with Jerry Lawler and Jerry Jarrett in Memphis. In fact, with the history between the two promotions, bouts between Lawler and Savage in Memphis were at the time drawing big money. My understanding is that Lawler, who Vince also asked about Savage, praised his old foe to the hilt.

When Randy Savage made the leap to the WWF, it also made his wife an international star. Liz Hulette became Randy's manager and was billed as the Lovely Miss Elizabeth. She had actually been with Randy that first night in St. Louis. She was so pretty and young that I did not want her wandering around The Checkerdome all by herself. I had Liz sit with my wife and some friends from the police department. Everyone adored her.

Liz became very smart — and maybe a bit disillusioned — about wrestling. In the summer of 1991, I helped Vince promote the only wrestling show ever at St. Louis's Busch Stadium. The card took place on July 14, but Randy and Liz came in a week early to make some PR appearances. At the time, they were still married and Turner's WTBS was starting to make big money offers in an attempt to lure away Vince's stars. Liz bluntly told Randy, "It's all about the money. We have to go where the money is."

Unfortunately, their marriage dissolved a few years later. And sadly, Liz met an untimely end — succumbing to a drug overdose in 2003 — after being involved with Lex Luger. When I first met Liz, she was a sweet, naïve, charming, innocent, beautiful young woman. She was the kind of girl everyone wants as a friend or a neighbor. Wrestling changed her. It's one of the sport's true tragedies.

As Liz cheered him on, Randy threw out the first pitch at a Cardinals game on that publicity swing in 1991. Before the game, the team let Randy see his old records and scouting reports. The Redbirds' Marty Hendin picked out the files for Randy, who shared them with his wife. As Marty remembers, "Randy was so happy, just like a little kid."

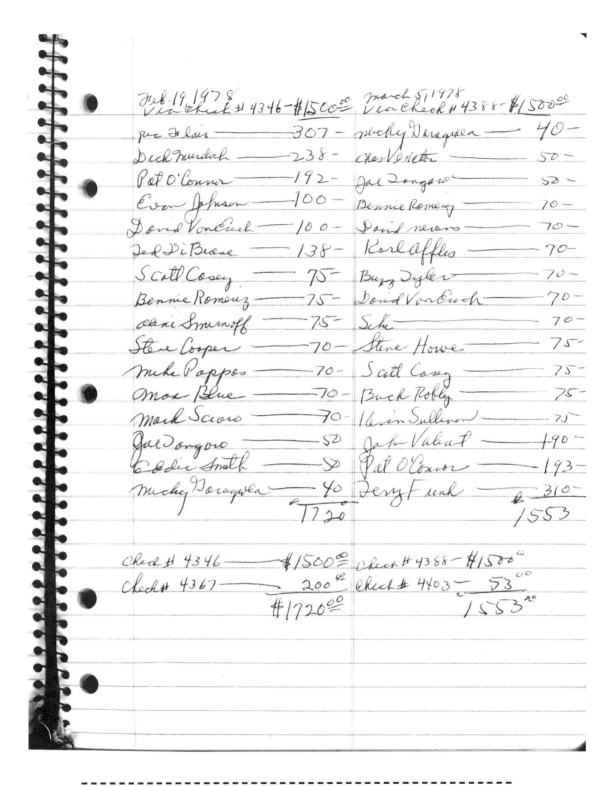

Feb. 19 1978
Via Check # 4346 - $1500.00

		March 5, 1978 Via Check # 4388 - $1500.00	
Ric Flair	307	Mickey Doragola	40
Dick Murdoch	238	Ches Veneto	50
Pat O'Connor	192	Joe Zongoro	50
Evan Johnson	100	Bennie Romeriz	70
David VonErich	100	David Nevara	70
Ted DiBiase	138	Karl Affles	70
Scott Casey	75	Buzz Tyler	70
Bennie Romeriz	75	David VonErich	70
Alexi Smirnoff	75	Sika	70
Steve Cooper	70	Steve Howe	75
Mike Pappas	70	Scott Casey	75
Mox Blue	70	Buck Robly	75
Mark Scioro	70	Kevin Sullivan	75
Joe Zongoro	50	John Valiant	190
Eddie Smith	50	Pat O'Connor	193
Mickey Doragola	40	Terry Funk	310
	1720		1553

Check # 4346 — $1500.00
Check # 4367 — 200.00
$1720.00

Check # 4388 — $1500.00
Check # 4403 — 53.00
1553.00

In Sam's own hand: here are television taping payoffs from 1978

Brody: The Sunday Morning Man

CHAPTER 8

SUNDAY

For countless fans, from 1959 to 1983, "Wrestling at the Chase" was both an institution and a right of passage. In truth, the show originated from the Khorassan Room of the Chase Park-Plaza hotel for only eight years, from May 23, 1959, until November 4, 1967. It returned, briefly, for about three months at the end of 1972.

Why did the television taping move? For one thing, it was difficult to obtain dates in the Khorassan Room. Having wrestlers come to St. Louis for a Friday evening Kiel Auditorium card and stay for the Monday taping (when the program was originally recorded) at the Khorassan Room was inconvenient and costly. Covering transportation costs and personal expenses, and securing available dates for talent became difficult. Finally, the costs and demands of setting up a television production at the Chase itself became prohibitive. After all, the KPLR studio was easier to work with, and it was right behind the stage wall of the Khorassan Room. That's why I always opened the show by saying, "From the KPLR studio in the Chase Hotel complex." Because that's literally where we were. And although the Saturday evening time may have bounced around over the years, wrestling on Sunday at 11 a.m. became a "can't miss" proposition.

After Joe Garagiola left "Wrestling at the Chase" to do the "Today" show in 1963, Don Cunningham took over for a brief period. Then, in January 1964, George Abel got the play-by-play honors.

Starry-eyed and pleased as punch, I first appeared beside George on February 12, 1972. Later that fall, I became the "color commentator" for Sam Menacker. By October 13, 1973, I was paired with Mickey Garagiola. From my viewpoint, not one episode of "Wrestling at the Chase" was less than special.

Ted Koplar had a unique perspective as the son of the owner of both KPLR-TV and the Chase. Growing up running around the hotel and the station, Ted was a director before eventually moving into management. Of course, KPLR was later sold and Koplar moved on to other ventures. Ted understood that the announcer could shape the public's enthusiasm. He realized that Joe was an integral part of its early success, and that Abel had been a solid, reliable professional.

In 2000, when we did an interview for a Channel 11 special called "Wrestling at the Chase — A Look Back," Ted paid me a great compliment, even though he may not have realized it. "You had a great knowledge of the sport," he said. "The fact that you loved wrestling as much as you did showed when you were on the microphone. It was like a singer naturally loving the words of a song. We could feel your emotion and share it. That is what you achieved on 'Wrestling at the Chase.'"

Koplar also noted, "Mickey was a real human being, not Mr. Slick. He was very, very popular."

"Popular" doesn't really do "Wrestling at the Chase" justice. Ratings, at that time, showed us regularly attracting more than 100,000 viewers per weekend. Of locally produced television shows, only the 10 p.m. news and baseball's Cardinals ever topped that figure.

But I had another, different way of knowing how well a show had gone. On most Monday mornings, I would go downtown to check our ticket office in the Arcade Building at 8th and Olive. Parking a few blocks away, as I walked, I would gauge the show's success by how many people stopped me to talk about the weekend's card. If they were excited about Dick Murdoch battling Dick "The Bruiser," or David Von Erich surprising Harley Race, or "King Kong" Brody making his debut, I knew we had a winner.

By 1973, we were taping three programs at a time in the Channel 11 studio on York Street, beginning at 12:30 p.m. Sunday. Sam and I would arrive by 10 a.m., but the engineers and stagehands had already turned the studio into a mini-wrestling arena. Wrestlers would be hustling in all morning. Mickey and I would have three different sport coats and ties ready for three different programs. Some fans were lined up for admission by 8 a.m.!

Ted DiBiase said, "Doing three shows in one day was just brutal. Most of us wrestled Friday in St. Louis, but then traveled somewhere else to wrestle Saturday night. Oh, those early Sunday morning flights in were tough! Then you'd have to get out for either a late Sunday night card somewhere or at least for a Monday booking. You also had the same crowd in person for all three shows, so you had to be versatile. It was just an exhausting day. Still, it was St. Louis. If Sam gave you the ball, you had to run with it and produce."

There was something else that demonstrated how dedicated and determined the wrestlers were. In that era, the real money was made or lost at Kiel or The Arena. That's where the paydays were for both the promotion and talent. Television was a break-even deal in St. Louis — unlike most other towns, where the promoter had to pay the station for the air-time.

The talent appearing on "Wrestling at the Chase" seldom got more than $75 or $100 for an *entire* day, after travel expenses — that's for all *three* programs. But everyone understood that television was the most important marketing tool a promotion, and a wrestler, had.

As announcer, I was paid the grand total of $150 ($50 per show) by KPLR. For booking, Pat O'Connor was paid the same, by Sam, whether he wrestled or not. No wonder we were all keyed in on drawing money at Kiel or The Arena!

Admission to "Wrestling at the Chase" was free, though a ticket had to be ordered from KPLR. The station generally had a waiting list three or four months long. The Khorassan Room itself seated close to 900 fans at its cloth-covered tables. It was cozier (or is that tighter?) at the studio, as just 350 fans could jam themselves in between the news set and the control room.

Ted Koplar and Jim Herd were the first directors I worked with, but eventually Bernie Corno, Jim Winkle, Randy Palubiak, and John Baker all spent time at the show's helm. The entire crew was professional and knowledgeable. All Sam or I had to do was suggest an idea and somehow, magically, the folks at Channel 11 made it happen.

The quality was first-rate, superior to virtually any other wrestling program in the country. More than once, the World Heavyweight Championship would change hands after a show had been recorded. A tape of the title change would be sent overnight to the office. With the help of the eager and interested people at KPLR, I would edit (often late at night) the upcoming edition of "Wrestling at the Chase" so it reflected the sport's latest happenings.

Eventually, we even produced early music videos. It took time, because digital recording was not yet available, but our directors and technicians choreographed wrestler's bumps to the beat of the music. The work, using "Hot Stuff" for Ric Flair, or "Let's Get Physical" for Ted DiBiase, for example, was superb for its day.

"Wrestling at the Chase" actually featured 45-and-a-half minutes of on-air product after commercials and station breaks. Sam always believed that more than one interview per show watered things down, taking away from the impact of a wrestler's words. The so-called "script" was nothing more than the lineup for three cards, the air dates, and a list of who was going to be interviewed.

Unlike today's version of wrestling, dialogue was not spelled out. Here's a typical example of how I prepared someone like Dick Murdoch for an interview: "Dick, you've got three minutes. I'll try to nudge your elbow at about two-thirty. The Kiel card is 'next Friday' when this tape is shown."

Murdoch would say, "Okay."

That was it.

The task of the wrestler was to get himself over and create demand for the upcoming match. Sam wanted an interview with questions, with give-and-take. Great talkers could do themselves infinite good. What viewers saw on "Wrestling at the Chase" was not someone playing a character. Dick "The Bruiser" *was* Dick "The Bruiser." And it was true of every wrestler we interviewed.

Some guys went in with a definite idea of what they wanted to say. Harley Race would always wonder what I wanted to talk about. Beforehand, he might say, "Ask me about . . ." because he'd want me to set the stage for him to tell a story. The Funks, Terry and Dory Jr., usually had a clear idea of where they wanted to go and how to get there.

Of course, Terry loved to talk, and in the process spun some memorable tales. On May 29, 1976, after pinning Lanny Poffo, Funk got himself worked up about an upcoming match. He was about to defend the NWA laurels against Gene Kiniski.

"We had this ole mongrel dog that hung around our ranch," Terry explained. "Somebody must have fed it once, because this ugly old mutt kept coming back. Barking, snapping, mean ole cuss. He was vicious and he scared all the little kids. So we'd kick it, chase it, throw rocks at it, but it just wouldn't go away. What a miserable, nasty hound . . . Gene Kiniski is like that dumb dog! Just because he had this gold belt once, before my brother put him in the dog house and took away the title, Kiniski thinks he can keep coming back and get something to eat. He thinks he can regain the championship! Kiniski is more stubborn and ugly than that dog ever was. . . . Finally, we ran that filthy animal away and never saw him again. Well, I'm going to run off Gene Kiniski the same way. He can bite me all he wants, but I'm going to whip him, pound him, kick him, and hurt him worse than we did that dog."

Terry capped it off by snarling, "I'm going to find out if Kiniski has as much brains as that mutt, because he might as well go away. He's never getting the World Championship from me!"

Murdoch was hilarious and I spent many interviews biting my tongue when he got on a roll. Normally, Dick would blame Sam for whatever problems he faced. Once, though, he started praising Sam in every possible manner.

"Sam is the greatest promoter of all time. He belongs in the Hall of Fame. He's the best of the best," he said, before working himself up. "Except Sam Muchnick is a thief, a cheat, and a crook! Old Sammy has been trying to steal from me since I first got here. Slammin' Sammy! You know it's a conspiracy and, Larry, you're part of it!"

Murdoch truly earned the wrath of viewers. While talking about Kevin Von Erich, who was watching at ringside, Murdoch sneered, "You're a snotty-nosed little punk. I'll give you a spanking and send you home crying to poppa, boy!"

"The Bruiser" gave a great interview when he was preparing for a title match against Jack Brisco. Dick knew they were both big favorites in St. Louis. "Jack Brisco is my friend," he said. "He's my best friend! I love him. There is nobody in wrestling I respect more than Jack Brisco. But he's the World Champion. I want that title more than anything."

And then his voice became eerily quiet.

"I'm going to take that gold belt from him," Dick "The Bruiser" whispered, then paused. Soon, he'd built back up to a roar: "But remember, when they wheel out Jack Brisco's bloody, beaten carcass on that stretcher, I still love him and he's still my best friend. I'll put the belt around my waist and help load my friend's body into the ambulance!"

"King Kong" Brody scared director Jim Winkle once. Brody's voice really projected and he established his personality easily, forcefully. During this interview, he was predicting a victory. Tying in what he said with our Sunday morning time slot, he screamed, "I'm the Sunday morning man! When I promise something, it's gospel!"

Suddenly, Brody dropped to his knees — actually out of the shot. I reacted by dropping down to my knees as well. "Wink" was shocked, but only momentarily. He, along with his cameraman, quickly caught up with Brody, who was still spinning his tale.

"I knew you guys were still alive, even for the second you were out of the picture, because I heard Brody and he sounded like one of those fire-and-brimstone preachers," Jim laughed.

Ric Flair has always been able to talk. The energy level might get turned up extra-high, but Ric could always tell his story and make sure key points were front and center. Johnny Valentine, on the other hand, was a slow, intense speaker. Nobody shared emotion better. Another blond who could "get heat" with his mic work was Buddy Rogers. He personified arrogance.

Gene Kiniski was a whirlwind. A bare introduction would start "Big Thunder" on a three-minute tirade that stressed every main point while leaving no room for an announcer to interrupt. Gene would always finish with: "Thank you for doing such a great job interviewing me."

Pat O'Connor, Ted DiBiase, and Jack Brisco each came across as very serious athletes. They fed off good questions about tactics and strategy. Every viewer sensed these men were determined competitors. Lou Thesz had a regal bearing all his own; he was unbelievably eloquent and articulate.

Rocky Johnson was a great character, but he was surprised when we first discussed doing TV in St. Louis. Unfortunately, wrestling often played to racial stereotypes, and Rocky was used to doing interviews in a way that played off those expectations. Luckily, he asked me about it and I told him just to be himself. It's easy to see where The Rock got his mic skills.

"Crusher" Blackwell was a 450-pounder who moved tremendously well in the ring. Though lacking in the way of formal education, "Crusher" could talk. "I'm not fat! Don't say I'm fat!" the 5-10 tough guy once bellowed. "I weigh the same as Andre the Giant! I'm in shape! I'll crush Andre until he's my height!"

A wrestler's charisma, or lack thereof, almost always came across in an interview. Dewey Robertson, at that point close to earning main events, never quite clicked on the mic and it probably hurt him in St. Louis. He just couldn't weave words together in a colorful fashion. Similarly, Ron Starr always seemed nervous and seldom looked at the camera. Meeting the viewer's gaze was vital.

Sgt. Slaughter, though, had no such problems. An excellent worker, big and mean, Slaughter's drill sergeant delivery was powerful. I slotted him with David Von Erich for Kiel on October 23, 1981. It made sense, the free-spirited young star against the demanding Marine. At the box office, though, it flopped. Looking back, maybe Slaughter was too cartoonish for our audience. Perhaps they sensed that Sarge was role-playing. Whatever it was, the chemistry was all wrong.

Kerry Von Erich was always a challenging interview. He could never remember dates or the history of a feud. I would try to prompt him — but unfortunately that usually resulted in a minute-long question. But maybe that was the lesser of two evils; and at least it was honest. Kerry was an athlete, handsome, with a quick and easy smile. And not being too glib or polished might have helped him get over. On the other hand, his brother David, whether he was angry with an opponent or happy about a victory, always came across like Huckleberry Finn.

"Ox" Baker, a lumbering 320-pounder with a huge, bushy mustache, once did an expensive interview. Before he began talking to me, he grabbed Mickey Garagiola's tie and twisted it, tearing the fabric. In the control room, Sam was incensed. The next time "Ox" came to the studio, he was the recipient of an angry ultimatum. Humbly, "Ox" apologized to Mickey and handed him a new, expensive tie. "The doggone tie was too fancy for me to wear to wrestling," Mickey said. "I saved it for weddings."

Even at tapings, Sam was clearly the boss. The dressing room was really a large conference room on the second floor, and each wrestler carved out his little corner. Before the session began, Sam or, at his request, O'Connor, gave the troops the same stern speech: "St. Louis is the only town that doesn't have to pay to be on television, so keep it clean but tough. No two men on the floor at the same time. Don't use the furniture. Stay away from the equipment. Don't get us kicked off TV."

DiBiase was not much more than a rookie when he and Rocky Johnson took on Murdoch and Bob Sweetan for "Wrestling at the Chase" on January 21, 1978. The match had barely started when Murdoch pitched Ted from the ring and followed him to the floor.

"No two men on the floor!" barked Dick, punching Ted in the jaw.

"Don't use the furniture!" he then said, slamming DiBiase's head into the table where Mickey and I were sitting.

"Stay away from the equipment!" he screamed as he took the long camera cable and wrapped it around Ted's throat to choke him.

DiBiase was positive Dick was going to get him fired.

Then Murdoch whispered, "Now it's your turn, kid."

Dick turned the tables and had Ted do everything he'd just done. The scrap ended as a no-contest, with Rocky and Dick both counted out while fighting on the announcer's platform.

"We went up the steps and I was scared to death that I'd be fired," Ted said. "Sam came right up to me and my heart just sank. Then he smiled, shook my hand, and told me, 'Great match, kid! Way to go!' I caught Murdoch's eye and he just winked."

It was not long before DiBiase figured out the reason behind Sam's apparent change of heart. "That speech kept the new guys or the inexperienced people from messing up. If everybody did it, when the stars did it, it wouldn't mean a thing." Naturally, that philosophy carried over to Kiel/Arena programs as well.

As it was, roughnecks like Brody, Murdoch, or "The Bruiser" found our table often enough that Mickey told me, "If another head gets bounced off this table, it will have more hits than Stan Musial. And he had 3000!"

Doing commentary came naturally to me. If the crowd got excited, I would too. If the spectators were quiet and on the edge of their seats, it was a chance to talk about personalities and strategy. If anything, my style was probably more radio-friendly. Growing up in St. Louis, great talkers like Jack Buck, Harry Caray, and Joe Garagiola ruled the airwaves. The gentleman who influenced me the most, though, was Buddy Blattner. Listening to him describe the exploits of basketball's St. Louis Hawks, and talking about stars like Bob Pettit, Cliff Hagan, Clyde Lovellette, and Slater Martin was spellbinding.

Buddy never trampled the talent or became bigger than the game. He was another good friend of Sam's, so it was truly an honor when I got to know him and his wife, Babs. He was vastly underrated as a radio and television commentator.

The lessons I learned from Blattner applied to our show as well. "Wrestling at the Chase" *was* the athletes. The goal was to help get them over with the public, not to make yourself a star. When the product got over, you got over. As the show earned a place in viewer's hearts, I went along for the ride.

A carnival barker eventually becomes boring. Wrestling, like baseball, football, or any other sport, has ups and downs. Trying to yell and sell the entire program only turns off viewers. Instead, a good wrestling announcer follows the rhythm, has an ear for the people, and feeds off their energy. He simply has to help tell the story.

Sam often pointed out that my job as announcer was to "educate our audience about the St. Louis style." He liked how I picked up on the little details of booking and that subtle intricacies were clearly explained. Just as important was the background material that added depth to the personalities in the ring. Making everything fit together seamlessly was the goal; it was a soft sell, cool, comfortable, and oh so effective.

Mickey and I were fans who happened to have a bit more inside knowledge. We were the conduit between the wrestlers and a public kind enough to invite us into their homes. And the bottom line is that it was just plain fun.

One of my favorite moments came when we were building to a title match between Ric Flair and Dick "The Bruiser" at The Checkerdome on June 12, 1982. The two had a history of combat, so I had plenty of facts to remind fans about while explaining why this showdown was special. It also helped create the sense that almost anything could erupt, especially considering Dick's volcanic personality.

What took place on "Wrestling at the Chase" on June 6, 1982, is still talked about by anyone who watched. As Flair was wrestling Art Crews, "The Bruiser" came to our table — where, incidentally, Flair had placed both his gorgeous, expensive robe and the gold belt. Fans started to react as Dick snapped the belt around his waist and, insult of insults, put on Flair's robe.

Ric went berserk and tried to get at "The Bruiser." Crews cut him off, still wanting to battle. As Flair got to the floor, with Crews hanging on for dear life, "The Bruiser" crawled into the ring. Dick pulled off the robe and threw it to the canvas. Then he stomped on the robe and did a little dance on the outrageous garment. Ric desperately tried to reach "The Bruiser," but Crews clawed, punched, and held him back.

Next, Dick waved the robe like a matador, and then heaved it into the studio's bleachers. Before Flair could get at him, he scooted out with the gold belt still around his waist. Flair then ripped Crews apart and charged my table. By that time, a referee had somehow retrieved the gold belt.

In the next bout, Dick absolutely destroyed Ray Hernandez (later Ray would add "Hercules" to his moniker). He whipped his hapless foe toward our table; Hernandez sailed over it, just past my right shoulder, and crashed into the canvas wall behind our platform!

Imagine the interviews that followed. Flair was enraged, shrieking that his pride had been assaulted, and that he'd get his revenge. Dick followed up by growling that he'd wanted Flair to "see how stupid he looks, prancing around like a sissy in a bathrobe." I was left to put the incident into perspective, pointing out that "The Bruiser" was playing mind games with the champion, putting him off-balance just before their showdown.

Setting up that angle was tremendously satisfying, and as I've said, Flair was always generous and open to creative new ideas. Ric suggested the robe, I added the belt, and Dick did the rest. Flair told young Art Crews again and again, "This is a shoot" — which meant it was for real — "hold nothing back . . . I'm going after him, and if you don't stop me, I'll get him. Don't worry about hurting me. Do what you have to do, because, brother, I'm going to be on fire!"

And he was.

The unbridled intensity of what happens inside a wrestling ring has never failed to amaze me. On October 13, 1972, Harley Race won a savage best-of-three falls duel from Gene Kiniski to become the new Missouri State Champion. Afterward, as I interviewed Race, Kiniski came back into the ring to challenge for a return bout. One thing led to another and "Big Thunder" walloped the new champ. The heavy thud almost knocked me out: it was that powerful. The pop sounded tremendous because I made sure the microphone was right there.

Harley was once again on the receiving end when he and Lord Alfred Hayes squared off with Dory Funk, Jr. and O'Connor on May 4, 1974. Dory Jr. was bleeding badly before he made a stirring comeback and knocked Race to the floor. The sight of blood dripping off Funk's forehead and onto Race was compelling, to say the least.

Many still recall September 9, 1978, when Ted DiBiase, in street clothes, was guest commentator for a match between Flair and O'Connor. Flair strutted toward us, verbally insulting Ted and his late father. Finally, Ric threw a cup of water in Ted's face. Despite being in shirt and slacks, DiBiase went after Flair. He even blasted Ric with a drop kick while in street shoes. Half of the dressing room had to help the referees pull them apart.

Countless moments like these stick out for St. Louis fans. Maybe it was Rogers and Valentine in 1961, or the Funk brothers against the Brisco brothers in 1971, or Von Raschke and David Von Erich in 1980. But it would be a shame to forget the many solid, meat-and-potato wrestling matches that were the foundation of the show. Not everything was structured around yelling and brawling, and more often than not the best matches were a test of skill and endurance.

Sam hated what's called a "squash," where one hapless grappler gets in zero offense while being pounded into oblivion. "Even if you're in over your head," Sam would instruct, "fight back. We don't want wash rags on this show!" Newcomers who followed the edict, in due course found themselves with more opportunities.

When the entire package was in place, the show documented the sights and sounds of what St. Louis wrestling had become. Two decades after its demise, "Wrestling at the Chase" still enthralls many loyal fans. To be a part of this history is, for me, nothing short of awesome. It's true. St. Louis was in fact the capital of the sport, and "Wrestling at the Chase" was its crown jewel.

So what if I had to do three shows in one day? When it all worked, from Friday at Kiel, to Saturday's writing sessions, to Sunday's studio tapings, it was absolutely electrifying.

Andre the Giant hoists TV's Mike Douglas

THE ONE AND THE ONLY . . .
ANDRE THE GIANT

"Hey, boss!"

With a voice that rumbled like a freight train, that's how Andre the Giant would greet his dressing room peers. Because Andre traveled so much and met so many different people, he probably never bothered to remember a name — except perhaps for Sam Muchnick.

Billed at 7-4 and 424 pounds, Andre made his St. Louis debut on February 15, 1974, with a victory over Baron Scicluna at Kiel Auditorium. What an incredible sight he was, even if he really stood a bit under seven feet. A huge head, and massive hands, a mop of curly black hair, his proportions were truly those of a giant.

And Andre could move. In that bout with Scicluna, the Baron went behind Andre. Instead of doing the usual strong-man spot of pulling Scicluna's hands apart, Andre executed a sit-out and switch so he ended up behind Scicluna. Then, Andre pulled Scicluna to the mat, clamped on a body scissors, and bounced Scicluna right on his butt.

I clearly remember the moment of silence that followed as everyone in attendance realized The Giant was not just another freak show.

Andre Rousimoff was born in Grenoble, France; he got involved in wrestling after playing rugby and soccer and doing a bit of boxing. Wrestling legend has it that Edouard Carpentier discovered Andre and engineered his move to Montreal in 1970. Billed as Jean Ferre, Andre immediately leaped into main events against the likes of "Killer" Kowalski and Don Leo Jonathan. Pictures of the ever-smiling Giant in wrestling magazines quickly gained attention around the globe.

By 1974, Andre was being booked by Vince McMahon, Sr. and following a schedule perhaps even more demanding than that of the National Wrestling Alliance champion.

He would visit every circuit once or twice a year, almost always drawing sellout crowds. St. Louis was no different. Twice he headlined in 1974, once in 1975, twice in 1976, once in both 1977 and 1978, three times in 1979, once in 1980 — and so it went.

To keep the record straight, Andre worked twelve Battle Royals (his specialty) in St. Louis. In keeping with Sam's booking philosophy, not even Andre would win every match. He did capture five Royals (the first victory did not come until 1978), including a shared victory with Dick "The Bruiser" on January 25, 1980, and another shared triumph with "Butch" Reed on January 23, 1981. Fittingly, Andre won his last ever Royal in St. Louis alone, on February 25, 1983.

I was introduced to Andre at the airport before the Scicluna match, and then drove him to the KSD-TV studio for an interview on John Auble's "Newsbeat" program. Just getting Andre into my car was a chore. The poor giant had to fold himself forward until his chin was almost resting on the dashboard. The interview was terrific; Andre was comfortable and funny on the air.

My wife Pat was amazed to find how gentle Andre could be when she met him. "I could barely feel his touch when we shook hands," she said. "It was like he was holding a little bird egg." Ed Merschen, a manager at the Chase Hotel, recalled that when he shook Andre's hand, "My arm disappeared below the elbow." Jeannie Venn, the Chase concierge, described Andre as "The most enormous human being I've ever seen."

His hands *were* like hams. Once I was interviewing him for an upcoming battle with "Crusher" Blackwell. He finished by putting his hand over my face. The heel of his hand was at my chin, the base of his fingers at my hairline, and his fingers curled over the top of my skull. His thumb and little finger were actually spread and over my ears.

My head was like a grape in his grasp.

Sam loved to take Andre for lunch at Jack English's popular bar, a hangout for political and media types in Belleville, Illinois. Stories of how many catfish Andre could eat and how much beer he could drink are the stuff of legend. Nobody in the St. Louis area was surprised by how successful he was in Billy Crystal's movie *The Princess Bride*. His personality truly sparkled in that role.

When I was helping Verne Gagne with his television, I traveled with Andre from Minneapolis to Winnipeg. We met at 7 a.m. for breakfast at the airport — Andre drank wine, and lots of it. In Winnipeg, I joined Andre for lunch at the Polo Park Inn with hockey greats John Ferguson and Serge Savard — they knew The Giant from a Montreal restaurant he owned. Again, Andre drank wine and lots of it.

After the show, Andre went with me and Wally Karbo to an exclusive steak house. After eating most of the beef in central Canada, Andre drank more wine. Lots more. But despite all the alcohol, he was never drunk, not in the slightest. It really must have been his giant capacity!

The road, though, was especially hard on Andre. Being wedged into airline seats and the struggle to find a decent bed took their toll. He never married, but he had a daughter. He suffered from acromegaly, which causes abnormal growth and proportions. His weight would balloon to well over 400 pounds. And the excessive drinking did, in fact, hurt him in the long run.

After one card at Kiel, I had my friend Dave Kraus sneak Andre out and give him a ride to the hotel. Dave was with his wife Sandy, older daughter Kathy (who was maybe eleven at the time), and one of her buddies. Sandy remembered: "Andre was so nice and gentle with the kids. He put his hand up next to theirs to compare size. He gave them his bag to carry, but they couldn't lift it and he laughed. So did they. When he got in the front seat, Dave had to help push the door closed. Andre took up the entire front seat. It was bizarre to see him trying to fit in the car. The girls were howling. He scrunched down and it was so hard for him to get out. He was very sore.

"We got a slight taste of what it was like to be a celebrity when he left," Sandy added. "Fans were just clawing all over him and yelling for him. They were everything from obnoxious to adoring. He acknowledged people, but just kept walking. It's hard to comprehend what his life must have been like."

Once, in the mid-1980s, Andre was shooting a live television angle from Indianapolis for a match with Hulk Hogan at WrestleMania. "King Kong" Brody toyed with the idea of sneaking into the building and jumping into the ring to get publicity, even if it would have made life-long enemies of Vince McMahon, Jr. and the WWF. Some rival promoters urged Brody to pull the stunt.

In the end, Brody decided against it. "First, nobody messes with The Giant," Brody said. "All he has to do is fall on you to crush you. Mostly, though, I respect him. He has a hard life doing what he does. He's been good for wrestling. Andre deserves respect."

Andre was just 46 when he passed away, in 1993. Though he had asked to be cremated when he died, no crematorium in Paris was big enough to accommodate him. A 300-pound casket was constructed for Andre — who was himself well over 500 pounds in the end. Finding a flight to return his body to the United States was difficult, because most cargo holds were not big enough. A forklift was needed to remove his casket from the plane in North Carolina. He was finally cremated there, and his ashes were scattered over a ranch he owned and loved.

More than a decade later, we all know that Andre was truly "the boss."

*Dick "The Bruiser" battles Dick Murdoch
in a tag bout on February 15, 1974, while
partner Bobo Brazil looks on*

Look at his eyes — precisely what makes
"The Bruiser" a legend

ONE OF WRESTLING'S TRUE LEGENDS . . .

DICK "THE BRUISER"

The reason Dick "The Bruiser" was "over" for so long is simple: he scared people.

When Dick made his St. Louis debut, crushing Emile Dupre on the January 19, 1963, edition of "Wrestling at the Chase," he was already a monster. "The Bruiser" was built like a tank, with slabs of bulging muscle, a snarling face, and angry eyes. The crowd in the Khorassan Room parted when he jumped out of the ring, poured some fan's beer over his own head, and then stalked out of the room and through the Chase lobby! It was unplanned and spontaneous.

Many in wrestling believed that Sam Muchnick would never be able to work with "The Bruiser," who had a checkered reputation. Dick, it's true, had been involved in more than his share of business disputes. "The Bruiser" had also been part of the riot that nearly got wrestling banned from New York's Madison Square Garden, when he and Jerry Graham got out of control in a tag bout against Edouard Carpentier and "Argentine" Rocca.

But then the strangest thing happened. Sam and "The Bruiser" became close friends.

His reputation certainly preceded him. Dick claimed to have attended five colleges — and that he'd been booted out of four. "The Bruiser" was also said to have been a feared bouncer at the famous Harold's Club in Reno, Nevada. And he definitely was a wildman when he played for the Green Bay Packers in the National Football League.

Sam Muchnick wasted no time in giving "The Bruiser" a push back in 1963. On February 1 at Kiel, Dick dismantled Ray Gordon. On February 15, "The Bruiser" and John Paul Henning were involved in a Pier Six brawl that saw them both disqualified. "Wild Bill" Longson and Bobby Bruns needed the help of three referees, 350-pound Gino Marella (who would later become Gorilla Monsoon), and other prelim wrestlers to restore order.

Hall of Fame football star and former wrestling champion Bronko Nagurski was brought in to be the special referee for the return bout on March 1. A sellout of 12,000 saw "The Bruiser" pin Henning and nearly get into a fight with Nagurski.

"The Bruiser" was disqualified in his first championship bout against Lou Thesz on March 15. Dick earned another crack at Thesz by whipping Rip Hawk, in a battle of the "bad boys," on April 5. Before "The Bruiser" and Thesz could square off again, though, Dick got himself involved in another predicament.

Alex Karras of the Detroit Lions and Paul Hornung of the Green Bay Packers had been suspended from football for betting on games. Karras had wrestled a bit in the off-season, and there was a good payday in a match pitting "The Bruiser" against him in Detroit. That showdown was set for April 25; "The Bruiser" was then to head to St. Louis to tackle Thesz on the following night.

A few nights before the Detroit event, "The Bruiser" decided to visit a bar Karras owned, with the hope that he might stir up some local talk. Dick succeeded, far better than he intended. Somehow, he instigated a full-fledged brawl, and allegedly assaulted several policemen who came to restore order. A nightstick split "The Bruiser's" head open (though he reportedly injured seven officers before being subdued). There were lawsuits pending for years.

Nonetheless, amid a storm of media attention, a bloodied "Bruiser" defeated Karras in Detroit. The next night, in St. Louis, Thesz got the verdict, reopening Dick's barroom wounds so badly that the ref had to stop the match. This provoked a monumental tantrum from "The Bruiser."

By this point, Sam and Dick had learned they could trust each other. "The Bruiser" would be a major attraction in St. Louis from then on. Even as his career waned, he never lost the aura which made everyone, even some wrestlers, afraid.

Sam was a stickler for punctuality, but Dick had special dispensation. He'd usually roll in right after a Kiel card had started. Sam would just grin and say that was for the best, because "the crowd at the stage door would crush him otherwise." Over the years, Dick never once let Sam down. He even made a couple of treacherous journeys through ice storms, above and beyond the call of duty, so he wouldn't fail to appear as advertised.

Sam thought he found a soft, sentimental side of "The Bruiser" in the mid-1970s when Dick's daughter Michelle married "Spike" Huber. "Dick had tears running down his face during the ceremony," Sam recalled. "Afterward, I hugged him and told him that he was just a big teddy bear inside.

"Dick frowned and growled, 'I was just crying about how much money I spent on the damn wedding!'" Sam laughed. "But he didn't fool me."

St. Louis fans weren't fooled either. By 1970 they'd started to cheer "The Bruiser," although his disdain for the rulebook had not changed. He was just being himself, a rowdy rebel — the element of fear, of Dick truly snapping and losing it, kept everyone on edge.

Nick Bockwinkel remembers a story he'd been told by Wilbur Snyder, who was "The Bruiser's" business partner in the Indianapolis operation. Snyder had tagged with Nick in California. "Wilbur agreed to ride with Dick to a show one night, and afterward they stopped in a terrible part of some town to have a beer. Wilbur was worried, but Dick fit right in with the other customers. When they went out to their car, the door was open and their wrestling bags were gone from the back seat. Wilbur said Dick started cussing, opened the trunk, and got out two .45 caliber pistols," Nick chuckled.

"Dick fired a couple shots in the air and told Wilbur to do the same. Now Wilbur thinks they're going to be killed for sure. People came out into the street and Dick bellowed, 'We're going back into that bar for an hour. When we come back, our bags better be back in this car or somebody is going to get hurt bad!' Then he stalked back into the bar, with Wilbur sticking close. When they came back out an hour later, their bags were intact in the back seat. Dick said, 'Told you so.' But Wilbur told me he made sure never to ride with Dick again. . . ."

Dick really cemented his "cult favorite" status in St. Louis after he and "Black Jack" Lanza opposed Luis Martinez and Tommy Martin on the October 25, 1969, edition of "Wrestling at the Chase." Bobby Heenan, Lanza's manager, was right in the middle when "The Bruiser" and Lanza got into a skirmish that ended in fisticuffs. "The Bruiser" loved smacking Heenan around, almost as much as the fans loved watching it.

On January 9, 1970, "The Bruiser" was disqualified for blasting NWA champ Dory Funk, Jr. with a chair. It led to an athletic commission suspension (which Sam instructed them to impose), which only made Dick even more of a rebel hero to most fans. Yet it wasn't until November of that year that Sam finally went with the flow and booked "The Bruiser" against other heels. Dick was cheered whether he wrestled Dory Jr., Lanza, Jack Brisco, or Von Raschke.

Once, when Sam was hospitalized during the 1970s, Dick became frustrated because he couldn't get in to visit his friend. Somehow, "The Bruiser" finally convinced the front desk that he was actually Sam's rabbi. He was cleared. Sam was very sick, but he couldn't stop laughing at Dick's guile. From then on, whenever I placed a call to Dick for Sam, I would ask for "Rabbi Bruiser."

In the ring, however, it was still always wise to be wary of "The Bruiser." On January 3, 1975, after being disqualified in a match against champion Jack Brisco, Dick first threw referee Bobby Whitlock, and then me, out of the ring. I ended up with a dislocated knee. Later, Dick apologized, but added, "I told you to get out, but you didn't move fast enough."

A not-so-classic donnybrook took place on August 27, 1982, when Dick defended the Missouri State Championship against Harley Race. The referee stopped the first fall, disqualifying both Race and "The Bruiser" for wielding chairs. But Race was already battered when I went into the ring for the announcement.

Dick headed towards me, but stopped cold when I said, "The first fall." "The Bruiser" snapped, "It's only one fall!"

I responded: "No, it's best-of-three. We said it on TV and it's in the program."

"Oh, hell!"

Thinking quickly, but staying nimble, I said, "Just do it again, another DQ! It'll be a helluva story."

Dick liked that. Poor Harley, he got beaned seven — yes, *seven* — more times by the chair Dick was swinging. It was definitely cause for a disqualification.

"The Bruiser's" last major hurrah — an event I'd argued for — came when he got into a feud with flamboyant Ric Flair in 1982. The climax came before 19,027 at The Checkerdome on June 12. "The Bruiser" might have been past his prime, but that night he was dangerous, mean, and explosive. In Flair he found the fountain of youth. Dick looked like "The Bruiser" of old, the monster who'd battled Thesz and Henning.

Flair took the first fall in 12:01 with a front rolling cradle. Dick used a piledriver to earn the second stanza in 7:28. Flair clinched it with a back body drop and bridge off Dick's attempted piledriver after 10:01. "The Bruiser" performed like the superstar he had always been, bouncing off the ropes and giving the fans chills with his unique brand of violence. He gave Ric a beating to remember before ultimately succumbing with dignity.

Even if fans noticed the mileage, he was still the unpredictable warrior who struck fear into their hearts. Legends like Dick "The Bruiser" never die.

"King Kong" Brody was right in the middle of the 1983 wrestling war

CHAPTER 9

THE WAR

This book just wouldn't be complete without a consideration of what happened in 1983 and 1984. The promotional battle that proved to be the last gasp of the National Wrestling Alliance also marked the World Wrestling Federation's rise to absolute power. Make no mistake, Vince McMahon, Jr. and the WWF were going to change the face of wrestling no matter what happened in St. Louis. But developments here hastened the process.

As I've noted, when a nasty promotional battle with Tom Packs finally came to a head after World War Two, Sam Muchnick consolidated power. Why Sam left his former partner to strike out on his own has never been clear to me, though I suppose it's the same old story. Money and who was doing the work were probably at issue. Still, their dispute eventually led to the formation of the NWA, the birth of "Wrestling at the Chase," and an incredibly stable, profitable period in wrestling history.

Somehow, I always sensed that I might be faced with a similar situation once Sam retired. By 1981, Muchnick's partners in the St. Louis Wrestling Club were Harley Race, Bob Geigel, Pat O'Connor, and Verne Gagne. Only six years earlier, when Sam stepped down as NWA president, it was Race who took me to lunch and said, "With the old man out of the picture, the whole thing will come crashing down. We need to keep him involved." Down deep, Harley must have recognized that Sam actually kept wrestling's power brokers from going too far — both in terms of the business and in matchmaking.

There are those who feel Sam was pushed out as NWA president by a small but persistent group that disliked how he tried to protect the champion's off-dates, battled over controversial finishes, and collected a 3% booking fee for doing the time-consuming job. Personally, I wonder if some talk traces back to the Dory Funk, Jr. controversy of 1973, when Sam demonstrated he could be fiercely, and successfully, independent.

Sam himself told me he was tired of the constant irritation he'd get from certain members as he looked out for the business in general. In 1975, he wanted a vote of confidence. When he realized that some of his peers were reluctant, he resigned. If they weren't happy with his methods, let them try doing things their own way. Nonetheless, Sam was instrumental in getting his friend Jack Adkisson (Fritz Von Erich) the presidency.

While the office passed between different hands, Jim Barnett was the man booking the champion. Barnett took no booking fee, but he was adept at using the power of his new role. The titleholder's off-days started disappearing, and Barnett worried little about championship match finishes. The various presidents looked the other way while the stature of the kingpin dwindled and the gold belt became tarnished.

Sam contemplated retirement often after he gave up the presidency. He frequently said that the St. Louis partners needed me desperately, that I should have a large amount of control, and that I should never — absolutely never — put up my own money to buy shares in the company. "Use other people's money," he'd laugh; it was the exact method he himself had employed. Muchnick also openly floated the idea of me running the promotion, suggesting that O'Connor should remain as the booker.

What finally pushed Sam to step down was the sudden death of his wife Helen in February 1981. She literally collapsed in front of him during a dinner at Norwood Hills Country Club. As tragic as this was, the outpouring of support from the often iron-hearted wrestling community was amazing.

Gene Kiniski from Vancouver, Fritz Von Erich from Dallas, Dick "The Bruiser" from Indianapolis, Wally Karbo from Minneapolis, Frank Tunney from Toronto, Jim Barnett from Atlanta, Jim Crockett from North Carolina, Eddie Graham from Tampa, plus all the St. Louis partners (Harley had just buried his father a week before) came to town to support Sam. Vince McMahon, Sr. and even Shohei "Giant" Baba from Japan were in constant contact.

Something else passed away with Helen. She was a strong woman who understood Sam better, perhaps, than he understood himself. Being older than his wife, Muchnick had always prepared for something happening to him first. With Helen gone, Sam sold off his shares. He retired officially on January 1, 1982. A fire had been extinguished.

He stayed as an adviser to the St. Louis Wrestling Club for another year, and that proved to be what kept me in the fold. I became the general manager. My philosophical differences with Kansas City, about how to run the business in St. Louis, became undeniable in the winter of 1982. First, Geigel and Race switched accountants, going with a firm in Kansas City. It made no sense, considering what Richard Kawanishi knew about how Sam operated. They also changed the method of distributing profits, which in turn caused the balance of our checking account to fall dramatically. This made it extremely difficult for me to promptly pay the bills for which I was responsible.

Ultimately, it was the wrestling itself that brought things to a head. I resigned for the first time after the finish to a March 26, 1982, title match between Ric Flair and Dick "The Bruiser" was changed. There was supposed to have been a clean pin, in the tradition of St. Louis; instead, there was a ref bump, a missed three-count for Dick, and then a victory for Flair after simultaneous flying tackles. The heat was bad, and the 10,000 plus in attendance were ready to riot. I felt, and Sam supported me, that it would be next to impossible to have another challenger ready for a June date at The Checkerdome after a legend like "The Bruiser" was treated so unjustly. Besides, it simply wasn't what we'd all agreed upon. In St. Louis, no rivalry, especially one involving a star of Dick's experience, could ever culminate with a blatantly missed call.

When Geigel, Gagne, and I met to discuss my disenchantment, we talked about the public perception of wrestling in St. Louis and methods of promoting, as well as matchmaking and finances. Bob said he would see that changes were made and I agreed to remain — but nothing happened. At the same time, Pat O'Connor was encountering personal tax problems, further complicating the situation and essentially making him invisible. After tensions continued to escalate, on November 19, I resigned once more.

Sam brokered a truce, and I wound up with more power over match direction, as well as a bigger percentage of the profits and a larger operating budget. But the end was still inevitable. Looking back, it was the kind of sad divorce where a couple just cannot communicate.

One of our biggest problems was that the partners believed I should "open it up, like Kansas City." Well, the truth is, Kansas City was never a model promotion. Pay was mediocre, trips were long, television was poorly produced, and established stars seldom wanted to work there. Weekly K.C. shows produced nowhere near as much revenue as just 17 Kiel/Arena programs a year.

Naturally, I argued that there was no reason to fix St. Louis when it wasn't broken. Verne Gagne seemed to understand my point of view. Of course, Gagne had a territory that included Chicago, Minneapolis, Milwaukee, Denver, and other big towns. The Kansas City office ran Topeka, Wichita, St. Joseph, Quincy, plus small Iowa and Missouri towns. The size of their venues was completely different. I always felt that Verne would have liked to have seen me with more control, since our interests were more simpatico — although he obviously joined in the attempt to prevent me from booking talent when the divorce finally occurred.

Remember, in the NWA's heyday, St. Louis was the cherry on top of the ice cream sundae. Sam did not have a territory, in the conventional sense, by personal choice. Part of the reason was Sam's commitment to the National Wrestling Alliance. He wanted St. Louis and only St. Louis. All of his promotional energy was concentrated on making his one town as powerful as possible, and because of this the NWA was unlikely to be compromised by any of his decisions.

Thanks to our big crowds and Sam's generous and honest payoffs, we could pick and choose, literally, from any star in the wrestling universe. And then there was the fact that in St. Louis wrestlers were regarded with respect — as professionals and athletes — by the media, as well as the fans.

Even with Sam's retirement, the potential to keep the tradition alive, and trade on its success for years to come, existed. I was happy to be visible, the person out front, but I was not willing to do that job without authority. If St. Louis floundered under my command, then I *should be* removed. But if business fell off because I could not do my job in the tradition of Sam Muchnick, I doggone well was not going to be the scapegoat.

When Sam gave up being a consultant at the end of 1982, I knew it was over.

I liked Harley, Pat, and Bob. And I respected them. Race and O'Connor, in particular, helped teach me things about wrestling that I could never have learned anywhere else. But on the other hand, I knew things about promotion and the status of wrestling in the St. Louis community that they did not. It wasn't their fault, but the fact is they never truly tried to understand what made St. Louis unique.

I grew up in St. Louis (well, Belleville), listening to my dad's stories about matches between Jim Londos and Hans Kampfer at The Arena in 1937. I could remember the St. Louis House television shows of the 1950s. I saw the first "Wrestling at the Chase" in 1959, and watched every single show thereafter. I read every morsel of publicity and I believed it.

Most importantly, each and every day I worked with Sam Muchnick I learned a subtle history lesson. I wasn't just told how to do things; I absorbed the knowledge necessary to create respect for professional wrestling by osmosis. It was in my brain, my blood, my very soul.

How could someone like Bob Geigel, who had been educated in wrestling's more usual, ragged form, have the same sense and emotion for St. Louis? Harley and Pat should have understood, Sam believed, because they'd both worn the belt and worked for promoters in big, successful cities. But that really wasn't the case. Often, a champion got into a town at 3 p.m., wrestled that night, and was gone again by 10 the next morning. The in-ring work of Race and O'Connor was impeccable; their understanding of a champion's role was solid. But fitting the entire package together, grinding it out day after day, spinning publicity, making match development fit a long-term plan, handling the calls from fans, media, and political powers were things they never learned.

One item that particularly disappointed me was the way Harley protected himself on finishes. Probably no star benefited more from Sam's win-lose system than Race in the 1970s. He won *and* lost, *cleanly* (usually on more than one occasion), against Johnny Valentine, Jack Brisco, Terry and Dory Funk, Jr., O'Connor, Gene Kiniski, Bob Backlund, and "The Bruiser." Every match was a main event and all paid big money. His great work fit perfectly with Sam's booking philosophy.

Yet after losing the NWA prize to Dusty Rhodes on June 21, 1981, Race systematically rejected any finish where he "did a job," one-two-three, in the middle of the ring. Actually, that's not entirely accurate — he lost cleanly, once. That lone pinfall defeat was at the hands of "Giant" Baba on February 11, 1983, at The Checkerdome. Ironically, that decision, while helping Harley's personal affairs in Japan, hurt St. Louis because at the time Baba had no real status in town, and the match itself was below Race's normal standards.

Mostly, Harley had been booking himself into a slew of disqualifications, with an occasional count-out thrown in for good measure. In the long run, none of these matches served to make either him or St. Louis stronger. When he lost the Missouri title to Kerry Von Erich by disqualification January 21, 1983, it set a precedent and nicked some credibility from that honor. Never before had a stipulation been made that allowed the championship to change hands on a disqualification. . . . But that was the only way Harley would drop the belt to Kerry.

Of course, Race did not want to become someone who lost every featured match, but that was never the idea. Consider instead how Kiniski or Dory Jr. had been used. They were former champions who won and lost main events while also getting many lucrative title shots. The fact also remained, of course, that as a partner, Harley could reject any finish.

Two decades later Dave Meltzer, editor of the *Wrestling Observer* newsletter, told me he had talked in detail with every major star of the era, and that all of them agreed: "St. Louis was how wrestling should be. Sam did it right and that was how it should work." Dave also pointed out, though, that each of those same wrestlers behaved in exactly the opposite manner when they themselves became bookers. According to Dave, none of them learned anything about why St. Louis worked.

Looking back, I wonder if power truly does corrupt. The inbred distrust of almost everyone in wrestling apparently causes grapplers who achieve booking power to make decisions for themselves first, and the business second. Perhaps it's inertia, created by a long, sad history of unsound business dealings, which fosters that type of thinking and decision-making. Or was the St. Louis way, even though it seemed so simple, so unique that it could not be duplicated?

Meltzer believes Muchnick's way of doing business seems simple and logical to me because I grew up with it. Maybe he's right. Dave argues, "It wasn't simple and logical to people who came from other systems where logic wasn't adhered to." His words remind me now of how Nick Bockwinkel attributed Sam's success to his pragmatism.

So when I talked with the partners, and Geigel, in particular, there was some missing element we could never find, struggle though we did. I recall our last conversation, in a Kiel Auditorium dressing room on February 25, 1983.

"What can we do to make you stay?" Bob asked.

I could not give him a clear explanation of why I felt as I did and, in retrospect, maybe that's my fault. It was like I was speaking a foreign language — one only Sam Muchnick understood — when I complained about public image, paying bills, and booking.

It's taken me all these years to understand how unique St. Louis wrestling was. Back then, I just couldn't find a way to articulate how deeply I believed that my role had to encompass more than being a general manager.

When my resignation became public, Ric Flair called me at home. We talked for two hours. Flair recognized how special St. Louis was. "I'll do anything to keep you guys together," he offered. "You understand how the town works, Larry. You have to be there." But he had no way to resolve the situation. Nonetheless, I will always remember his call and his concern. Ric Flair will always have my respect and gratitude.

Of course, by this point, something had already begun to percolate with Charlie Mancuso, the manager of The Checkerdome. Charlie knew of my frustration, and of my dreams. He also had seen how successful Muchnick-style wrestling could be.

As a representative of one of the companies funded by Delaware North (also known as Sports Service), Charlie was willing to put up the money for a new promotion. He was a bright, high-energy operator and one of the youngest building managers in the country. At one point, in February 1983, our new entity even offered to buy out the Kansas City faction. We were, of course, turned down.

Another person knew about all of this too — Vince McMahon, Jr. We were speaking on a regular basis, and I had traded many promotional ideas with his sharp assistant, Howard Finkel. Vince was just two years older than me, and we both broke in as commentators in our respective markets. While cautious, he urged me to move forward as well, since, as he put it, "Wrestling always changes." Little did anyone know what Vince himself was concocting.

From the start, Sam knew of my plans. While he felt he needed to be publicly neutral, his heart was with me. Looking down the road, as he always did, Sam probably felt a beneficial compromise could be reached. Sam spoke with Charlie and gave his personal blessing for the new promotion, but stressed he could not be a financial part of the venture because he feared that a legal conflict with the St. Louis Wrestling Club might ensue.

The stage was set for a promotional war — in, of all places, the home of the NWA. In the old days, I would have been squashed like a bug in a matter of weeks. But things, in 1983, weren't like they used to be.

Securing talent wasn't a problem, though I had been prepared to scrape the bottom of the barrel. This was when my friendship with "King Kong" Brody really blossomed, and that rebel was happily surprised to discover how much spunk I had. From day one, Dick Murdoch said, "Count me in." Quickly, Tully Blanchard, Adrian Adonis, Jerry Oates, Tiger Conway, Jr., Chavo Guerrero, and Scott Casey were on board. Joe Blanchard helped me get wrestlers, and Debbie Combs helped with the lady competitors.

Bruno Sammartino put me in touch with Dominic DeNucci, who also agreed to help. Professor Toru Tanaka and Nikolai Volkoff (the best dressing room magician I have ever seen — imagine doing sleight of hand card tricks while naked!) were brought in through Brody. Even Vince Jr., quietly and behind the scenes, gave me names — though perhaps not for the reasons I originally believed.

A future Minnesota governor named Jesse Ventura set aside dates for me starting in November of 1983. All-time great Lou Thesz quickly agreed to be a special referee, a guest commentator on television, and a private sounding board for ideas and problems.

"Spike" Huber, unsure of what coming with me would do to his relationship with father-in-law Dick "The Bruiser," agonized but said "Yes" — and in the process found he could headline. It was great watching "Spike" finally step out of the shadows to shine. Soon Dick started using some of my undercard television talent on his shows. Maybe Sam said something, or maybe another old renegade just appreciated what was going on.

I had grown close to David Von Erich, and spoke with all of the brothers. David wanted to work for me, saying he needed to move out on his own and that he couldn't think of a better place to headline. Kevin was more cautious, but promising; Kerry did not really grasp what was happening. Like a nitwit, though, I held off cinching a promise from the boys, pending a visit to their father. Isn't it amazing that in the middle of a war I was still worried that having his sons work for me might put Fritz in a bad spot?

In fact, on April 19, 1983, I flew to Denton, Texas, and spent a long day on the Von Erich ranch. Fritz drove me around his incredible property and explained how he had used wrestling money to buy real estate all over Dallas. He even said he could not have done it without Sam and St. Louis.

A powerful personality, and a guy I'd always admired, Fritz then told me the story of the Dallas wrestling war of the 1960s. Like me, though for different reasons, Fritz believed he was the one who should be in charge and started a conflict with the territory's long-time promoters. At that time,

Muchnick was *the* power in wrestling. Sam subtly swung his influence behind Fritz, but only after he agreed that once the air cleared he'd make peace with his former partners.

Fritz wanted the same promise from me, believing that history was repeating itself twenty years later. He offered to help with talent (he sent me Terry Gordy of the red-hot "Fabulous Freebirds," and put me on the trail of "Macho Man" Randy Savage) — if I promised to make peace with Bob, Harley, Pat, and Verne once I'd solidified my position. They were friends, and I essentially had no problem with what Fritz suggested.

We shook hands. David and Kevin stopped by — and David wanted to appear on my very first card. He reluctantly accepted that things should move more slowly, however, and chomped at the bit for the call. Now I wish I had taken him for that first show — and for every one thereafter.

McMahon led me to "Black Jack" Mulligan, a former New York Jets football lineman whose real name was Bob Windham. Of course, Bob's son was Barry Windham, who many predicted would someday be a champion. I booked Mulligan to meet Brody in my first Checkerdome show on June 18, 1983. With quintessential wrestling intrigue, rumors flew fast and furious. My talent, including Brody, many speculated, was going to be bought off and my card ruined.

On June 14, Sam was visiting my office when Mulligan called to let me know that Harley told him not to show. "Black Jack" claimed that Harley had said, "Think of your son's future in this business before you go Saturday." Mulligan said this had made him angry and that he would be there for sure.

When I told him what Mulligan was calling about, Sam urged me to begin composing a request for the Anti-Trust Division of the Justice Department to investigate. It was what Sam described as a violation of the consent decree signed by the National Wrestling Alliance — the consent decree he himself had engineered decades earlier. "Hopefully it won't lead to a lawsuit," Sam said, "but just informing Anti-Trust could stop stuff like this." He was also aware that Kiniski, Bob Orton Jr., and Greg Valentine had been pressured to not work for me.

Brody came in a day early so we could do publicity and, amazingly, that night at the Tenderloin Room in the Chase Park-Plaza Hotel we ran into Pat O'Connor. Pat nodded politely but stayed away. He'd survived his financial difficulties and was then running the St. Louis office of my former colleagues.

Brody had a drink sent to O'Connor. We stopped by his table and had a friendly, animated conversation for the steak room patrons. Since Pat had been the one saying Brody wouldn't show, it was amusing.

Instead, it was Mulligan who failed to appear.

The call came on the afternoon of the 18th from a woman claiming to be Mulligan's wife. Supposedly, Jack had been in an accident near Tampa and was in rough shape. Charlie Mancuso began calling every hospital in Florida, but Mulligan-Windham could not be found. Later, two stories floated around. One said he'd been bought off; another that he had been told his son Barry would become NWA champion if he stiffed my card.

While it was a headache notifying the media and fans, overall, the no-show meant nothing. We had to refund only $18! Better still, the week after the show I struck a TV deal with Channel 30. We'd broadcast on Saturdays at 5 p.m., beginning on August 6, 1983. I quickly discovered that my real problem would be keeping *all* of the talent happy. I simply had too many offers.

Rocky Johnson called to bawl me out for not having him on the card. I mentioned that McMahon had said he'd be working around New York in July, and that he wouldn't have time for other towns. Rocky said, "I could have done the June shot for you and made room on my schedule down the road."

Speaking of Vince, he quickly called to apologize about Mulligan and claimed he had no inkling that Mulligan would cave to the pressure and no-show. In fact, Vince was the one who provided me with the theories about why Mulligan had failed to appear. I believed him, and still do today, because Vince truly wanted me to succeed. Again, he had his reasons. . . .

We definitely showed life. The crowds were decent, ranging from 3000 to 6000, and the television ratings were surprising. By September 30, our show had moved to 10 a.m. on Sunday mornings. At the same time, Fritz's blazing "World Class Wrestling" program had started running head-to-head with "Wrestling at the Chase," and my old show's ratings were sinking fast. It was in early October that Ted Koplar said KPLR wanted me back.

Similarly, attendance figures for my old partners had begun to plummet. On April 15, they drew 2972. An NWA title bout on April 25 lured just 4355. Rock-bottom came on May 13, when only 1590 paying customers were in attendance. The St. Louis Wrestling Club was staggering even before my show made its Channel 30 debut.

The tide of war had turned in just a few months. Our first-ever two-ring Battle Royal, won by "Spike" Huber, was a huge success. Brody and Volkoff shot an angle to develop an exciting feud. The talent gave more than one hundred percent for me every time the bell sounded. We gathered all sorts of press by putting Brody on The Checkerdome marquee. In a promo worthy of King Kong from movie fame, he climbed the marquee and lifted Angie Werner, one of Charlie Mancuso's secretaries, to his shoulders. The television spot snarled traffic on Highway 40.

Mancuso's company *was* losing money, but this was expected. It was more than they had anticipated, however, despite my warnings. Over and over, I had said, and Sam had confirmed: expect to lose money for a year or so, until things stabilize. I personally never took a penny past expenses.

It was a tremendous amount of work, not that I'm complaining. In fact, I wish I could do it again! But I was booking, calling everyone from talent to radio stations, working out angles, writing the program, going to too many meetings, and supervising television production with Bernie Corno and Parvin Trammel.

My wife Pat was a saint, juggling the late night calls and never ending details with me. Maybe I should have found someone to mentor and delegated some of those details. But again, finding someone who could understand all the intricacies of St. Louis was a chore in itself, and there simply wasn't time.

Pressure was building from Mancuso. I was exhausted when talks started with Koplar, my friend and the owner of KPLR-TV, Channel 11. When he discovered there was no contract with Channel 30, just a week-by-week letter of agreement, Ted wanted me back.

By the middle of October, a couple of critical things had happened. Mancuso's bosses wanted to change what was originally a 50-50 deal to 80-20 in their favor. I balked. Don't tell me how naïve I was, not having a written contract in a venture like this. I was just discovering that not everyone would honor a handshake deal like Sam Muchnick.

Talking with Channel 11, it became clear that the old St. Louis Wrestling Club would be finished by the end of the year. Ted Koplar said he felt that a partnership which included Vince McMahon, Jr. would be in the town's and station's best interest, because of the established nature of Vince's company.

I was stunned. My buddy Vince had been talking with Koplar all along, no doubt realizing that the NWA was all bark and no bite *because* I was still very much alive and (if only I'd had my legal ducks in a row) on the verge of victory. With the benefit of hindsight, it's easy to see that Vince had plans to take advantage of the changes cable, closed circuit, and pay-per-view would be making to the wrestling landscape. He was already, in fact, attempting to establish the national promotion others had only dared dream about. What was happening in St. Louis, I am sure, told him that the NWA was collapsing. Taking over would be easier than he had anticipated.

If the NWA couldn't manage their own affairs, how could they stop the WWF? Ruthlessly and efficiently, McMahon took advantage of every crack in their foundation. The existing structures of wrestling began to crumble.

On the morning of October 23, I called Fritz and filled him in on what was happening: that Vince intended to go national and crush, by any means necessary, anyone who stood in his way. Fritz, who was close with Vince's father, refused to believe it. I pleaded with him, trying to make him see that this was undoubtedly where the war in St. Louis was heading.

I proposed we strike up our own alliance, in the process answering Koplar's concerns about a stable core of talent — something that Vince had obviously and rightly convinced Ted was crucial since my wrestlers were independents. With Fritz and me doing a St. Louis-style show on one channel, and Von Erich's "World Class" program airing on another, we might have been able to derail Vince's plans.

Fritz said, "You don't need me. You are going to win and the best thing for this business is that you do, and then make peace with Bob, Harley, Verne, and Pat." I could not make him understand that our struggle had taken a totally unexpected and dangerous turn.

On the evening of October 23, Mancuso and I met with both Koplar and Vince McMahon, Jr. As angry as I was, I understood Ted's thinking. In his eyes, I was still the young, green kid he first directed on television. Vince, on the other hand, was already romancing TV execs worldwide. He'd put an unbelievable offer on the table for KPLR and confidently expressed revolutionary ideas. I was worried about little ole St. Louis; Vince was going to conquer the world.

A deal was struck that allowed Charlie to escape from the situation without financial damage — an agreement that was never honored. I was to be Vince's partner in St. Louis. The arrangement lasted about a week. It ended when Vince's right-hand man, Jim Barnett (who had been pushed out of the Atlanta office by his partners), called to say McMahon had to have one hundred percent control. Of course, by then I had cancelled my agreement with Channel 30; conveniently, Vince had already signed his pact with Koplar and Channel 11.

Immediately after our talks in St. Louis, Vince flew to Minneapolis and signed a contract with Verne Gagne's number one star, Hulk Hogan. He was

McMahon's hand-picked champion and the future face of professional wrestling. The war was on. Everyone knows how it ended.

My final card took place on October 29, 1983, and I told all the talent that the television taping scheduled for the next day had been cancelled. Brody was devastated. We sat in his hotel room later and he begged me to continue the fight, arguing that I was in fact winning.

The talent was really starting to flow, Brody insisted. Michael Hayes, the other half of the "Freebirds," was going to join Gordy. Fritz had acknowledged David would have his blessing to come in January. Ventura was booked. Stan Hansen, a Brody ally and Japanese superstar, was on the way. The likes of Murdoch, Blanchard, Adonis, Oates, Volkoff, and Huber were in place. Savage and I were learning to trust each other and it was time to cut Randy loose and let him fly.

But I was exhausted, emotionally drained by my battles with Delaware North and the shock of the McMahon-Koplar alliance. My fatal failure was on the business end.

That important and very underestimated Vince operative, Howard Finkel, kept in contact with me after the coup. So did Vince. Once the St. Louis Wrestling Club was booted by KPLR, I was invited to the first taping of Vince's new show at the Khorassan Room of the Chase-Park Plaza Hotel. Bobby Heenan and Jesse Ventura both spoke at length about why they had jumped to Vince from Gagne's AWA, and both said that they thought it would be a good spot for me.

Vince flew me to New York to see the coronation of Hogan as champion. When Hulk beat the Iron Sheik in Madison Square Garden on January 23, 1984, it was indeed impressive. Reluctantly, I began thinking about joining the WWF.

Harley called me on January 30, 1984, to renew our connection. On the afternoon of February 3, 1984, Sam arranged a meeting between Geigel, Race, and me at Sam's condo in Clayton. Race and Geigel were involved in an attempt to go into McMahon "territory," and had scheduled a show at the Meadowlands in New Jersey. They would be working with Gagne, Jim Crockett from North Carolina, and Bill Watts of Mid-South. They said everyone wanted me in the fold, especially for television.

It was a good meeting, but there was definite confusion as to who would make decisions about finishes, payoffs, and future dates — it was simply the nature of that headstrong group. After Race and Geigel left, Sam asked what I thought.

"I'm worried. Nobody seems to be in charge. If they're fighting each other," I said, "it won't work."

Wisely, almost sadly, Sam nodded. "I think Vince is the more stable option. You're probably better off with him."

Finally, I gave in and made the deal which brought me to the WWF. I told Vince I was with him on February 5. It was the beginning of a wild ride, especially with Vince taping his early "Superstars of Wrestling" program in St. Louis.

The war for wrestling supremacy in North America was vicious. Vince bought television stations away from established promotions and lured talent with big money or, at least, big promises. On November 22, 1983, as we talked about whether or not I'd work for the WWF, Vince had said, "Wrestling is a rotten business, with rotten people, and the only way you succeed is to be more rotten than the other guy." Anyone who lived through the tumult would say Vince had to prove himself right in order to land on top.

Once, as I drove Vince from the St. Louis airport to KPLR, I mentioned how surprised I was at the bumbling efforts of experienced NWA promoters in response to Vince's assault. "It looks like they're trying to go out of business," I marveled.

Vince loved that. He slapped my knee and laughed, "That's it! It's not me. They're putting themselves out of business." But of course, thanks to Sam and the strength of the alliance, none of these promoters had ever faced real competition.

Eventually, the WWF moved its studio show out of St. Louis, although for a while production for syndication was still done from Channel 11. Finally, after staving off bankruptcy with the first WrestleMania, Vince's company became so big that it could produce its own television: the WWF was on the road to becoming the monster marketing machine it is today.

As for me, when I joined the company Vince said, "be ready to work harder than you ever have in your life." He never understood that was an impossibility. I'd already given St. Louis wrestling my heart and my soul.

My ten years with the WWF provided me with countless stories, a chance to work from home, and the opportunity to watch my daughter Kelly grow up. I wouldn't have traded coaching basketball and softball and organizing select volleyball for anything. I still remember Kelly's smile when she started throwing blazing fastball strikes as a 10-year-old, or when she scored her first game-winning basket at Emge school, or when Belleville Momentum, her 18-under select volleyball team, earned the right to go to the Junior Olympic Nationals. They eventually finished 11th in the country.

Parents are allowed to brag, so please indulge me here. In college, Kelly was a two-term captain at Oglethorpe University, where she achieved the rare career feat of a Triple Thousand — 1000 assists, 1000 kills, 1000 digs. And she got her degree in International Studies!

A serious offer did come in, however, that could have ended my amateur sports coaching career. It was from World Championship Wrestling.

In the fall of 1988, Jim Crockett was selling his collapsing promotion to WTBS and Ted Turner in Atlanta. Jack Petrik, who managed Channel 30 in St. Louis during the 1970s, was the point man for Turner. He'd put Jim Herd, my first director on "Wrestling at the Chase," in charge of wrestling.

The problem was that Herd knew virtually nothing about wrestling and needed somebody to make all the pieces fit. After he was turned down by Sam, who suggested contacting me, I began the process of "smartening up" Herd. How difficult was it? Well, I suggested to Jim that WTBS sign Ricky Steamboat since he'd just left Vince and was a free agent.

Herd said, "Who's he?"

We met often. During a conference with Petrik on November 29, 1988, at the Media Club in St. Louis, I asked if they wanted to be a standard wrestling promotion or a promotion that was primarily television-based. Remember, at the time, pay-per-view was really just beginning to blossom. I explained angles, discussed talent, and proposed payoffs by percentage or guarantee. In detail, the St. Louis wrestling model was mapped out. Today I realize that they had no idea what I was talking about.

Just as WTBS was taking control, an internal argument broke out in Crockett's organization between booker Dusty Rhodes and champion Ric Flair. As a result, Rhodes decided to take the belt off Flair and put it on Rick Steiner, quickly, before the sale was complete. When Herd called to tell me this I was in bed, shaking my head in amazement. I asked, "Who owns the company right now?"

Herd said, "WTBS." I told him to order Rhodes and Crockett to leave the belt on Flair until WTBS was actively running the show. A completely amazing back and forth dialogue ensued, spanning at least six calls, with me briefing Herd, him calling Crockett or Rhodes, them calling back, and then Herd updating me.

At any rate, I eventually balked at the idea of moving to Atlanta, for the simple reason that there were far too many sharks swimming in that pool. My wife Pat had taught for years at Belleville West High School and Kelly was getting into the sports scene. It was a terribly risky proposition, especially without serious money and other guarantees on the table.

Still, at one point I felt that Herd and I had come to a verbal agreement, starting at $70,000 per year plus travel expenses until we could assess how things were working out. I was to have a major say in booking decisions, along with Herd's ear in most aspects of the promotion. Unfortunately, my old "buddy" Jim Barnett had landed with WTBS after being fired by Vince. Once Herd met with Barnett, he returned to St. Louis to tell me: "Jim says that's too much. We'll do $50,000."

On my idealistic high-horse, believing a man's word should be his bond, I turned him down, taking it as a sign of how WCW would do business. Besides, if Barnett had that much influence, was Herd really calling the shots? Who was the ultimate authority in terms of wrestling? Did they ever really figure that out?

Barnett knew me, and understood how like Sam I was. In my mind, he purposefully manipulated the situation to get to a point where he knew I'd have to turn them down. Working with him at the WWF, I always sensed that Barnett never trusted me — probably because of the independence I'd demonstrated after Sam's retirement.

Supposedly, he felt I wasn't qualified to be a booker, and, in standard wrestling terms, I wasn't. (Neither was Sam.) In fact, I'd told Herd and Petrik they would need a dressing room man (like Bob Brown had been in St. Louis) to be on the road, working live shows. Again, Sam's methods were the model of what I suggested.

I often wonder what would have happened, and what I would have done, had my friend Brody, that other side of my personality, lived. My misgivings about Atlanta might have been overcome. At any rate, I would have had a powerful ally. The end result might have been the same, considering the cast of characters at WCW, but it could have been fun.

WTBS went on its merry way, plowing through many managers and bookers, and even enjoyed one tremendous run in the late 1990s, before finally going under and being bought out by McMahon. I parted ways with Vince after being a fish out of water for nearly a decade.

For a while I was bitter about wrestling, and it often showed. I'd gripe to Brody in our 2 a.m. phone calls, when we were plotting and planning during the 80s. I would ask how Vince could know my feelings and still put up with me. Brody would laugh and say, "Better to have you inside the castle, pissing out, than outside, pissing in."

It's too bad that, despite our history together, Harley Race, Bob Geigel, and I could not find the common ground for a compromise. In the end, though, it probably would not have mattered.

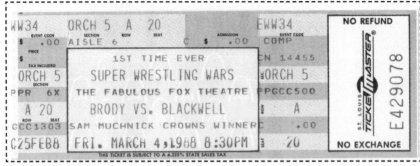

Brody and "Crusher" Blackwell collided in, of all places,
"The Fabulous Fox Theatre"

CHAPTER 10

BRODY

In St. Louis and New York, he was "King Kong." In Japan and other wrestling venues around the globe, he was "Bruiser." At home, he was Frank Goodish.

To me he was simply Brody.

But who was he, really? Was he the wildman with blood streaming down his face? Was he the serious businessman, studying the stock prospectus for a computer company? Or was he the proud father, bragging about the first essay his son ever wrote? He was always a complicated man, a mix of all these elements, equal parts "King Kong," "Bruiser," and Frank.

Like any professional wrestler, Brody was an athlete, a husband, a performer, a father — and a manipulator. Unlike almost any other grappler, however, Brody was independent (often to the point of rebellion), intelligent (his mind was perhaps more intimidating than his considerable strength), and explosive (often to the point where serious injury was imminent).

Most promoters in wrestling were, at best, leery of my friend Brody. At 6-5 and 280 pounds, a mass of fury, he would twist situations to his benefit. In business, he could create havoc over confirmed dates; inside the squared circle he always marched to the beat of his own drummer. If he felt wronged in any way, he would move heaven and earth to extract money from a promoter. Grudges were typically forgotten, however, because he could deliver the big house.

But who had the best working relationships with Brody? Shohei "Giant" Baba, the owner of All Japan Wrestling, and Sam Muchnick, the legendary ruler of St. Louis and the National Wrestling Alliance. By almost unanimous accounts, Baba and Sam were the two most honest promoters in the history of the business. They got along with Brody just fine.

Perhaps the wisest thing Sam ever said to me was, "Judge every individual yourself. Don't listen to rumors or opinions. Make a decision based on the merits of what you see." That's what I did with Brody, and he became a loyal friend and trusted business partner. Considering his reputation, and my background, few, if any, would have expected it.

Raised in a Detroit suburb, in high school Brody was an All-State football and basketball standout. After a brief stint at Iowa State, where he generally ignored his classes, Brody landed at West Texas State University, which produced the likes of the NFL's "Mercury" Morris, and a number of other football players who would later move on to professional wrestling, including Dusty Rhodes, Bobby Duncum, Terry Funk, Ted DiBiase, Scott Casey, and Stan Hansen.

After college, Brody spent a year on the taxi squad of the Washington Redskins. There, he learned a difficult lesson. "I always got by just being a great athlete and tough as hell," Brody told me. "I could beat people up, so I never bothered to learn the fundamentals. When I got to the Redskins, I was as tough as everyone else, but they knew the fundamentals."

Bouncing between the Edmonton Eskimos in Canada and semi-pro football in Fort Worth and San Antonio, Brody met wrestler Ivan Putski and began serious power lifting. At one point, he could bench press 540 pounds and squat 700. Putski also convinced Brody to try wrestling. He began under the tutelage of Leroy McGuirk in the old Tulsa territory, and then eventually came under the influence of Fritz Von Erich in Dallas.

Brody was a natural. Totally uninhibited, he did things in the ring few his size were willing to try or able to pull off. He grasped the fine art of ring psychology and created a character who struck chords of both fear and passion. Visually, he was nothing short of terrifying, a huge powerhouse whose long, curly hair and beard framed ice-cold eyes.

After a good run in Florida, he moved to New York to work for Vince McMahon, Sr., who actually gave him the name "King Kong." Our many late night trips into little towns during the 1980s gave Brody a chance to reminisce.

"I got off a plane in Allentown, Pennsylvania, for television and got into a cab," Brody laughed. "The first thing that happened was the driver stuck a gun in my face, robbed me, and tossed me out. That woke me up."

He eventually battled World Wide Wrestling Federation champion Bruno Sammartino in the ring. "Strong as a bear and a class guy," said Brody.

Brody also noted how often Vince McMahon, Jr., then the television commentator, talked about becoming a wrestler, but that his father would hear none of it. "Think the business would be different now if Senior had let the kid wrestle?" he asked in 1987.

In the end, he had an argument with Vince McMahon, Sr.'s right-hand man, Gorilla Monsoon (Gino Marella), and work became hard to come by. Bouncing around, Brody met his wife Barbara in Australia before returning to work for Von Erich in Texas. Soon, he was firing on all cylinders. He became a superstar in Japan just as he was making his debut in St. Louis.

When he came in for the "Wrestling at the Chase" show that was to air on July 29, 1978, Pat O'Connor penciled him in as "Bruiser" Brody. Since Dick "The Bruiser" was already an established headliner, and because O'Connor also wanted me to call tough Bob Sweetan by that moniker (a directive I pretty much ignored), I suggested to Sam that we bill Brody as "King Kong." St. Louis did not need three "Bruisers," especially when the newest guy had serious box office potential. I dug out publicity photos that McMahon had made, with Brody standing next to a huge movie poster, and Sam made the call to go with "King Kong."

He got over instantly. Weighing about 320 at the time, Brody could still launch an incredible drop kick and had frightening intensity between the ropes. Personally, we hit it off right away, as Brody told me how important Fritz said it would be for him to click with Sam in St. Louis. With his Japanese invasion still in its infancy, St. Louis was clearly important to him. Brody's Kiel Auditorium run began with a bang — he beat Jack Brisco on September 16, 1978, and O'Connor three weeks later.

"Wrestling at the Chase" on October 28, 1978, really set Brody apart. He was scheduled to meet a gentleman named Ed Schaeffer in what would obviously be a decisive squash. Referee Lee Warren remembered it best. "Brody would always bark and stalk around when he got into the ring. All of a sudden, Schaeffer started barking too. Brody told him to stop it and Schaeffer barked right in Brody's face. Brody got close to me and told me to stay out of the way unless I wanted to get hurt bad," recalled Lee. "He was steaming."

The next five minutes can be summed up with two words: sheer brutality. Schaeffer threw but one slap before Brody shoved him (he was Brody's height and weighed maybe 260 pounds) into a corner. The first punch struck Schaeffer's face like a bolt of lightning, opening a gash under his eye that quickly swelled to the size of a golf ball. Then came the boot — right to the bridge of Schaeffer's nose. Vicious kick after vicious kick rained down upon Schaeffer's side and back. Forearm smashes slammed into him, nothing was held back. When it was over, Schaeffer did not know what town he was in. Two referees tried to guide him toward the dressing room.

Brody was already there. Lee Warren said, "Brody stormed in and went to the two wrestlers who had driven in with Schaeffer. He asked them if they wanted a piece and both said, 'No way.' Then Brody threw Schaeffer's bag and clothes out the door and into the hallway. 'He's got no business in here,' Brody yelled. Nobody argued."

A few weeks later, Schaeffer or his representative contacted Sam to ask about reimbursing Schaeffer's emergency room bill. To this day, I don't know if Sam paid it or not, but he did say, "Brody was right. The guy got what he deserved."

By 1980, Brody was one of the top box-office attractions in Japan and that lucrative spot made him even more independent. He worked Kansas City fairly often, mainly because his friend "Buck" Robley was a booker there. He had various disagreements with promoters over payoffs and O'Connor often carried tales back to Sam. To his credit, however, Sam judged Brody by his personal dealings with the man.

I set Brody up with a couple of zany television commercials for appliance store owner Steve Mizerany. When the shoot was over, Mizerany took us to lunch with his business friends. Brody was completely at ease and accepted — because he was a student of the stock market. Clearly, he grasped how to present a different side of his personality to the people Sam knew.

The commercials got Brody over with a new audience. We began to talk often and without restraint about what might happen to St. Louis wrestling as Sam phased himself out of power.

When it came to finishes, Brody was never a problem. His St. Louis matches were fierce, fast, and smart. Ted DiBiase recalled defeating Brody on October 24, 1980, at Kiel: "Brody was strictly business and would never put his shoulders down for just anyone." Ted added, "Before the bout, Brody came to my room and told me he was doing this because it was me and it meant something. St. Louis was special, Brody told me."

Brody also worked Indianapolis for "The Bruiser," who had his own reputation for fiddling with payoffs. In 1981, a dispute began to simmer because Brody felt Dick had shorted him money from a main event. Things came to a head in Peoria, where the two were at a "spot" show. Apparently, there had been a heated verbal dispute earlier in the night. And then Brody stormed into the dressing room after his match.

On his way in, Brody ran into Dick's son-in-law, "Spike" Huber. "You want any of this?" Brody growled. "Spike" said no, it wasn't his battle. There were only a few angry words before Brody and "The Bruiser" went at each other. A row of lockers was turned over, a door ripped off, and Dick's head was opened up and bleeding before other wrestlers could quell the donnybrook.

Just a few days later, Brody was slated to tag with Dick and "Spike" against Dick Murdoch, John Studd, and "Bulldog" Bob Brown in a six-man match at Kiel. I know O'Connor wanted to remove Brody from the lineup. I also know Sam spoke with Dick about what had happened. No change was made.

The Kiel dressing room was usually relaxed, but not on February 6, 1981. It was tense, and things became even worse when "The Bruiser" showed up an hour early. I was at the top of the steps when Brody came into view only minutes later. At that moment, Dick came around the corner. He held out a hand with his thumb cocked and forefinger and middle finger extended, like a gun. Between his fingers was a check.

"Here!" Dick snapped. Brody looked at the check, nodded, and said, "That's fine. Thanks."

Dick smiled. "We're square then." The evening went on without a hitch.

A few years later, on another one of those late-night drives, Brody talked about the incident: "I'll fight for what I got coming. Dick was the same way. He had to be fifty years old when we had that fight! Brother, did he battle. He was as tough as nails. Dick must have been something when he was thirty. We had an argument, we settled it, and that was that."

When the spring of 1981 arrived, Brody was in such demand in Japan and across the United States that he could pick his spots. But he'd also incurred the wrath of O'Connor, Harley Race, and Bob Geigel by no-showing towns in response to what he felt was a Geigel swerve. Because of this, Brody disappeared from St. Louis for more than a year.

I argued for Brody's return and finally had enough power to swing it in 1982. What really tipped the scale was the realization that no other star was strong enough to draw against then NWA Champion Ric Flair at The Checkerdome (Arena) on February 11, 1983. Brody was the only performer dynamic enough to be ready for such a big date on relatively short notice.

My relationship with Sam's successors was fraying on a daily basis, and I explained this to Brody when he came back on November 19, 1982, to begin the run leading to the title bout. I said I'd be history by the time he took on Flair. Brody implored me to stay through the Flair bout. "Hey, you'll get a great payday for that card [I was getting a percentage of profits] and I need you here to engineer the thing," Brody said. I agreed and told him I'd announce my departure after the Flair duel.

There were extra pressures on that date because Baba's television station in Tokyo planned to tape both the Flair-Brody battle and a match between Baba and Race. I had to organize the entire production with KPLR-TV. It was going to be a major, national event on Japanese television.

In early 1983 I learned something about how Baba took care of his bills. On February 9, Baba's production people came in to work with the crew from KPLR and I took his head man to meet KPLR General Manager Hal Protter. Baba's man asked if Protter would like to be paid in advance for the shoot. Protter, of course, said that would be fine. Hal was as surprised as I was when the polite gentleman opened his briefcase and counted out $7500 — *cash*.

What a night of wrestling it was. Brody and Flair went to an astounding one-hour draw before 16,695 psyched fans. Flair has often called this his favorite one-hour stalemate because of the crowd atmosphere. Brody took the first stanza with a flying knee drop in 21:04, before Flair evened things when Brody was counted out after 22:40. Time expired with the entire audience standing and screaming for near-fall after near-fall.

I had kept my word to Brody, and he would always keep his word with me. "If you go on your own, I'll be there. You can take it to the bank," he said.

As the St. Louis war of 1983 began to heat up and the wrestling world discovered what I planned, Brody and his wife called my home one evening. "You need to know what dirty tricks these people will pull," Brody said. "If you have trouble at home, you'll be easier to stop. I know, because these guys did it to us. Let us talk to Pat."

Brody and Barbara then explained what Pat should expect — calls from women whenever I was out of town, crass rumors being spread to anyone who'd listen, maybe even threats. If Pat knew it was coming, Barbara explained, she could handle it. It was a timely warning. The following week the calls started.

In addition, Brody gave me another heads-up. Wrestling has always been known for partners who had become enemies becoming partners again. "Yeah, that'll probably happen," Brody scoffed. "But some people will never forgive you for going out on your own and being independent. They'll be spreading lies for twenty years! I know."

During the portion of 1983 when I was running Greater St. Louis Wrestling and the old promotion was falling into disarray, Brody was a rock. His work in the ring and on television was, naturally, superb. I also found out from other sources (Lou Thesz in particular) that Brody had heard someone who had a reputation as a tough guy griping about his part in what I was doing in St. Louis. During a Japanese tour, my friend confronted the complainant and challenged him to settle any differences then and there. The offer was declined.

Privately, Brody and I developed a healthy respect for each others' particular knowledge of different elements of the business. Personally, he was there to pick up my spirits in tough times and I, well, maybe a little, helped smooth some of Brody's rough edges.

When Vince McMahon, Jr. delivered his knockout punch and began his move to conquer the entire wrestling world, Brody was crushed — mostly by the failure of my effort. He had enjoyed every moment of the battle as much as I had. But then, reality set in. I had not prepared myself, legally, as well as I should have. Instead of damaging our friendship, however, the development simply opened another door for both of us.

Dave Meltzer was a young man I met in Houston in the spring of 1983. Fresh out of college, in 1982 he'd started a newsletter called the *Wrestling Observer*. Over time, it would become incredibly influential and challenge Dave with demanding, fulltime work. From the outset, though, I found him to have an impressive understanding of the sport and its participants.

When I went to work for the WWF in 1984, Dave and I began to talk often. He was an absolute sponge for information. His outlook was unlike any other newsletter writer — most did not want to rock the boat. Meltzer was what a young Sam Muchnick must have been like as a baseball reporter, digging for every little fact.

He did not want to "expose" wrestling; he didn't want to harm it in any way. He just wanted to cover it like any other serious journalist who reports on a demanding, complex business. Brody and I were still talking regularly, and he too became a tutor for Dave. He particularly loved to hear about the reactions of those skewered by Meltzer's astute criticism.

The *Wrestling Observer* was blunt, opinionated, *and* accurate. When Meltzer made errors, he corrected them in his next issue. When he was misled by a source, he admitted it. His pieces were nothing like the occasional "straight" media articles that simply harped on about wrestling not being "real." Naturally, many wrestling insiders were enraged by Dave's new type of coverage. To be honest, I too had misgivings.

"Kayfabe" is a word that even most casual fans know today. The term was a catchall and warning, a reminder that insiders were never to expose industry secrets. Even though Sam seldom used "carney" talk, he was a strong believer in "kayfabe." It was not that Muchnick was trying to trick fans, he simply felt it was better for the spectacle if certain inside information never went mainstream. Does the audience really want to know how David Copperfield makes the elephant disappear — or is it more important that they simply enjoy the show?

Some promoters actually shied away from reporters, fearing they'd write something negative. Muchnick wasn't one of them. Once, before a feature appeared in the *St. Louis Globe Democrat*, O'Connor asked Sam if he was worried that the writer might question the results of a match. Sam just shrugged.

All publicity, in Muchnick's mind, was good publicity.

What *would* make Sam irate was when someone questioned the athletic ability or professionalism of his wrestlers. He wanted to see details about the athletic careers of performers like Ken Patera or Jack Brisco even if the writer also expressed a negative opinion about the sport in general. If someone questioned a wrestler's toughness, Sam countered by saying, "Sign a waiver and I'll put you in the ring."

What quickly became obvious to me was that the people who wanted the kind of news Dave Meltzer provided were serious fans who would always buy tickets — until they were driven away. Brody and I encouraged Dave to look beyond the "con," to consider why and how wrestling worked, to treat it as the serious, intricate operation — with a boatload of colorful characters — it really is.

That was the direction Meltzer was following instinctively. As insiders discovered he truly loved wrestling and that he was absolutely serious about providing meaningful news and analysis, he soon developed many other contacts. The stories he uncovered *were* fascinating. At one point in the mid-1980s, Brody, Dave, and I joked that we might be the only people who knew where every wrestler was working or wanted to go, or when every television taping and house show was scheduled.

Brody and I also got deeply involved in the independent scene. Herb Simmons, a wrestling fanatic who also operated an ambulance service in the St. Louis area, was partially the catalyst. Herb approached me about getting talent for some small cards he wanted to run in Illinois and Missouri. I suggested Brody and we struck a satisfactory financial deal. The alliance led to several years of fun, and we presented many shows with Herb as the licensed promoter.

Before Brody's first outing for Simmons, he and I grabbed something to eat. Brody's flight had been delayed and we were running a bit late. We arrived about ten minutes before the show to find Herb pacing in the parking lot. "I was sweating bullets," Herb said. "Brody asked me, 'Did you think I wasn't coming, big man?' Then he shook my hand."

Simmons and Brody became good pals. Brody often told me how much he respected Herb's hard work and honesty.

Of course, Brody was bouncing all over the map. The territorial promotions were going under as the WWF grew, but Brody was able to combine those struggling towns with independent dates and Japanese commitments to forge a strong base that allowed him more time at home in Boerne, Texas, with Barbara and his son, Geoffrey.

It was during this period that Brody jumped to Antonio Inoki's New Japan Wrestling. Going with Baba's rival boosted Brody's weekly pay for a Japanese tour to around $16,000, but he eventually decided he'd made the wrong decision. Inoki's operation did not pay attention to details as well as Baba's.

When an opening came, Brody returned to Baba. Wanting to regain his old employer's trust, he agreed to put over Tommy "Jumbo" Tsuruta in the middle of the ring. Brody was so concerned about whether the match had clicked that he sent me a tape. It was a terrific duel, fitting perfectly into the classic modes of Japan and St. Louis.

Across the United States, Brody would pick and choose his spots as various promotions reeled and finally crumbled under the McMahon onslaught. When the independent scene showed any life, it was because Brody, one of the mainstays, was always able to draw a crowd.

Brody's non-traditional approach to booking himself also created a couple of notable confrontations. While working in Georgia, Brody came across a loud, obnoxious manager billed as Paul E. Dangerously. Fans today know him as Paul Heyman. Brody really liked Paul's potential. "Good, sharp mind," he told me. "That kid will go somewhere in this business."

Paul, though, was young, with a lot to learn. According to Brody, on one occasion he arrived at a show where the office was set up in a trailer. It was early in the evening, but fans had started to gather. Brody spotted Paul just as he arrived. In this particular promotion, they were bitter rivals. Paul, though, ran to Brody, happily yelling, "Hey, Frank! How are you? What's going on?"

When Paul extended his hand, Brody smacked him, knocking him silly. Paul fell down the steps as Brody stalked inside the trailer. "I really like the guy," Brody said. "It's one thing to go out quietly and eat together, but it's another to come right up in front of fans. Can't let that happen, brother!"

In Florida, early in 1987, Lex Luger was riding the wave of magazine publicity as the next Hulk Hogan. He was cocky, but still not very smooth. And while he was a fine athlete, Lex had an inflated opinion of his own in-ring toughness. In the simplest terms, he believed his own hype. There had already been tense moments between Luger and some more seasoned grapplers who resented his attitude.

Luger and Brody were paired for a few matches, and none of them had been very good. Lex was the baby face, but he didn't sell at all. This made it difficult for a heel like Brody to generate heat for the baby face comeback. Brody, who was the real deal when it came to toughness, was always careful, but fair, about when, and for whom, he sold. Accordingly, he gave Luger nothing. Brody knew their matches suffered because of Luger's refusal to cooperate, and the action started to get pretty stiff.

When the two were slated to collide inside a steel cage, Brody suggested I keep my ears open. "I'm not putting up with any of his bullshit," he said.

I've seen the tape. Brody deployed what, years later, would become a strategic move in so-called "shoot" fights. When Luger charged toward him and began firing punches meant to maim, Brody just blocked the assault with his forearms and shoulders, bobbing and weaving.

Within a minute, Lex was gassed. Sucking for air, he stepped back. Brody reared back and — stared. The look on Luger's face can be translated into a few words: "Oh my God, what have I done?" What would happen next was obvious. Brody intended to make sure that Luger's reluctance to sell wasn't an issue. He was going to hurt him, for real.

Lex turned, ran to the cage wall, crawled over the top, and sprinted to the dressing room. Brody stalked around the ring for a long while, then kicked open the cage door and headed for the same destination. By the time he got to the back of the building, Luger had grabbed his bag and disappeared. All things considered, it was probably one of the best decisions he ever made.

Brody found life well structured when he visited the St. Louis area to wrestle for Herb and me. The working environment, however, tended to be unusual at times. One memorable bill was presented at the Casa Loma Ballroom, a famous dancing and concert location. Brody tackled "Killer" Brooks, a good guy and a solid professional, while "Spike" Huber faced Scott Casey, another extremely reliable hand.

"Big Daddy" was a St. Louis area manager Brody loved to chase. Better known to his friends and family as Roger Bailey, "Big Daddy" had presence and the gift of gab. If wrestling had been different in the mid-1980s, Roger might have established himself full time in the mat world. Brody and I both liked his potential.

Brody bumped into Roger on one of Herb Simmons' cards in Belleville, Illinois, at the fair grounds and auto racing track. After Brody had nailed the wrestler "Big Daddy" managed that evening, Brody ripped off Roger's trousers. The crowd roared when they saw he was clad in pink boxer shorts with red hearts.

Another evening, at the Carondelet Sunday Morning Athletic Club, a tiny hall in south St. Louis, Brody smacked Roger's grappler The Assassin (Joe Zakibe) with a chair. Then Brody charged "Big Daddy." Roger ran out the door, figuring Brody would break off his pursuit. Wrong. Probably weighing more than 300 pounds at the time, "Big Daddy" discovered a sprinting ability he never knew he had. Brody came charging through the door and half the crowd excitedly followed him through the parking lot. Gasping for wind, Roger hissed, "Run me into that tree!"

"Run back!" snarled Brody. With Brody hot on his heels, "Big Daddy" rounded a tree at the edge of the parking lot. Fearing for his well-being and finding new motivation, "Big Daddy" scurried back into the hall to hide behind the woozy Assassin.

Afterward, still huffing and puffing in the dressing room, Roger asked Brody what he would have done if he'd caught him. Brody just smiled, "I'd have beat your ass in the parking lot."

In dismay, Roger turned to me and asked, "Why didn't you come outside, Larry?"

I could only laugh. "Roger, I knew you'd be back. One way or the other."

The evening of August 18, 1985, at the Fairmount Race Track in Collinsville, Illinois, was also memorable. Brody took on "Ox" Baker — in a ring set up right on the infield — before the horse races began. After the wrestling, Brian Zander, the track manager, treated us to dinner in the facility's first-class restaurant. Brody also cashed in on winning bets he placed thanks to tips from the jockeys in the locker room. We were just as successful when, two years later, on August 20, 1987, Brody took on John Nord.

The most unusual venue we used, however, was definitely the Fabulous Fox Theatre. The Fox was a gorgeous, ornate facility that seated more than 4000 fans. Originally a cavernous movie theater, the Fox had been remade into a location for stage plays, including traveling Broadway shows, and concerts. Mat wars at the Fox? Never before. Never again. But on March 4, 1988, our sport nearly recreated the glory days of wrestling at the Chase Hotel.

Geri Couch, who had been a partner with Charlie Mancuso at The Checkerdome, had started her own PR company. I was doing some promotion for Geri's new Working Women's Survival Show and we came up with the idea of putting on a card at the Fox, a venue Geri was also using for some stage productions.

The logistics proved relatively simple. The orchestra pit was brought up to the level of the stage to accommodate the ring. A few rows of seats fit ringside and on the stage. Our main event would be for the Sam Muchnick Trophy. Sam was happy to appear and loved the idea of wrestling at the Fox. Brody clashed with 460-pound Jerry "Crusher" Blackwell for the honor.

Blackwell was actually someone who walked away from the WWF at the start of "the war." When I began working for McMahon in 1984, interviews for his syndicated television show were often taped at KPLR's studio. Many standouts from Verne Gagne's promotion had made the jump to McMahon, and it looked like Blackwell would join the list.

In order to begin working for Vince, Jerry was to cut interviews for upcoming telecasts. As a long day of endless promos progressed, Vince's production crew methodically lined up wrestlers like marching soldiers. I watched as Blackwell's agitation mounted.

Suddenly, Blackwell called me over and began gathering his bags. "Larry, when you see Vince, tell him thanks but no thanks," Blackwell said. "I didn't get into wrestling to punch a time clock. This is going to be like working for a corporation." And then "Crusher" Blackwell walked out the door, never to test the World Wrestling Federation waters.

I told the story to Brody, who always had a huge amount of respect for Blackwell. Naturally, he loved the big man's independent streak and whenever we could use him, we did. He fit perfectly at the Fox, where another semi-main event pitted Kimala, the Ugandan Giant, against Chris Adams. Hot local newcomer Ron Powers, John Nord, Bobby Fulton and Tommy Rogers (known as The Fantastics), and midgets were also featured.

There was one problem we had to solve before the Fox extravaganza. If Sam himself was to be on hand, we could hardly have him just crawl into the ring to shake hands with the winner after the main event. There had to be something, something very special, for him to present. Brody came in a day early to visit radio stations and drum up interest, so we had time to think about it. That evening, the Fox invited us to be guests at a Stevie Ray Vaughn concert and for dinner in the Fox Club.

As we pondered our problem with Sue Nickrent, the Fox's sharp stage manager, we spotted the answer to our prayers. Overlooking the glittering lobby, we discovered a huge spittoon, filled with sand. Or was it an overgrown ashtray? At any rate, it was gold, well-shaped, shiny, and large.

Sue started laughing when we told her our idea. But she delivered. The next evening, when Brody squeaked out a tough victory over Blackwell, Sam Muchnick handed Brody a polished, gleaming, three-foot tall trophy that only hours before had served in anonymity in the Fox lobby. It may, in fact, be in the same location this very day.

The wrestlers were in awe as they roamed the historic Fox dressing rooms. Performers from Bob Hope to Smokey Robinson to Ann Margret had signed the ancient walls. Now Brody's name and a few others are on those walls as well. While my wife Pat worked under the stage counting out cash for the payoff, we darkened the entire Fox, played classical music, and then, in one burst, turned on the blazing spotlights as "Spike" Huber and Steve Regal bounced off the ropes for the opening bout.

Not all of our promotions, of course, were quite so unusual, but Brody liked working with those small, independent groups. We both sensed that places where young talent could learn and be discovered were drying up. A major international star headlining the program was one way to help keep grass-roots wrestling alive.

In the St. Louis area alone, Ron Powers (Plummer) got a Ph.D. in professionalism from Brody. Gary Jackson gained the nickname "Night Train" because he was smooth like "Night Train" Dick Lane, a famous defensive back for the Detroit Lions football team. Joe Zakibe (The Assassin) was instructed by Brody to drop to the floor after getting whacked on the back with a chair. The cool concrete helped ease the sting.

One of our favorite guys to work with was Larry Irwin, who owned a funeral home in Centralia, Illinois. Irwin had run spot shows in Illinois for the dying Kansas City office and earned a reputation for being fair and efficient under trying circumstances. Not surprisingly, he was happy to connect with us. Along with Herb Simmons, we put together cards all over Illinois.

Larry remembers meeting Brody fondly: "I was surprised how smart he was. At first, he was in character, talking about 'rassling.' Then, as we got to know each other, suddenly he was seriously discussing the financial problems of the business and what wrestling had to do to change and thrive. I really admired Brody. He was brilliant, when he let you see it."

Larry, whose dry sense of humor might be unexpected in a funeral home operator, discovered what was perhaps Brody's only weakness after a show in Centralia. We were back at Larry's office eating pizza when Brody asked how bodies were prepared for funerals. Larry explained the practice of keeping spare body parts, frozen, just in case. It was about 2 a.m., in a dark building with real corpses in real caskets, when Brody growled, "No, you gotta be kidding!"

"Follow me," Larry ordered. We walked through a black, spooky hallway to the garage. And then Larry opened up a large freezer. "Here are the legs." I was hiding behind Brody, who freaked and nearly ran me over getting back to the office. Larry couldn't stop laughing.

"I knew he wasn't that tough! I should have shown him the eyes."

Brody did Larry Irwin a favor he never forgot. The son of a friend in little Irvington, Illinois, was a big Brody fan, and Larry asked him if he'd go to the boy's fourteenth birthday party. Brody was coming in for a show, but even I was surprised when he agreed. "Hey, Larry's been a great friend," Brody insisted. Naturally, he was a huge hit.

"The boy's father dropped dead, suddenly, of a massive heart attack just two weeks later," Larry explained. "The boy is an adult now, but he's still got those pictures of Brody and his dad from that day."

Reminiscing with Irwin and Simmons, they both recalled a trip we made to Taylorville, Illinois. Everybody was starving after the matches and we could only find one little place — optimistically called a bar and grill — still open. "We walked in about midnight and they had maybe six people in the place," Larry said. "Hardly anybody would talk to us or even make eye contact. Gee, we had Brody with us, plus Debbie Combs, 'Spike'

Huber, and Abdullah the Butcher. . . . They probably thought we were attackers from Mars!"

On our travels Brody and I would dissect the business: Which promoter was shooting the best angles? Who was Vince going to hire next? Was Verne Gagne getting a cable slot on ESPN? Jim Crockett had an interesting idea. . . . Who had good ring psychology? Who was injured? How was Brody himself, in particular his hip and elbow? Dave Meltzer just blasted another promoter for advertising talent he knew would never appear. . . . We talked endlessly.

"Vince Junior is going to win this battle in the long run," Brody had already predicted in the mid-1980s, while others still held out hope for the territorial system. "His style of wrestling is different, and it may not always be what some of us want or like. If he has all the television, though, new fans are going to grow up thinking: this is what wrestling is. They won't even know what Sam did, or Verne, or Paul Boesch, or Baba. Wrestling will be whatever Vince says it is."

And then he smiled, wryly. "I may have to revamp my image. Get a flat top, trim down to 240, wear silver tights, and call myself the Space Invader."

We talked about the stock market, politics, our kids, and baseball. Brody was a Detroit Tigers fan whose hero was Al Kaline. After one show, while we replayed the night in the bar of the downtown Marriott, we met Curt Flood, the former Cardinal whose refusal to accept a trade had opened the door to the legal battle over free agency. Outlaw greeted outlaw. Flood and Brody got along great.

On some of our long treks, Brody talked about wrestlers who confused their in-ring personality with their true self. "It's tough sometimes, but I have to remember I'm really Frank Goodish," he admitted. "Some of these guys start to believe their own hype. Of course, there's always Murdoch. . . ."

We both laughed. Dick Murdoch was Dick Murdoch at all times — in a wrestling ring, a bar, or at home.

Brody also acknowledged that life on the road had become increasingly difficult: "If you have any weakness at all, whether it's booze or drugs or women, traveling all the time will find it. The road will break anybody. Sometimes I wish I was just a school bus driver so I could see my son every day."

And yes, he realized he'd probably work for the WWF someday. There was money in Hulk Hogan versus "King Kong" Brody. Even Vince knew it. At some point, there was even some informal contact. The question was whether or not the parties involved would risk the kind of upheaval that would result if something went wrong.

Brody even spent several months booking for Fritz Von Erich's "World Class Championship Wrestling" in Dallas. "Thank goodness I don't have to deal with anyone like me," Brody laughed one night on the phone while I served as a sounding board for ideas. One of the youngsters he enjoyed working with, while doing a masked gimmick as "Red River Jack," was Mark Calaway — a man better known today as The Undertaker.

When most fans think of Brody they also think of blood. By now, the truth about how wrestlers blade has been well documented. A tiny piece of razor blade slicing across a forehead can make a bloody mess — but a "hard way" punch will produce the same effect just fine. Brody agreed with promoters who argued "red means green." Blood could draw at the box office. Sam, too, would grudgingly admit that there was some truth to the theory, but only when it wasn't overdone.

In St. Louis, Sam always carefully avoided going overboard with gore. When someone bled, Sam wanted it to matter. For what it's worth, I can count on one hand the number of times Brody got color for a St. Louis program. "I'm a blade freak," conceded Brody. "Must be something weird somewhere, but I like it. I like the reaction I get when I fight through the blood and the crowd is with me. I can tell when I'm going to bleed good. If it sounds like a scratch, that's a scrape and it won't be much color. If it sounds like paper tearing, it's going to bleed buckets. I did it a few times, and then it was what most promoters expected from me. So I did it again."

That was one side of Brody: the cold, hard man doing what he had to for business. Another side appeared when Sam had me invite him to the annual St. Louis Baseball Writers' Banquet. With a prominent table, Sam knew he'd generate attention with someone like Brody seated there. Brody's wife Barbara shipped her husband's suit and tie to me so he would fit in with the likes of Jack Buck, Stan Musial, and Bob Costas.

One of Sam's sons, Dr. Richard Muchnick, was at our table, as were well-known local attorney Bob McGlynn, Boston Red Sox scout Don Lenhardt, and their wives. McGlynn said, "Brody was a nice guy, down to earth. He surprised me with how classy he was."

His hair back in a neat ponytail, Brody was the hit of the night. He told wrestling stories, discussed finance, and signed autographs. Sam beamed; it was an impressive performance.

Of course, I had also been handling some St. Louis and regional business for McMahon while Brody and I were doing independent cards. I did not have an exclusivity agreement with the WWF, but by 1988 the end game was clear. Wrestling was undergoing a seismic alteration. Brody and I began to discuss something different.

Our working name was BAM! — "Brody Athletic Management." Between our various contacts, we were investigating the possibility of representing athletes in other professional sports. It was Brody's baby, and he'd already started to develop the project. If we could obtain the proper legal and financial support, pair that with Brody's hardball negotiating philosophy and my public relation skills, our honest belief was that we could make something successful for ourselves in a different field.

In May 1988, Brody had a few hours between flights. I met him for one of our discussions, but he was distracted. His schedule was becoming more difficult. "Geoff just wrote a little essay for school about what he and Mom would do if Dad never came back from a trip. I was really proud of how mature it was. He said, 'We would be sad, but we'd get through it and go on because that was what Dad would want.' That's really smart for Geoff's age," Brody said, and then paused. "But it kind of scared me."

On July 9, 1988, Brody did an autograph session for our friend Herb Simmons, who at that time owned a bar and grill in Cahokia, Illinois. Herb remembers it vividly — Brody ended up staying most of the day and evening. He asked whether the travel and inherent risks bothered Brody.

"Frank said it did bother him, that it was tough and he hated not being with his son," Herb recalled. "He said that was the business he was in, though, so he had no choice."

And then Brody got on a plane to make dates in Puerto Rico. ("Man, that's a tough buck to earn," he had said.) My wife Pat and I left for a quick vacation in Las Vegas. Brody and I had made plans to get together before he left, again, for dates in Japan.

I returned to St. Louis on July 16. On the 17th I was working out on a stationary bike when the phone rang. It was Dave Meltzer. "Something bad happened last night with Brody in Puerto Rico," Dave said. "I think he's dead."

I tried to call Barbara but there was no answer. In my gut, I think I knew before Dave called back with more information: wrestler/promoter Jose Gonzales had murdered Brody in a dressing room at Juan Lobriel Stadium in Bayamon.

Barbara, in shock, called from Puerto Rico. Devastated, she'd just flown out. "He was so cold when I touched him," Barbara agonized. "Did he ever talk about cremation with you?"

It was the worst, most helpless moment of my life.

Barbara was trapped, alone, except for her 7-year-old son, in a foreign place with her murdered husband. Stunned, I said I would fly down immediately. She refused my offer.

"I'll be okay, but I don't think it's safe here," Barbara said. "Stay there."

I got details about what had happened from Bobby Jaggers, Tony Atlas, and especially "Dutch" Mantell. They all told the same basic story. There had been no problems, whatsoever, at the shows. Years earlier Brody and Gonzales had butted heads while working in New York, but who even remembered that? When Brody got backstage on July 16, Gonzales, who had a big towel over his arm, said they needed to talk about something. They both moved into the bathroom area.

Suddenly, there was a terrifying scream. The other wrestlers ran in to find Brody clutching his stomach. Blood spurted everywhere. Gonzales ran from the building. The knife he used was never found. Everyone present now believes that Gonzales had the weapon hidden in the towel he carried.

Wrestlers heard Brody whisper to Carlos Colon, the principal owner of the promotion, to take care of his son and tell Barbara he loved her. It took nearly thirty minutes for an ambulance to arrive. Brody died in the hospital, on the morning of July 17. Because he had been working with what was essentially a broken elbow for months, Brody had been taking large amounts of aspirin. This had thinned his blood, and made his injuries even worse.

Various wrestlers wanted to testify. But the trial took place without any of them being notified until two weeks *after* a verdict was delivered. Gonzales alone testified. He claimed that Brody was the attacker — a much larger man with a violent reputation — and that he had happened to "find" a knife to use in self-defense. Allegedly, someone heard Gonzales boast that he would "get Brody" earlier in the week, but nobody was on hand to testify to that either.

Jose Gonzales was found not guilty.

The *Sporting News* ran an article on Brody's death, calling him the "Last of the Outlaws." Love him or hate him — and many did both — a part of wrestling's soul died with "King Kong."

After Dave confirmed the worst that afternoon, my daughter Kelly played in the living room. I pedaled furiously on that stationary bike in my den. It was shock; there was nothing I could say or do or feel.

My daughter was only six. She liked Brody because he had gotten down on his knees to play catch with her and let her pull on his beard. Only Kelly, running into the den to say she smelled smoke, brought me back. I looked down. The tires of the stationary bike were actually smoking.

I told my daughter about the horrible thing that had happened. And then we both cried.

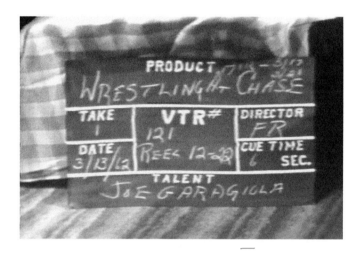

- -

The business certainly has changed

CHAPTER 11

A DIFFERENT TIME

St. Louis had a ringside seat as wrestling changed. Every gimmick, every "hot shot," and every mistake affected us too. St. Louis became just another town on the circuit.

The St. Louis Wrestling Club vanished completely in 1985. Jim Crockett, Jr., who inherited the NWA name, struggled to run against my new employer, the WWF. Vince and I had our share of disagreements, though, as I tried to keep St. Louis on a separate track from the rest of the WWF. Looking back, I realize that this just was not feasible — he was trying to run a national operation. It was easier for Vince to run the same show, and the same television programs. Fine-tuning for certain markets just wasn't a viable option.

Our interaction did lead to another Sam Muchnick tournament. It took place on August 29, 1986. Harley Race (who had made the jump to the WWF) defeated Ricky Steamboat in the finale. The co-feature was a double disqualification between Hulk Hogan and "Mr. Wonderful" Paul Orndorff. Kiel Auditorium was completely sold out, with almost 11,000 fans in attendance. But when Hogan and Orndorff were put together in a rematch for the next show, only 7000 paid.

After decades of consistency with Sam Muchnick, it was very difficult for me to watch crowds fluctuate so wildly — from a sellout one night, to only 1400 the next. Vince and I still talked often, however, and I made trips to New York to go over areas of concern in person.

Truthfully? It *was* exciting. Vince had more imagination and energy than anyone I've ever met. Ideas spewed out of him, like lava from a volcano. No wonder he was able to discover and refine revenue streams previously untapped by the industry. Nonetheless, a few select others, with similar opportunities, could have been equally innovative.

It was also oddly like talking to a mirror. Vince acknowledged everything I'd suggest for St. Louis. Unfortunately, what we agreed to was seldom what happened. The ref bumps, screwy DQs, and walk-outs I abhorred continued. At one point, the same goofy finish was used on three main events in a row. Attendance tumbled.

Again and again, we'd come to terms on an upcoming match, or agree upon how St. Louis should be promoted. All that harmony went down the drain when Vince did something completely different.

Even though wrestling had an unparalleled position in St. Louis, the sport also had a rich and successful tradition in many other towns. The general philosophy might have been different from that of Muchnick's operation, but many places had well-known promoters and loyal fans. The changes Vince initiated were wrenching.

McMahon also seemed to enjoy taking shots at former NWA standouts. Dory Funk, Jr. was decorated with a Dan Blocker-style cowboy hat and billed as "Hoss" Funk — with no mention of what Dory had done as an NWA titleholder. Race paraded around in a shiny crown, a gaudy robe, and was called "The King." At the time, it seemed totally inappropriate.

Vince may have wanted to demean the NWA's past and portray it as inferior to the WWF. Obviously, the promotional war had been bitter. He may have also felt that those wrestlers were a product of a system Sam Muchnick had constructed and that they were not meaningful attractions on their own. Without a gimmick, to Vince they must have seemed flat — gone were the days when just having the NWA belt guaranteed box office appeal. The new characters forced upon Dory, Harley, and others created resentment among St. Louis fans.

No-shows and last-second changes in advertised lineups became even more pronounced over time. Sure, Hulk drew several sellouts — but on occasion he also failed to appear as announced, and this damaged whatever trust fans still had in the product. The situation became even worse when Crockett's operation staged the same type of finishes and announced cards that never happened as advertised.

There is such a thing as "good heat." Once in a while, when a baby face gets cheated, the crowd will erupt with a marketable anger — because they want to see the baby face get revenge. But when this type of thing occurs too often, the "heat" quickly becomes "bad." Fans littering the ring with debris are not looking for a baby face comeback; they're saying, "You screwed me and I won't buy any more tickets from you." With Vince running the show this became common — not only in St. Louis but across the continent.

Our loyal fans became disillusioned, tired of having their intelligence insulted. All the chemically-enhanced physiques in the world could not overcome these mistakes. Compounding the fundamental booking and business errors, wrestling itself was becoming unrecognizable. History no longer mattered. But the truth is, even if Vince had not made his radical bid for supremacy, the world of wrestling would still have had to change — television was becoming an entirely different entity.

Cable was already emerging as a remarkable cultural force. With more channels suddenly available, the influence of syndicated programming or any individual television outlet was reduced. Pay-per-view quickly began generating the industry's biggest single revenue stream. House shows, at venues like Kiel or The Arena, became less and less important. As well, merchandising income grew exponentially.

All of this would have happened anyway. Could someone else, perhaps Gagne, or Crockett, or Von Erich, have tried to become the dominant national provider? Of course. Could the pie have been chopped up between a consortium of promoters exploiting the cable outlets? Perhaps. And while Vince crushed many a career, he simply moved as many other good businessmen would have. His goal was to win, at all costs, and damn the ethics.

Finally, when Ted Turner bought the NWA from the failing Crockett enterprise in 1988, a new sense of urgency was brought to the struggle. In the process, it became clear that there were only two legitimate players left. I would have been on the other side had it not been for the bungled negotiations with Jim Herd — the first in a long line of Turner executives with no real knowledge of the wrestling business. Still, even when Turner brought in experienced wrestling people, the company was bamboozled by their egos. In general, Turner's operation failed to strike the balance between business and wrestling that's so vital to success.

By the early 1990s, the entire industry was in the toilet. My association with Vince floundered: we hardly ever talked. There was no acrimony, however, just the realization that we had a completely different vision of the sport. We really had nothing to talk about.

I remember Vince saying, "We have to realize that we are television producers who do wrestling."

I still believed that I was a wrestling promoter who happened to do television. It's a big distinction.

At the same time, Vince was distracted by various media and legal headaches, having to deal with a steroid scandal as well as running a national promotion. Attendance in St. Louis became so pitiful that in 1993 the WWF drew Arena houses of 4169, 4759, 3624, and 2313 (that's right, just 2313) in a six-month period.

Vince and I parted company after what was called a "C" show (where lesser talent was used for smaller markets) in Dupo, Illinois, on November 13, 1993. It really was the proverbial last straw. I had begged Ed Cohen, who did the exhausting job of booking dates for Vince, not to run "C" shows in the area because I knew they wouldn't draw flies. He had his marching orders, though, so I prevailed upon the friendship of Herb Simmons' wife Mickey, who was on the school board, to get Dupo High School for a program.

Of course, almost all the "C" cards the WWF booked in the area bombed; and eventually Cohen had to cancel programs, including two of the three I had arranged. I battled to keep the Dupo show in order to avoid double-crossing someone who had acted on my behalf out of friendship. It is worth noting that a future WWF champion, Bret "Hitman" Hart, was so low on Vince's pecking order at the time that he was co-featured on the Dupo bill.

When we drew only 628 spectators (actually, that was pretty decent for a lesser lineup at a small high school), I knew that my time with Vince was finished. The WWF was allegedly in dire financial straits. It just made sense for them to lop off a guy who clearly was disgusted with the way they operated. The truth is, I was as tired of them as they were of me. Besides, by that time the WWF was already using venue staff to do its promotion.

Exile gave me the opportunity to watch and evaluate the Monday night cable wars which eventually re-ignited interest in wrestling. When the

Turner operation, by then known as World Championship Wrestling, finally made use of its resources and the TNT network to go head-to-head against Vince's show on USA cable, I was, like everyone else, intrigued.

Eric Bischoff somehow managed to convince WCW to let him run with the ball, and he in turn convinced the parent company to open its wallet. By bringing in former WWF stars like Hulk Hogan, Randy Savage, Kevin Nash, and Scott Hall, along with many previously unheralded talents (mostly exciting, but smaller performers, and many Mexican luchadores), Bischoff forced Vince to develop a new stable of headliners. This, in turn, allowed both companies to explore fresh rivalries. With nothing less than survival at stake, both WCW and the WWF pulled out all the stops. Their hi-jinks both drew a new audience and resurrected part of an old one.

I had another WCW tease at this time. Zane Bresloff, a promoter I'd met during my time with Vince, had joined Turner's operation. Zane wanted a St. Louis connection for WCW, but at the time the Savvis Center was the only available local venue because both Kiel and The Arena had been shuttered. Since Vince had Savvis locked up, I suggested that Zane and WCW roll the dice by going to what was then the TWA Dome.

I put Zane in contact with Jack Croghan at the Dome. WCW promised that I'd be involved with the show, and even spoke about me going to work for them, full time, in some capacity. Of course, in typical wrestling fashion, the pledge was never kept. I did, however, find some solace in the fact that I was able to warn Croghan about exactly what would transpire. I accurately predicted a good start, a mediocre return, and then the emergence of serious problems — unless the promotion and matchmaking were sharp.

The first show was great. On December 21, 1998, they drew over 29,000. Ric Flair had the fans whooping and hollering when he cut an interview talking about Sam Muchnick, Dick "The Bruiser," and "King Kong" Brody. Their second card, as I feared, was a disappointment — a loser, financially, that still drew over 10,000 people. The final fiasco pulled in fewer paying customers than ushers. Flair again spoke about Sam, but no one reacted. None of the loyal St. Louis regulars remained.

The handwriting was on the wall. WCW destroyed itself with its incompetence and lack of foresight. The final Nitro aired on March 26, 2001; Vince had purchased the remnants of Turner's dream. He'd finally achieved his goal: total wrestling dominance.

As everything played out, I had the perfect vantage point from which to formulate a fair comparison of Muchnick and McMahon, by far the most influential promoters of their times. The two men could not have been more different.

With the creation of the National Wrestling Alliance, Sam Muchnick helped secure the framework of the business. He then used his political acumen and clout to save wrestling from serious legal trouble. In creating "Wrestling at the Chase" he helped move wrestling out of intensive care and into an era of prosperity. Had this foundation not been so secure, wrestling might never have been able to gather the national attention it eventually achieved later in the century.

Vince McMahon, Jr. cleverly took advantage of industry-wide confusion as the National Wrestling Alliance collapsed and died. He successfully anticipated and utilized new media technologies, and essentially created a monopoly.

Sam was an "old school" gentleman. He was frugal, always very careful with money, yet he tipped great (ask Mickey Garagiola) and always picked up the tab at dinner. He was reticent about the growing power of women in the workplace — but he eagerly praised someone like Geri Couch at The Checkerdome when he realized how efficient she was.

His honesty wasn't an act. Roger Deem, still a young photojournalist as Sam's career was winding down, put it into perspective: "I was just a kid, but I never thought Sam lied to me. He was not always forthcoming, yet he did not mislead. He just didn't tell you everything."

That's it: basic, logical Sam. Direct question. Simple answer. If he did not want to divulge information, nothing was offered. On any level, business or personal, it was nearly impossible to find someone who could claim Sam had lied or broken his word. For once, the word "integrity" and the term "wrestling promoter" could be used in the same sentence.

Sam could spin a yarn with the very best. He was cordial, humorous, and bright, and for the most part he kept the hard businessman he could be sheltered from public view. In the office, I saw both sides. Sam was terribly disappointed when Fritz Von Erich and Eddie Graham, who followed him as NWA Presidents, contributed to the organization's demise by making decisions that were good for their own territories but not for the business in general. When Jim Barnett took on the responsibility of booking the champion, Sam was upset by the titleholder being placed in the kinds of difficult circumstances he had battled against.

He was similarly dissatisfied with Bob Geigel. I remember him griping, "How can the NWA president wear flip-flops and blue jeans walking through the lobby of the Chase Hotel?" Perception *was* reality as far as Sam was concerned. Appearance mattered. He truly believed that making decisions for the good of wrestling, not one particular territory or person, would in the long run benefit everyone.

Vince McMahon, Jr. has a different kind of charisma. Smooth and smart, he too knows how to spend money in social situations. He can be funny, charming, and a great host. Make no mistake, Vince is a brilliant operator and a truly engaging man. He can look you in the eye and make you feel like the most important being on earth.

Whether or not this is real, however, is always the question. When is Vince "working" (many would say he's "working" all the time) and when is he "shooting"? With McMahon, agreements could be broken or forgotten because, as he once said to me, "It's business." I also remember him telling me, "Contracts don't work."

In Vince's defense, that *was* the way the wrestling business almost always operated. Still, there are those who trust Vince's word completely, those who have seen his generous, charitable side.

Sam used the power he had with grace. Those who were kayoed by his manipulations often did not know how they'd been decked — it was done so tactfully. Even today, there are still those who are unaware of what they achieved with the help of Sam's pragmatic juggling. Some still believe they were making decisions, when in fact Sam was laying the foundation of their success.

Vince utilizes his power like a sledgehammer. He can be brutal, nasty, and very effective. As he once told me, "The big elephant is going to sit wherever it wants to sit. And we're the big elephant." Sure, different times call for different tactics. Sometimes he needed to be blunt, ruthless to the point of arrogance. But other occasions call for finesse.

Vince throws a million ideas at the wall. The good ones, like The Undertaker and his gimmick, stick. Still, McMahon's pockets are deep, so he can afford flops. And there have been many.

His relentless energy sparks a company that can be unfocused and confusing, even as it generates millions of dollars. Just when praise is due for the greater emphasis on hot duels between superb workers, WWE jumps into the gutter with rape (further degrading a true Olympic gold medalist), sexual harassment, violence to women, and racism.

But give Vince's team credit. Their television is slick and state-of-the-art. Unfortunately, it's been so tightly scripted and choreographed that spontaneity and originality have, for the most part, been taken out of the equation. Today there is often less wrestling than soap opera time. Will a miscarriage ever really be entertaining? Is a long and tedious interview more exciting than a promising youngster showing his fire inside the squared circle? How many pay-per-view buys come from a star beating and bloodying an announcer? Wouldn't it be nice to have a commercial break during those long, yawn-inducing comedy skits, rather than during an exciting wrestling match?

Face it, the name of the game is making money, which WWE does hand over fist. Vince found, enlarged, and manipulated a big audience with his interpretation of wrestling. But it sure isn't "Wrestling at the Chase!"

Right now, WWE's in-ring product is changing, even perhaps trying to reach back into history for balance, resurrecting an era when psychology was a critical factor. Of course, the narrative and pace of wrestling must keep up with society itself. And that's meant a clear improvement on the lumbering product of the early 1990s.

But the high-flying, bump-taking, risky days of the "hardcore" style of the late 1990s led to a huge number of injuries, some of which have put stars who should be in their prime on the sidelines. And the emphasis on "pretty" bodies has also caused problems. A huge, chiseled physique is not always the best body type for a grappler — and this emphasis and what it requires athletes to do has led to a horrible catalogue of drug and health disasters.

Without question, Vince has become the master of using the promotional tools at his disposal. My experience, however, tells me that Sam, in his day, would have expertly embraced, explored, and exploited the changes in the ring, in television, and in revenue opportunities. That is, after all, what he did with "Wrestling at the Chase." Why wouldn't he be just as perceptive today? He was, first and foremost, a sharp businessman — one without a hint of sleaze.

Still, it's interesting to speculate about how well Vince would have done fifty years ago, when house shows and coherent booking were the only things that mattered in the struggle for financial success.

It's ironic, and at times pathetic, that many of those writing about wrestling today ignore Sam's accomplishments. Worse, I sometimes wonder why so much ink is spilled — without critical balance — about McMahon. Is it because, as pretty much the sole proprietor of wrestling today, he controls who may or may not find work in the industry?

Ultimately, I don't want to diminish what Vince has achieved, but I do want to acknowledge that others in the right situation might have had similar success. Just as the true history of wrestling cannot be bought, the facts behind its ups and downs should not be buried.

Today, McMahon has the power to control and spin wrestling's legacy — and polishing his image and smoothing off jagged edges for posterity is apparently important to him. It's true, of course, that survivors get to write history. Luckily for Sam, St. Louis, and wrestling itself, Vince is not the only survivor. There are a few of us still among the living.

And just as it's fun to speculate about whether Vince and Sam would have been successful in each other's era, there remains the question of how the likes of Lou Thesz, Jack Brisco, and the other superstars of the past would fare in the current climate. Would the sad truth come down to whether or not they'd take enough steroids to have the beautiful (some would say freaky) physiques they'd need to find themselves being pushed by the lone organization promoting wrestling on a national level?

If the answer is yes, then we're not talking about skill, athletic ability, or even wrestling. Instead, we'd be debating the pros and cons of the kinds of medical risks a man is willing to endure to become a star.

But if you're asking me about whether or not Brisco and Thesz could adapt to a faster pace or different style, well, no answer is necessary. They were great athletes. They'd adapt. In fact, guys like Thesz and Brisco would have led the revolution.

That assumes, of course, that the powers-that-be chose to give main events to guys with talent — not just cartoon muscles. If WWE wants to keep faith with its public pronouncements regarding steroids, this should be its policy. It's not what you say, it's what you do that matters. If only wrestlers who are juiced get pushed, what is the alternative for young talent?

Bluntly, WWE is a monstrously powerful organization, with the kind of television presence that can easily convince a substantial portion of the audience that bigger is indeed better — or *whatever* it is they believe. "King Kong" Brody foresaw it all years ago.

I wonder, too, if the likes of Triple H, Kurt Angle, The Rock, Steve Austin, Randy Orton, and Shawn Michaels would have been smart enough to develop the psychology a grappler needed to be on top in the glory days of the NWA. I truly believe that most of them would be main-event stars in any era. Others, however, who have found themselves in the spotlight solely because of their physiques or gimmicks would find themselves relegated to the prelims.

Styles change in all athletic endeavors, but truly great competitors transcend the vagaries of what's fashionable. Still, in the vicious world of professional wrestling, the space at the top, where the big money awaits, is limited.

The truth has always been the same; in wrestling, genetics count. Looks matter. Thesz and Brisco were handsome guys who looked like superb athletes without artificial enhancement. They had "it." Like Wilt Chamberlain, Michael Jordan, Mickey Mantle, Willie Mays, Walter Payton, and Johnny Unitas, they were natural stars, and because of "it" they got special attention.

Today, it's growing more difficult to find grapplers with genuine "star" quality. Gimmicks and steroids only go so far.

When Pat O'Connor came from New Zealand in 1951 with just $250 in his pocket, there were many opportunities for him to learn and grow as a performer. Many different promotions, each thriving, with a revolving door of new faces, prospered around the country.

But when Ron Powers and Gary Jackson, who both grew up idolizing old school St. Louis wrestling, tried to break in during the late 1980s, those kinds of opportunities were drying up. The territories, where a promising youngster could learn his craft and earn a living, were dead or close to extinction. Gary jokingly calls himself "the most famous unknown wrestler in the world" because he worked for several promotions just as they went under.

How often did I tell Ron, Gary, Joe Zakibe, and Roger Bailey that their lack of opportunity had nothing to do with their ability; that it was, instead, all about politics and business? Over the past fifteen years, how many other potential talents never got the chance?

Because WWE visits most markets only once or twice a year, there's little local opportunity for promising athletes. The pool in which future stars are created has evaporated. Besides, there are other, less stressful ways to earn a living.

Do the math. When there were thirty offices, each with, say, six wrestlers earning main event pay, that meant there were 180 lucrative slots to fight for. Now there's one office, with two brands (Raw and Smackdown!), each with just a handful of featured positions. At best there are a dozen big pay spots. What's the incentive for new talent? And clearly, the competition within the company to land that star status is intense.

Furthermore, with WWE operating only a few training facilities, and with so little competition, it's almost impossible to learn the skills a rookie needs to be successful. Working for a struggling independent promotion, in shows that run once or twice a month, is nothing like being in the ring, under novel circumstances, twenty-eight days out of thirty. But the truth remains: there's room in wrestling for many different styles, and many different kinds of performers. The assembly line of numbingly similar duels can be stopped.

Now, even when someone like Michaels, Orton, or Chris Benoit does get into an exciting fracas with some different twists, the crowd waits for the inevitable referee bump. How disappointing it must be for the talent when they brilliantly execute a finishing move — only to realize that every eye is turned to the aisle, looking for the inevitable run-in.

No, the days of the territories are not coming back. And WWE is not going to collapse. The industry would be well-served by meaningful competition: wrestlers themselves would benefit from some kind of rivalry — at least they'd have options. Competing forces spark fresh ideas, and force the kind of attention to detail that, right now, is lacking. Perhaps it's time for wrestlers to finally unionize for their own benefit.

The state of wrestling today does not make the history of the sport in St. Louis any less valid, exciting, or important. Even if those of us who lived through that era tend to romanticize it, so much of what happened *deserves* to be remembered fondly. It was a once-in-a-lifetime experience.

St. Louis wrestling never died. The buildings were full. The ratings were high. It was simply swept away by the tides of change, as someone who had a different business philosophy took over and completely transformed the industry.

Would Sam Muchnick's version of wrestling succeed on the national stage? Without question. Naturally, it would have to adapt to new technologies, more sophisticated marketing, and different wrestling styles, but the basics are still the same. Exciting stars, colorful characters, smart booking, and efficient promotion still work.

But there's one other thing. For me, as for Sam, wrestling was never a job. It wasn't even a profession. St. Louis wrestling was a passion, something to be lavished with tender, loving care. The memories will last forever.

Sam with his "Boys" (left to right): Ox Baker, Baron Von Raschke, Pat O'Connor, Ric Flair, Gene Kiniski, Sam Muchnick, Harley Race, Dusty Rhodes, Greg Valentine, and Ken Patera

CHAPTER 12

EPILOGUE

The finest description of wrestling in St. Louis I know comes from Mel Hutnick, a loyal friend and brilliant attorney who also grew up as a fan: "Wrestling was a mesmerizing illusion into which we all willingly entered."

How wonderfully accurate.

It's true for the young girl, now a police officer, who skipped church to watch "Wrestling at the Chase" with her father on Sunday mornings. It's true for the elderly grandfather who laughed, cheered, and booed with his sons, now adults themselves. It's true for the mature businessman who recalls being so angry he wanted to punch Dick Murdoch in the nose. It's true for today's dignified teacher, who remembers a teenage crush so powerful that she trembled at the mere sight of David Von Erich.

It is true for thousands of people, for thousands of different reasons. St. Louis wrestling did not appeal to prurient interests and never offended anyone. It wasn't a freak show. An audience's intelligence was never insulted. Wrestling was, simply, magic. A "mesmerizing illusion" created by some of the most compelling characters ever. It was as real and alive as the pleasure we took in it.

On January 1, 1982, we presented Sam Muchnick's farewell card at The Checkerdome. It was a record-setting evening, and all 19,819 seats were sold days in advance. In fact, almost half the tickets had been purchased before we even announced a match — something that was unheard of at the time.

I wonder now how many of us sensed, unconsciously, that the event represented a turning point for a business that was about to be reinvented.

The action, of course, was stellar. What else could be expected of Sam's final program?

One last time, Sam's logical booking prevailed in a main event: Ric Flair successfully defended the NWA prize by winning two-of-three falls from Dusty Rhodes. Former champion Gene Kiniski was the special referee.

Just six months earlier, Rhodes himself had captured the title by defeating Harley Race in Atlanta. A rematch had been scheduled for October 2, 1981, at The Checkerdome, but Flair upset the apple cart by taking the gold belt from "The American Dream" on September 17 in Kansas City. It was Flair, therefore, who defended against Race in October. They wrestled to a one-hour draw before 18,055; Rhodes was the odd man out. It made perfect sense, therefore, for Dusty to go after Flair to start the new year.

That farewell card would have sold out even if the feature was Mickey Garagiola versus Larry Matysik. Our goal, though, was to present a night of wrestling that would make Sam proud. To the credit of every performer on the lineup, we succeeded.

Dick "The Bruiser" — just as he had promised on television — captured the Missouri State Championship from Ken Patera. The tag team duel which sent David Von Erich and Rufus R. Jones against Greg Valentine and Harley Race was ruled a draw when Harley and David were both disqualified. Dewey Robertson pinned Von Raschke. "Crusher" Blackwell won a handicap tag match from "Ox" Baker and "Butch" Reed by flattening "Ox."

Pat O'Connor beat Bob Sweetan in what was billed as the final bout of Pat's career. Luckily Sam was retiring — he would have had a fit when Pat made several more appearances in the Kansas City territory! Joyce Grable and Wendi Richter scored a triumph over Early Dawn and Sandy Partlow. "Bulldog" Bob Brown and Jerry Brown were both counted out.

January 1, 1982, however, was about something more than just wrestling. The outpouring of respect, and the appreciation for what Sam had accomplished, was unbelievable. The short ceremony I'd planned for Sam turned into a long one — simply because so many members of the community wanted to pay their respects. When all was said and done, the list of gifts and tributes was overwhelming.

Bob Burnes and Bob Broeg, the sports editors of the daily St. Louis newspapers, both entered the ring to salute Muchnick. So did the sports directors of the television stations. The weekly papers were represented by the likes of Morris Henderson and Roscoe McCrary. Other television and radio personalities joined representatives of the mayor's office, plus both the Missouri House and Senate, to congratulate Sam. Sports figures such as Dan Kelly, the famous voice of the Blues hockey team; Bing Devine, once general manager of the Cardinals; and Ben Kerner, the owner of the St. Louis Hawks who was then also involved with the Steamers soccer team, were on hand.

KPLR made a presentation. So did the Harlem Globetrotters and Fairmount race track.

The wrestling world, of course, was represented by the likes of Verne Gagne, Wally Karbo, and Frank Tunney from Toronto, as well as magazine guru Bill Apter. George Abel, Sam Menacker, and Joe Garagiola joined me, as the announcers for "Wrestling at the Chase," in honoring our "boss."

In what other town could this incredible mix of sports, politics, business, and media come together to celebrate wrestling?

Sam, clearly surprised and moved, expressed his feelings in a sincere speech that ended, "I owe it all to you. A promoter cannot do well unless he gets people in the building. . . . I'll make this short. Thank you, St. Louis."

After the in-ring ceremony, which Sam knew nothing about in advance, he told me that he most appreciated the plaque that many of the season reservation holders had put together to say thanks.

Following the show, a private party was held in the Dome Club. Everyone who had honored Sam in the ring was invited to attend. His children were there, plus a few hundred other friends who just wanted to say "congratulations" and "thank you" in private. Wrestlers mingled among the audience and earned a huge amount of respect for how professional and friendly they were. Charlie Mancuso, the manager of The Checkerdome, and Geri Couch, his assistant, were absolutely marvelous in helping put all the pieces together.

The police department, represented by Ken Gabel, gave Sam an inscribed nightstick. Oscar Roettger and Frank Torre from Rawlings Sporting Goods gave Sam a huge five-foot bat made specially by the Adirondack bat company — because, according to Oscar, Sam "spoke softly and carried a big stick."

The highlight of the night came when I introduced Joe Garagiola and he invited Gene Kiniski to the microphone. Their comedic "improv" was hilarious. But then Gene got serious.

"Every great man in the world has always had somebody behind him," Kiniski solemnly declared. "Tonight there's a lady who's not with us in person. But I know she's here in spirit. That's Helen Muchnick. I miss her and I think that all of Sam's friends and I realize how much of an asset she has been to Sam, and how much she has done for the world of professional wrestling. I only wish this lady could be with us in person."

Turning to Sam, Gene continued: "And Sam, I know you've been a super promoter, and I just want to say this: may the best things that ever happened to me in this life be the worst things that ever happen to you and your family."

Finally, Gene hugged Sam, kissed him, and shed a tear.

Everything went right that evening. Nobody was paid to be there — they wanted to be involved in the moment. Everyone came because they wanted to be part of the magic spell wrestling and Sam had cast over St. Louis. It would never be surpassed, and only very rarely equaled.

For a promoter, it was the epitome.

When the dust settled and the lights went out, and everyone except the ghosts had left the old Arena, Kiniski and Gagne needed a ride back to the Chase Hotel. Gentlemen always, Gene and Verne made sure my wife, who was within six days of giving birth to Kelly, was comfortable in the front before they squeezed into the back seat.

These two great warriors, who had seen and done it all, were babbling with as much excitement and satisfaction as Pat and I were. That night of wrestling really had been perfect.

As we drove away from the building, there was a sudden silence, then muffled whispering behind me.

And then, in voices strong and powerful, Gene Kiniski and Verne Gagne began singing.

There's no business, like show *business . . . There's no business I knoooow . . .*

They serenaded us through the twinkling St. Louis night, deep into the heart of the magic city of wrestling.

Thanks!

To my wife Pat, whose love and stability made the crazy world of wrestling fit in the proper place. It certainly has never been dull, has it?

To my daughter Kelly, who enjoyed all of the silliness even if some of it had to make absolutely no sense whatsoever to her.

To my parents, for their love and support from the very start.

To Mel Hutnick, a tried and true friend who always insisted there was value in my tales about wrestling. By golly, Mel, I think you were correct!

To Herb Simmons, another loyal friend who has always been upbeat, helpful, and certain that people wanted to hear these stories. Herb's "elf" Mickey has been invaluable too.

To Charlie Ragle, for new ideas, energy, and plenty of laughs.

To the late Frank Goodish, for helping me to learn so much more about wrestling and about myself. To his wife Barbara, for showing everyone what true poise and courage really are in the face of tragedy.

To Dave Meltzer, for helping me keep my passion alive when it might have died.

To Keith Schildroth, who helped start the St. Louis nostalgia craze with his feature in the St. Louis Post-Dispatch.

To Mickey Garagiola, the late Ray Gillespie, Steve Horn, Randy Liebler, Dave and Sandy Kraus, Bob McGlynn, Wayne St. Wayne, Tom Wheatley, Bart Saracino, Doug Dahm, Joe May, Mitch Hartsey, Jimmy Hart, and all of the others who have supported me.

To Michael Holmes and Jack David at ECW Press, for their enthusiasm and professionalism. Michael understands this unique sport, in addition to being a marvelously patient and perceptive editor.

To every wrestler who risked life and limb to entertain us with the spectacle. To every fan whose energy helped make the magic real.

To Sam Muchnick, who made it all possible.

Thank you, one and all.

From the personal collection of Larry Matysik come 12 two-hour videos of great moments from "Wrestling at the Chase" and the stars of St. Louis.

Here is a brief look at some of the highlights:

Volume One

"The Bruiser" vs. Murdoch, DiBiase vs. Brody, O'Connor vs. Murdoch

Volume Two

David and Fritz Von Erich vs. Race, Kevin Von Erich vs. Murdoch, and from 1962 with O'Connor, Johnny Valentine, and Joe Garagiola

Volume Three

Murdoch & Raschke vs. DiBiase & David Von Erich, Brody vs. Abdullah, Thesz interview from 1980

Volume Four

Rocky Johnson & O'Connor vs. Brody & Patera, DiBiase vs. Studd, 2004 interview with Mickey Garagiola

Volume Five

Flair vs. O'Connor, Kerry Von Erich vs. Patera, Brisco vs. Baba

Volume Six

The Race-DiBiase feud, Brody vs. Dory Jr., plus Orton, Blackwell

Volume Seven

Race vs. David Von Erich, Greg Valentine vs. Kerry Von Erich, 2004 interview with Von Raschke

Volume Eight

The Flair-"Bruiser" feud, Kiniski wins tag elimination, 2004 interview with Jack Brisco

Volume Nine

Brody vs. Murdoch, The 1983 War in St. Louis, Terry Gordy, Randy Savage, Tully Blanchard, Adrian Adonis

Volume Ten

Sam Muchnick's final card January 1, 1982, the private party, Flair vs. Rhodes (with Kiniski as referee), Patera vs. "The Bruiser"

Volume Eleven

Dory Jr. & Patera vs. Blackwell & Flair, from 1969, "Cowboy" Bob Ellis

Volume Twelve (Special Edition)

Flair and Brody, The Hour (plus Patera, Murdoch, Kevin Von Erich and more)

To purchase the entire collection or individual VHS/DVDs, call **618-286-4848** or e-mail **stlouiswrestling@juno.com**

For information about obtaining the entire raw and unedited sixty (60) plus total hours of the Matysik collection, contact the above number or e-mail address.